# Relationship Marketing in the Digital Age

The concept of relationship marketing has been discussed among marketing academics and managers since the early 1980s. But instead of reaching its maturity stage, relationship marketing is nowadays encountering its next upsurge. Due to a confluence of trends driving the global business world—including the transition to service-based economies, faster product commoditization, intensified competition worldwide, growth among emerging markets, aging populations, advertising saturation, and (above all) the digital age—strong customer relationships are more than ever vital to company strategy and performance.

*Relationship Marketing in the Digital Age* provides a comprehensive overview of the state of the art of relationship marketing, offering fruitful insights to marketing scholars and practitioners. In seven chapters, divided into two main sections on understanding (Part I) and effectively applying (Part II) relationship marketing, an introductory and a concluding chapter, readers learn how to successfully manage customer–seller relationships.

**Robert W. Palmatier** is Professor of Marketing and John C. Narver Chair of Business Administration at the Foster School at the University of Washington. He founded and serves as the global research director of the Sales & Marketing Strategy Institute (SAMSinstitute.com), a global organization focused on linking business and academics for knowledge.

**Lena Steinhoff** is Assistant Professor of Service Management at the Institute for Marketing and Service Research at the University of Rostock in Germany. She is also an affiliated faculty member of the Sales & Marketing Strategy Institute at the Foster School of Business at the University of Washington.

# Routledge Studies in Marketing

This series welcomes proposals for original research projects that are either single or multi-authored or an edited collection from both established and emerging scholars working on any aspect of marketing theory and practice and provides an outlet for studies dealing with elements of marketing theory, thought, pedagogy and practice.

It aims to reflect the evolving role of marketing and bring together the most innovative work across all aspects of the marketing 'mix'—from product development, consumer behaviour, marketing analysis, branding, and customer relationships, to sustainability, ethics and the new opportunities and challenges presented by digital and online marketing.

# Relationship Marketing in the Digital Age

Robert W. Palmatier and
Lena Steinhoff

NEW YORK AND LONDON

First published 2019
by Routledge
605 Third Avenue, New York, NY 10017

and by Routledge
2 Park Square, Milton Park, Abingdon, Oxon, OX14 4RN

First issued in paperback 2021

*Routledge is an imprint of the Taylor & Francis Group, an informa business*

© 2019 Taylor & Francis

*Library of Congress Cataloging-in-Publication Data*
A catalog record for this book has been requested

ISBN 13: 978-0-367-78692-2 (pbk)
ISBN 13: 978-1-138-31002-5 (hbk)

Typeset in Sabon
by Apex CoVantage, LLC

# Contents

# Figures

# Tables

# Author Biographies

**Robert W. Palmatier** is Professor of Marketing and John C. Narver Chair of Business Administration at the Foster School at the University of Washington. He founded and serves as the global research director of the Sales and Marketing Strategy Institute (SAMSinstitute.com), a global organization focused on linking business and academics for knowledge.

He earned his bachelor's and master's degrees in electrical engineering from the Georgia Institute of Technology, as well as an MBA from Georgia State University and a doctoral degree from the University of Missouri, followed by postdoctoral research at Northwestern University's Kellogg School of Management. Prior to entering academia, Robert held various industry positions, including president and COO of C&K Components (global electronics company) and European general manager and sales and marketing manager at Tyco-Raychem Corporation. He also served as a U.S. Navy lieutenant on board nuclear submarines. Robert's research interests focus on marketing strategy, relationship marketing, customer loyalty, privacy, marketing channels, and sales management. His research has appeared in *Harvard Business Review*, *Journal of Marketing*, *Journal of Marketing Research*, *Marketing Science*, *Journal of Academy of Marketing Science*, *Journal of Retailing*, *Journal of Consumer Psychology*, *Marketing Letters*, and *International Journal of Research in Marketing*. He has also published a number of leading textbooks including *Marketing Channel Strategy*; *Marketing Strategy: Based on First Principles and Data Analytics*; a monograph entitled *Relationship Marketing*; and chapters in numerous books. His research has been highlighted in *Nature, New York Times Magazine, LA Times, Electrical Wholesaling, Agency Sales*, and *The Representor*, as well as on NPR and MSNBC. In a recent AMA study, he was shown to be the 10th most productive scholar in marketing (across the top four marketing journals) over the past 10 years.

He has served as editor-in-chief of the *Journal of Academy of Marketing Science* and presently is the co-editor for *Journal of Marketing* and also sits on numerous editorial review boards. His publications have received multiple awards, including the Harold H. Maynard (twice) and Sheth awards at the *Journal of Marketing* and Robert D. Buzzell Award (twice), Lou W. Stern Award (four times), selected as both MSI Scholar and Young Scholar, Varadarajan Award for Early Contribution to Marketing Strategy Research, and the American Marketing Association Best Services Article awards. He also has won multiple awards as a teacher of advanced marketing strategy in the doctoral, EMBA, and MBA programs at the University of Washington.

Among the numerous industry and governmental committees on which Robert has served, he chaired proposal selection committees for the National Research Council (NRC), National Academy of Sciences (NAS), and the Wright Centers of Innovation, which awarded grants of $20 million for the development of a new Wright Center of Innovation based on joint academic–industry proposals. He has served in NASA's Computing, Information, and Communications Advisory Group with the AMES Research Center. This advisory group assessed the current state of technology development within academia, governmental agencies, and industry related to NASA's information technology activities and space exploration requirements. He also consults and serves as an expert witness for companies including Alston+Bird, Paul Hastings, Microsoft, Telstra, Starbucks, Emerson, Fifth Third Bank, Wells Fargo, Genie, Cincom, Tableau, Concur, World Vision, and Belkin.

**Lena Steinhoff** is Assistant Professor of Service Management at the Institute for Marketing and Service Research at the University of Rostock in Germany. She is also an affiliated faculty member of the Sales & Marketing Strategy Institute at the Foster School of Business at the University of Washington. Prior to joining the University of Rostock in the fall of 2018, she held a position as Assistant Professor of Marketing at the University of Paderborn in Germany. Lena earned her bachelor's and master's degrees in international business as well as a doctoral degree in marketing from the University of Paderborn. In 2015 and 2012, she was a visiting scholar at the University of Washington's Foster School of Business, funded through scholarships awarded by the German Research Foundation (DFG) and the German Academic Exchange Service (DAAD).

Lena's research interests are service management, marketing strategy, and relationship marketing, with a particular focus on managing customer relationships through loyalty programs and rewards. Specifically, she explores the intended as well as the unintended effects diverse relationship marketing instruments might spur and looks at their impact on company performance. Her research has appeared in *Journal of the Academy of Marketing Science, Journal of Service Research, Journal of Service Management, Journal of Service Management Research,* and the *Marketing Science Institute (MSI) Working*

*Paper Series*, where she has received the 2016 Robert D. Buzzell MSI Best Paper Award. Lena serves on the editorial review board for *Journal of the Academy of Marketing Science* and as an ad hoc reviewer for *Journal of Service Research*, *Journal of Retailing*, and *Journal of Business Research*. She held invited research presentations at numerous international schools, such as Florida State University, HEC Paris, ETH Zurich, and Copenhagen Business School.

Lena served as a consultant and research advisor to several firms in business-to-consumer as well as business-to-business industries. In 2016, she conducted a workshop for 60 executives on understanding and designing effective loyalty programs at the Sales & Marketing Strategy Institute. Lena has considerable experience in teaching relationship marketing, service management, consumer behavior, and experimental research to undergraduate and graduate students at the Universities of Rostock, Paderborn, and Wuppertal, where she received temporary teaching appointments.

# Preface

The relevance of relationships in business exchanges has continuously been documented ever since Homeric Greece. Yet it was not until the early 1980s that the concept of relationship marketing had its first mention in the marketing literature. Since then, over the past decades, we have observed an explosion of research papers and popular business books, with academics and managers agreeing that strong customer relationships are vital to company strategy and performance.

But instead of reaching its maturity stage, relationship marketing is nowadays encountering its next upsurge. Due to a confluence of trends driving the global business world—including the transition to service-based economies, faster product commoditization, intensified competition worldwide, growth among emerging markets, aging populations, advertising saturation, and (above all) the digital age—the critical impact and effectiveness of idiosyncratic relationships, relative to other marketing mix factors, continues to increase at an ever-growing pace.

This research monograph provides a comprehensive overview of the state of the art of relationship marketing, offering fruitful insights to marketing scholars and practitioners. In seven chapters, divided into two main sections, an introductory and a concluding chapter, readers learn how to successfully manage customer–seller relationships. The introductory chapter educates the reader on the scope of the domain of relationship marketing and details why and how relationships are key for firms to succeed in the digital age.

Part I equips the reader with a profound understanding of relationship marketing. While Chapter 2 focuses on a multitude of relevant theories that have informed three different types of customer–seller relationships (i.e., interpersonal, interfirm, and online), Chapter 3 weaves these theories and their focal constructs into a comprehensive relationship marketing framework.

Part II focuses on successful applications of relationship marketing. Based on key empirical research findings, we review different research-based approaches to relationship marketing dynamics (Chapter 4), strategies for building and maintaining relationships (Chapter 5), and targeting

(Chapter 6) and provide actionable guidance on how to leverage these approaches in today's relationship marketing environment.

The concluding chapter compiles current issues and trends in relationship marketing research and practice, putting forward a research agenda evolving around 14 research tenets that we hope will help shape the future of relationship marketing.

# Acknowledgments

Robert W. Palmatier thanks his colleagues and doctoral students, whose insights into relationship marketing have helped inform this book in multiple ways: Denni Arli, Todd Arnold, Joshua T. Beck, Abhishek Borah, Daniel Claro, Andrew Crecelius, Eric Fang, Gabe Gonzalez, Srinath Gopalakrishna, Dhruv Grewal, Rajdeep Grewal, Colleen Harmeling, Conor Henderson, Mark B. Houston, Brett Josephson, Vamsi Kanuri, Frank R. Kardes, Jisu J. Kim, Irina V. Kozlenkova, Justin Lawrence, Ju-Yeon Lee, Kelly Martin, Jordan Moffett, Stephen Samaha, Lisa K. Scheer, Hari Sridhar, Jan-Benedict E.M. Steenkamp, Park Thaichon, George Watson, Scott Weaven, Stefan Worm, and Jonathan Zhang. His debt to past MBA, EMBA, and PhD students is large; they were key in developing many of the insights in this book. He is also extremely grateful to Charles and Gwen Lillis for their support of the Foster Business School and his research, which helped make this book possible. Finally, Rob would like to acknowledge the support and love of his daughter, Alexandra, which made this effort worthwhile.

Lena Steinhoff thanks her co-authors and colleagues for enriching this book with their insights and inspiring her academic work in various ways: Denni Arli, Joshua T. Beck, Eva Böhm, Andreas Eggert, Eric Fang, Ina Garnefeld, Colleen M. Harmeling, Conor M. Henderson, Gary L. Hunter, Jisu J. Kim, Irina V. Kozlenkova, Ju-Yeon Lee, Stephen S. Samaha, Lisa K. Scheer, George F. Watson, Scott Weaven, Carina Witte, and Marcellis M. Zondag. She appreciates her master's students' fruitful contributions to engaging classroom discussions on relationship marketing. Finally, Lena is deeply grateful to Julia; her love, support, and belief are a constant source of encouragement.

Both authors extend their appreciation to Elisabeth Nevins for editing and often rewriting the chapters to enhance the readability of this book, Nicole Obermann for her contributions to the graphical layout of the figures and tables, and Jisu J. Kim for her support on the proofreading of this text. We also thank our research assistants at Universities of Washington and Paderborn, Johanna Horsthemke, Pia Kallen, Sereen Kallerackal, and Chuangzuo Liu, for their help in researching materials for and formatting this text. Finally, we are indebted to the vast number of authors whose work we cite throughout this work. Without their dedicated efforts and valuable contributions, we could not have written this book.

Robert W. Palmatier
Seattle, Washington, USA

Lena Steinhoff
Rostock, Germany

# Introductory Chapter

# 1 Relationship Marketing and the Digital Age

## Learning Objectives

- Understand relationship marketing as an important source of sustainable competitive advantage for companies, with increasing relevance in today's world.
- Define relationship marketing.
- Identify the conceptual differences between relationship marketing and other strategies, such as branding or promotional marketing.
- Review the evolution of relationship marketing terminology over four decades.
- Outline various trends in the economy and society that have increased the relevance of strong customer–seller relationships.
- Analyze how the advancement of the digital age as a mega-trend has revolutionized customers' and sellers' lives.
- Evaluate the diverse characteristics that differentiate customer–seller relationships in the digital age versus the predigital age.
- Detail the growing importance of relationship marketing for firms striving to succeed in the digital age.

## Introduction

Relationships have defined business exchanges ever since Homeric Greece. Yet it was not until 1983 that the concept of relationship marketing first appeared in marketing literature (Berry 1983). Since then, relationship marketing has emerged as a specific priority for marketing academics and managers. We have observed an explosion of research papers and popular business books, with academics and managers coming to a consensus view: Strong customer relationships are vital to company strategy and performance (Morgan and Hunt 1994; Palmatier et al. 2006).

But instead of reaching a maturity stage, relationship marketing is entering its next upsurge. A confluence of trends driving the global business world—including the transition to service-based economies, faster product commoditization, intensified competition worldwide, growth among emerging markets, aging populations, advertising saturation, and (above all) the digital age—has prompted the continued expansion of the impact and effectiveness of strong customer–seller relationships relative to other marketing mix factors. Marketing thought leaders compellingly delineate how strong customer relationship value can trump brand value—one of marketing's most traditional home turfs—when it comes to determining the total value of an enterprise. For example, when Binder and Hanssens (2015) investigated and compared the dollar valuations of brand assets and customer relationship assets in 6,000 mergers and acquisitions between 2003 and 2013, they found that worldwide, while brand value declined by almost half (i.e., from 18% to 10% of total enterprise value), relationship value doubled (i.e., from 9% to 18%). These findings illustrate a substantial shift in investors' preferences, away from acquiring businesses with strong brands to businesses that possess strong customer relationships. We posit that this trend only will strengthen as the digital age proceeds, as we detail in this chapter.

Building their marketing strategy around relationships is a viable strategy for firms, considering the innate importance of relationships for human beings. As primates, we have evolved to be social animals, such that approximately one-third of the activity performed by an average human brain is linked to interactions. In addition, our capacity for empathy is among the most essential defining traits of humanity (Newman 2016; University of Virginia 2013). Relationships drive human behavior; along with cooperation, they enable evolutionary advances (Becker 1986; Trivers 1971; Trivers 1985). As we will discuss in this book, it is possible to explain how consumers respond to different marketing activities by considering psychological factors and perceptions related to relationships and interactions (e.g., gift–gratitude, anger–punishment, guilt–reciprocation, love–hate) (Cialdini and Rhoads 2001; Dahl, Honea, and Manchanda 2003; Dahl, Honea, and Manchanda 2005; Palmatier et al. 2009; Palmatier et al. 2007). In this sense, human evolution is a critical foundation for the effectiveness of relationship marketing.

Recognizing the innate need for relationships, customer-centric organizations devote substantial resources to connect with customers and maintain strong relationships with them, which ultimately may evoke relationship-based loyalty (Day 2006; Gartner 2014a). Companies employ relationship marketing tools to produce relationship equity, and from an overall marketing strategy perspective, this equity can be a source of sustainable competitive advantage, together with brand or offering equity (Palmatier and Sridhar 2017). Customers value and seek unique characteristics that emerge in relationship-based exchanges (e.g., reduced perceptions of risk, higher trust, enhanced cooperation, greater flexibility), especially in service, business-to-business, and complex offerings contexts. In many settings, both sellers and customers prefer to conduct business transactions embedded within mutually beneficial relationships.

This chapter therefore introduces the concept of relationship market-ing in four parts. First, we explain the very notion of relationship market-ing, highlighting how it can drive a company's sustainable competitive advantage. Second, with an overview approach, we describe what rela-tionship marketing is, how it relates to and is distinct from other market-ing domains, and how its meaning and terminology have evolved over time. Third, we review five key trends that have shaped and reinforced relationship marketing's role in recent years. Fourth, in line with the overall approach we take in this book, we focus on the digital age as a mega-trend that continues to determine relationship marketing practices while simultaneously augmenting the relevance of effective relationship marketing strategies for any firms striving to survive in the challenging modern marketing environment.

## Relationship Marketing as a Source of Sustainable Competitive Advantage

A basic underlying principle of marketing strategy is that no firm ever operates in isolation. Any strategy a firm follows—especially if it turns out to be effective in the target market—will prompt some reaction from competitors, either to mimic successful strategies or to come up with their own innovative approach (Palmatier and Sridhar 2017). To thrive in the long run, companies thus must develop barriers to competitive attacks, in the form of **sustainable competitive advantages**. Regardless of their source, these advantages indicate that the company can generate more customer value than its competitors in the industry for the same set of products and services, such that competitive firms are unable to imitate or surpass the focal company's successful strategy (Barney and Clark 2007). A sustainable competitive advantage thus meets three crite-ria: (1) The firm's customers care about it, (2) the firm is relatively better than its competitors in providing it, and (3) it is difficult for competitors to duplicate or substitute for, even if they invest substantially in trying to do so (Barney and Hesterly 2012).

From a marketing perspective, there are three main sources of sus-tainable competitive advantages: brands, offerings, and relationships (Palmatier and Sridhar 2017). A **brand-based sustainable competitive advantage** relies on brand awareness and the brand image built up in consumers' minds, which makes brands hard to imitate, promotes habit-ual buying, and offers identity benefits to customers. Brands and brand equity have long had pivotal roles in large consumer markets (e.g., soft drinks, beer, fashion, automobiles). **Offering-based sustainable competi-tive advantages** instead build on investments in research and development and resulting innovations, such that the offered products and services substantially improve the customer's experience through cost benefits, performance advantages, or supplementary services. This form of equity can be relevant across markets, particularly in domains such as software or electronics. Finally, a **relationship-based sustainable competitive advantage** relies on strong relationships between customers and salespeople, other boundary-spanning personnel, or the firm as a whole, which evoke hard-to-copy and high levels of trust, commitment, and reciprocal bonds. They thus encourage customer retention and loyalty, even when circumstances change, and they enhance financial performance. Relationship equity usually is most effective in service, complex offering, and business-to-business contexts.

Firms typically invest in efforts to obtain all three categories of sustainable competitive advantage. Together, brand-, offering-, and relationship-based equities synergistically constitute a company's overall customer equity, or "the total of the discounted lifetime values summed over all of the firm's current and potential customers" (Rust, Lemon, and Zeithaml 2004, p. 110). In a particular context, the weight and effectiveness of the three sources of sustainable competitive advantage vary cross-sectionally, depending on general market conditions, and also evolve longitudinally over time (see Figure 1.1).

Yet in a very broad sense, this three-pronged approach is relatively new, because relationships represented the dominant source of advantages for literally thousands of years (Palmatier 2008). During preindustrial eras, farmers and craftspeople took to local exchanges in nearby markets to get their products to consumers directly. These producers functioned as manufacturers, but they also performed retailing functions, and their familiar, embedded relationships with consumers established trust-based business norms. Few institutionalized rules or protections were in place. Even as they extended beyond immediately local markets, traders relied on relationships to ensure confidence in the quality of the goods. Many trade patterns in history only could have emerged from groups that maintained consistent, strong relationships; the historical "silk route" is a key example. In addition, to signal their trustworthiness, some of these groups started citing their family or group names—an early form of branded relational trust (Sheth and Parvatiyar 1995). Early

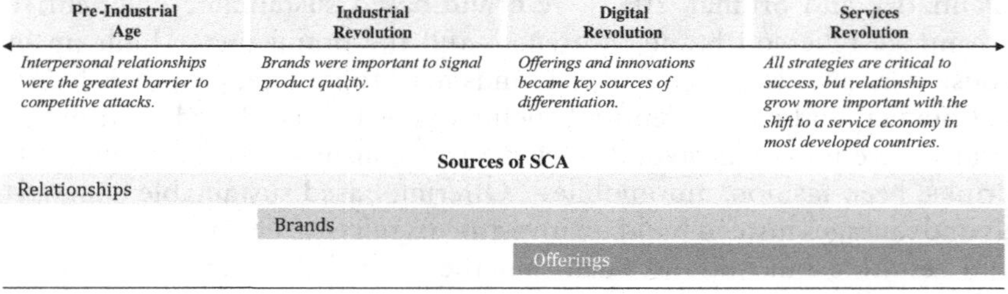

| Pre-Industrial Age | Industrial Revolution | Digital Revolution | Services Revolution |
|---|---|---|---|
| *Interpersonal relationships were the greatest barrier to competitive attacks.* | *Brands were important to signal product quality.* | *Offerings and innovations became key sources of differentiation.* | *All strategies are critical to success, but relationships grow more important with the shift to a service economy in most developed countries.* |

**Sources of SCA**

Relationships

Brands

Offerings

*Figure 1.1* Evolution of Sustainable Competitive Advantages (SCA) in Marketing "brands" derived from family names sought to spread their foundational or prototypical customer relationships, in which a store owner developed good relationships with customers (e.g., Ferrari, J.C. Penney, Adidas, Abercrombie & Fitch, Ben & Jerry's, Bentley, Campbell's, Gillette, Jack Daniel's, Yamaha, Suzuki).

Along with vast other shifts, the mass production supported by the Industrial Revolution prompted a change to the dynamic relations between producers and consumers. Mass production led to substantial volumes of manufactured goods, so to ensure sufficient demand for all these items, producers had to conduct more aggressive sales and promotions. It also allowed for vast economies of scale, such that as producers churned out large volumes of goods at low cost, they had to be stored, transported, and ultimately sold to a wider, more distant customer base. To meet these new market needs, people increasingly moved to urban manufacturing centers; in turn, more goods (especially agricultural production) had to be moved into the new population centers and held until the newly urban consumers were ready to purchase them. In aggregate then, industrialization created new channel members that could provide transportation, storage, selling, and retailing functions (Bartels 1962). Competition to sell similar products also led to more transactional exchanges, so brands gained a new and critical role, namely, as a means to distinguish the products and signal their quality. As these mass-production outcomes expanded, the effectiveness of local, long-term relationships as a sustainable competitive advantage diminished.

This evolution in the source of sustainable competitive advantage did not stop there, either. That is, such advantages relied largely on relationships in the earliest markets and turned more to brands following the Industrial Revolution; today, we find that innovative offerings represent the primary source of a sustainable competitive advantage, a shift that signals the evolution created by the digital revolution. Today the digital revolution refers to cutting-edge technologies, but it really began in the late 1950s, as analog or mechanical tools gave way to digital computers. As these techniques produced new and innovative offerings, CEOs came to regard a constant focus on innovation as the determinant of their competitiveness, allowing the firm to protect its existing status but also expand into new markets.

Each new source of a sustainable competitive advantage enhances the other, rather than just replacing it. Perhaps the next source will come from a service revolution (Vargo and Lusch 2004). Relative to products, services account for approximately 85% of the U.S. economy (Fang, Palmatier, and Steenkamp 2008), and because a single organization often produces and delivers them, they create "disintermediation"—eliminating the middleman from the channel and solidifying the producer–consumer bond. By definition, services are intangible, inconsistent, perishable, and hard to evaluate, so customers often must depend on boundary-spanning personnel to obtain and sometimes even coproduce them. Furthermore, the intangibility of service offerings increases the benefits of relationship-based trust for the customer (Palmatier et al. 2006).

---

**Example 1.1  Platform Business Models**

The sustainable competitive advantage of platform businesses heavily depends on the platform provider's customer relationships. Platforms represent a disruptive business model innovation where a third-party service provider operates a platform to enable exchanges between two groups of entities (i.e., users and providers of the focal service). As such, platforms represent two-sided markets where the platform company needs to effectively manage their relationships with two types of customers. Popular examples of platform businesses are Airbnb and Uber, which have transformed the hospitality and transportation industries, respectively. Without owning any one bed, Airbnb today represents the world's largest accommodation service. As the world's largest taxi service, Uber owns no cabs. Instead, through their platforms, Airbnb and Uber connect and match hosts and guests or drivers and riders. As such, platforms' success is reliant on the size of the community of service providers and service users, putting the management of customer relationships with and the provision of value to both parties at the forefront of managerial thinking for establishing sustainable competitive advantage.

Source: McRae (2015).

---

These more recent shifts—that is, the service revolution and the most recent advances in the digital age, as related to Web 4.0 (e.g., artificial intelligence, augmented reality)—have brought the evolution of sustainable competitive advantages full circle, back to relationships. The anonymity and geographic distance separating relational partners in online settings and the intangibility of digital products and services means that channel members strive to establish relational trust and strong bonds. Relationships are coming back *en vogue* as important sources of sustainable competitive advantage.

## A Brief Overview of Relationship Marketing

To answer the crucial and foundational question, "What is relationship marketing?," this section first delineates the scope and definition of relationship marketing. We compare relationship marketing with related areas to evaluate the potential overlap, and we also place relationship marketing within a historical context by describing the evolution of the discipline and its terminology over time.

## Definition of Relationship Marketing

> **Relationship marketing** is "the process of identifying, developing, maintaining, and terminating relational exchanges with the purpose of enhancing performance."
>
> (Palmatier 2008, p. 3)

We start with this definition, derived from the contributions of scholars who have established the very domain of relationship marketing as a specific field within marketing. In particular, one of the most widely used definitions of marketing in general, issued by the American Marketing Association, emphasizes relationships by asserting that "marketing is an organizational function and a set of processes for creating, communicating, and delivering value to customers and for *managing customer relationships* in ways that benefit the organization and its stakeholders" (Palmatier 2008, p. 3, emphasis added). Across various definitions of marketing, managing relationships thus appears in conjunction with, and as equally important as, traditional marketing mix elements (e.g., place, price, product, promotion), prompting a specific line of research into relationship marketing that leverages various research domains and perspectives to derive various definitions (Berry 1983; Harker 1999), as summarized in Table 1.1. Across these variations though, three features are common (Gronroos 1997; Sheth and Parvatiyar 2000):

1. Relationships are dynamic, and therefore so must relationship marketing be.
2. The scope of relationships is broad, as is the scope of relationship marketing.
3. Relationship marketing must generate benefits for both parties to the relationship.

With the clear recognition that relationships consist of various stages, often following a common pattern of growth, researchers establish that engagement develops over time. In turn, the relationship marketing tactics that are appropriate and that reflect the changing exchange must shift dynamically across stages (Dwyer and Oh 1987; Wilson 1995). Even when scholars specify different numbers of substages or adopt varying terminology to refer to similar ideas, we can identify four main stages in extant research: identifying, developing, maintaining, and terminating.

The breadth of a relationship defines the target of relationship marketing tactics, such that relationship marketing might not be limited just to customers but also could include various stakeholders—that is, anyone with an interest in or who might be affected by the firm's activities, including employees, suppliers, competitors, and wider society. Accordingly, relationship marketing might apply to individual entities, but it also might span groups or networks. For example, relationships might link individuals (person-to-person, person-to-many persons; network perspective, *interpersonal*), an individual with a firm or group (person-to-firm, firm-to-person), or firms (firm-to-firm, *interfirm*). Although the precise tactics differ for the different types of partners, the underlying theories and models remain fundamentally the same (Morgan and Hunt 1994). In this sense, relationship marketing practices can apply to virtually any "entity," or networks of entities and interfirm relationships (Rindfleisch and Moorman 2003; Sivadas and Dwyer 2000). Some decisions and efforts to enhance relationship development require modifications when applied to groups versus individuals, but according to extant empirical evidence, relationships constantly and simultaneously form at different levels (Doney and Cannon 1997; Palmatier et al. 2007). These unique, simultaneous relationships with various targets in turn exert specific and distinct effects on the firm's performance (Palmatier et al. 2007).

Finally, descriptions of relationship marketing often highlight its promise for creating "win–win" outcomes. Such language may come to seem unrealistically altruistic and "contradict the fact that the profit motive [is] still a principal business driver" (Egan 2004, p. 23). But in practice, for it to persist and support long-term performance goals, relationship marketing must provide benefits for both parties. Its success demands consideration of both parties' outcomes, not just those achieved by the entity that initiates the relationship (e.g., seller), even if one party's benefits might be solely social. Despite this clear and required feature of relationship marketing, many assessments and measures adopt the single perspective of the initiator, which adopts relationship marketing explicitly to achieve its goals. The unidirectional perspective can be beneficial, in that it reveals whether the actual practice of relationship marketing remains consistent with the underlying motivations that drove the partners to engage in the first place. For example, seller firms often measure the returns on their investments (ROI) in relationship marketing, and though they might include any new value generated for customers in these metrics, they do so mainly to determine whether their relationship marketing program is sufficiently effective. Moreover, the recognition that all relationships may enter a termination stage entails to some extent the use of a unidimensional perspective: A seller will need to terminate relationships on which it continues to lose money, even if they provide the linked customers with value. That is, even in the "win–win" context of relationship marketing, with its pursuit of value cocreation through cooperation, rejection of transactional exploitation, and long-term perspective, each party ultimately must achieve its profit goals, and unprofitable relationships will not often continue in business exchanges.

Table 1.1  Summary and Analysis of Relationship Marketing Definitions

| Citation | Definition | Stage | | | | Target/Scope | | Locus of Benefits | |
|---|---|---|---|---|---|---|---|---|---|
| | | Identifying | Developing | Maintaining | Terminating | Customer Only | All | Implementer | Bilateral |
| Berry (1983, p. 25) | "Attracting, maintaining, and—in multi-service organizations—enhancing customer relationships" | x | x | x | | x | | | |
| Morgan and Hunt (1994, p. 22) | "Relationship marketing refers to all marketing activities directed toward establishing, developing, and maintaining successful relational exchanges." | x | x | x | | | x | | x |
| Gronroos (1997, p. 407) | "[P]rocess of identifying and establishing, maintaining, enhancing, and when necessary terminating relationships with customers and other stakeholders, at a profit, so that the objectives of all parties involved are met, where this is done by a mutual giving and fulfillment of promises." | x | x | x | x | | x | x | x |
| Sheth and Parvatiyar (2000, p. 9) | "Relationship marketing is the ongoing process of engaging in cooperative and collaborative activities and programs with immediate and end-user customers to create or enhance mutual economic value at reduced cost." | x | x | | | x | | | x |
| Palmatier (2008, p. 5) | "Relationship marketing is the process of identifying, developing, maintaining, and terminating relational exchanges with the purpose of enhancing performance." | x | x | x | x | | x | x | |

Source: Adapted from Palmatier (2008, pp. 6–7).

### Distinguishing Relationship Marketing From Other Marketing Domains

As the previous discussion should make clear, relationship marketing overlaps somewhat with various other marketing domains and areas; in these related fields, academics study similar antecedents and outcomes. Yet important distinctions also arise when we compare the focus of relationship marketing strategies with the foci of other established marketing strategies.

For example, consider how relationship marketing and branding strategies overlap. Both relationships and brands are critical sources of intangible, market-based assets that can be leveraged to achieve superior financial performance (Srivastava, Shervani, and Fahey 1998). But brand equity refers to the differential effect of brand knowledge on customer actions, such that customers behave more favorably toward a product when they can identify its brand (Keller 1993). In this sense, brand equity may be "a fundamentally product-centered concept" that does not fully capture the drivers of customer behavior (Rust, Lemon, and Zeithaml 2004, p. 110). Thus, even if relationship marketing and branding activities both seek to build intangible assets that can encourage customer loyalty or purchase behaviors at lower costs, they differ fundamentally in their *unit of analysis*. Branding focuses on *products* (*i.e., product-centric*), with extensions to the firm; relationship marketing focuses on *customers* (*i.e., customer-centric*) and their extensions to the firm. This distinction at the core level of products versus customers thus appears clear, but as customers develop their attitudes toward and beliefs about the firm, these distinct impacts become more difficult to separate. The overall customer equity that results reflects both brand equity and relationship equity (as well as offering equity, of course). Their relative importance in turn depends on the context or the perspective. If a survey asks a customer to indicate his or her "trust in a firm," it might evoke both product- and relationship-based trust, for example. To differentiate the effects of brands and relationships pragmatically, we would need to identify specifically which constructs were being measured and their focal referent. With its focus on the relationship (not product), relationship marketing uniquely entails measuring relational characteristics such as relational trust, commitment, reciprocity norms, cooperation, or conflict.

Another comparison involves promotional marketing. The tactics and instruments employed may be similar (e.g., providing price concessions in a financial relationship marketing program or a promotional campaign), yet relationship marketing and promotional strategies differ in their *orientations*. By definition, relationship marketing takes a *long-term, relational orientation*, aimed at retaining a customer and stimulating repeated transactions that ultimately ensure greater customer lifetime value. Promotional marketing strategies instead reflect companies' efforts to spark consumers' interest in and purchase of a focal product rather than competitors' products, often to increase their market share (Wierenga and Soethoudt 2010). The focus is on attracting and acquiring prospective customers to stimulate their discrete transactions with the firm. Such promotional marketing strategies are characterized by their *short-term, transactional orientation.*

---

**Example 1.2  Amazon (USA)**

E-commerce giant Amazon invests in both relationship and promotional marketing. For example, Amazon introduced its Amazon Prime program to continuously provide recurring customers with convenient benefits of shopping at Amazon. In contrast, the firm uses online promotions to attract and acquire prospective customers and to stimulate and accelerate discrete transactions. As an example, Amazon offers special deals and promotions on Cyber Monday as an online counterpart to traditional offline retailers' Black Friday. Combining both instruments and enhancing Prime members' exclusivity and status feelings, Amazon gives their loyalty program members a 30-minute early access to Cyber Monday deals.

Source: Amazon (2018).

---

Finally, relationship marketing shares commonalities with services marketing, business-to-business marketing, and channel marketing, but distinctions also exist. For example, service, business-to-business, and channel marketing each reflect a specific focus on improving performance in unique contexts with distinct features (e.g., intangible services, exchanges between firms, channel members), whereas relationship marketing seeks to improve performance by changing all sorts of relationships, which take place in many different contexts. A meta-analysis of more than 38,000 marketing relationships shows that building strong links is more effective, in terms of improving performance, for services than for product offerings, in business-to-business (B2B) versus business-to-consumer (B2C) markets, and for channel partners rather than direct customers (Palmatier et al. 2006). As should come as no surprise, research and practice in services, B2B, and channels contexts thus tend to include relational constructs. We also note that early services research provides the foundations for many key relationship marketing concepts (Berry 1983; Berry 1995).

## Evolution of Relationship Marketing Terminology

Since its emergence as a separate academic domain in the 1980s, relationship marketing has spread and grown into an umbrella term for various concepts, strategies, and instruments that companies leverage in their efforts to strengthen, build, grow, and maintain successful relationships with customers. Figure 1.2 depicts the evolution of relationship marketing terminology, as used in marketing literature. In particular, customer loyalty, customer relationship management, loyalty programs, customer centricity, customer engagement, and customer experience represent relevant terms employed to denote aliases, subcomponents, or specific facets of relationship marketing.

The concept of customer loyalty, often referred to as brand loyalty before the 1990s, is older than the relationship marketing concept itself. **Customer loyalty** is "a collection of attitudes aligned with a series of purchase behaviors that systematically favor one entity over competing entities," which enhances relationship performance (Watson et al. 2015, p. 803). Customers that offer a seller loyalty engage in a limited search for alternatives, rebuy without soliciting competitive bids, and disclose competitive quotes so the favored company can have the final opportunity to win their business (i.e., last look). Increased customer loyalty represents one of the most valued and anticipated relational outcomes of relationship marketing efforts because of its strong positive effects on financial performance (Jacoby and Chestnut 1978; Oliver 1999; Watson et al. 2015).

The term "customer relationship management" emerged from IT vendor and practitioner communities in the mid-1990s (Payne and Frow

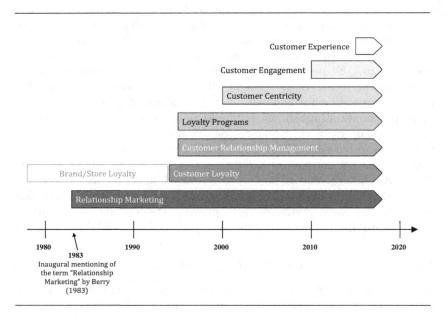

*Figure 1.2* Evolution of Relationship Marketing Terminology

2005). Although often used interchangeably (Parvatiyar and Sheth 2001; Payne and Frow 2005), this term actually tends to be a more focused, narrowly defined term, rather than the broad, holistic concept of relationship marketing. A synthesis of extant literature suggests a definition of **customer relationship management** as a subcomponent of relationship marketing that seeks to develop "appropriate relationships with key customers and customer segments," "unites the potential of relationship marketing strategies and IT," and focuses on tactical issues through the "integration of process, people, operations, and marketing capabilities that is enabled through information, technology, and applications" (Payne and Frow 2005, p. 168). In a sense, then, customer relationship management is the application of relationship marketing by managers across the organization using IT tools to ensure a persistent focus on customers and attain performance objectives.

Another tool for relationship marketing is loyalty programs. Employed by firms in diverse industries, such as retailing, travel and hospitality, and financial services, these programs count 3.8 billion members in the United States alone. The average household subscribes to more than 30 different programs; companies spend $48 billion annually to manage them (Fruend 2017; Gordon and Hlavinka 2011). Noting their ubiquity in practice, academic research on loyalty programs also has gained traction since the mid-1990s (Dowling and Uncles 1997). From this research stream, we derive a definition of **loyalty programs** as encompassing any institutionalized incentive system that attempts to enhance customers' attitudes and behaviors over time; they take myriad formats, such as bonus points, gifts, tiered service levels, or dedicated support (Henderson, Beck, and Palmatier 2011; O'Brien and Jones 1995).

The notion of customer centricity, throughout the organization, arose in literature published in the 2000s (Lemon and Verhoef 2016; Sheth, Sisodia, and Sharma 2000). **Customer centricity** refers to "a holistic organizational mindset or strategic approach that centers on understanding and delivering value to individual customers rather than mass or target markets" (Lemon and Verhoef 2016, p. 73). Regarding customer centricity as a managerial goal or customer perception about how well the firm manages to make customers the focus of the organization's overall behavior implies that it can be an effective relationship marketing strategy.

Emerging and gaining widespread reception only in the early 2010s, the customer engagement construct broadens the scope of relationship marketing–relevant customer behaviors, in response to developments of marketing relationships in the digital age. Capturing "a customer's voluntary resource contribution to a firm's marketing function, going beyond financial patronage," **customer engagement** subsumes a multitude of customer behaviors beyond purchase that benefit the company (Harmeling et al. 2017, p. 316). It thus represents a performance-relevant behavioral relational mechanism. A prominent type of engagement behavior is providing word-of-mouth or referrals. In the digital age, the reduced cost, increased availability, and widespread use of online referrals combine to make such behavior even more significant for firms.

Finally, the most recent entry into this list of related terms is **customer experience**, which is "a multidimensional construct focusing on a customer's cognitive, emotional, behavioral, sensorial, and social responses to a firm's offerings during the customer's entire [customer] journey," such that this new relational mechanism mediates the performance impacts of relationship marketing (Lemon and Verhoef 2016, p. 71). Its recent popularity results from recognition of the increasingly complex customer journey, in which customers face a multitude of new channels they can use to purchase or engage with the firm, often through technology-mediated interfaces. For relationship marketers, it has become increasingly important to ensure that the diverse touchpoints act in concert to provide a comprehensive and seamless customer experience throughout the entire relationship.

## Key Trends Increasing the Importance of Relationship Marketing

Instead of attaining maturity and staying stable, relationship marketing is undergoing a modern surge, shifting the very meaning of marketing. The convergence of multiple trends and drivers in global business has meant that strong customer–seller relationships are increasingly critical, especially relative to other marketing mix factors. We outline six key developments that contribute to the ascending relevance of companies' relationship marketing efforts.

### Transition to Service-Based Economies

Relationships are more relevant in service sectors, and in many developed countries, the economies are predominantly based on services. For example, services represent approximately 85% of the U.S. economy (Fang, Palmatier, and Steenkamp 2008). Because services often are produced and delivered by the same organization, the "middleman" disappears, so the bonds between producer and consumer are direct and close. In addition, services are more intangible, less consistent, more perishable, and harder to evaluate than products, so customers and sellers' boundary-spanning personnel already tend to be more involved in their production and consumption, sometimes even engaging in coproduction (Zeithaml, Parasuraman, and Berry 1985). These close interactions make high-quality customer–seller relationships critical for services; the intangibility of these offerings also makes the benefits of trust more important (Palmatier et al. 2006). Thus, when economies transition from product- to service-based designs, customer–seller relationships develop (fewer middlemen, more interaction) and become more important to customers (reduced risk, need for cooperation).

### Faster Product Commoditization

Advances in production technology are both a boon and a bane for manufacturers. Global competition and transparency and the increasing accessibility of production technologies have accelerated product life cycles, such that the velocity with which a product moves from launch to maturity is extreme. Generally, companies also compete in contexts that demand very high product standards. As the overall quality of objective product attributes increases, products grow more similar; according to product life cycle theory, as product categories mature, they become more susceptible to commoditization (Quelch 2007). When differentiated products transform into commodities, they offer smaller margins and suffer fiercer competition, particularly on price, which represents a strategic challenge for managers. Consider the grocery industry as an example. Private-label shares have jumped in recent years, such that they account for 45% of sales in both the U.K. and German grocery markets (PLMA 2017). Consumers perceive the objective quality of private-label products as fully comparable to that of national brands, so the latter have a hard time convincing them to pay price premiums to obtain their brands. Achieving sustainable competitive advantages solely by leveraging product features thus represents a rare exception rather than the rule. In both B2B and B2C realms, services must accompany the core product to appeal to customers, meaning that strong relationships become key to establishing and securing sustainable competitive advantages.

---

**Example 1.3  Michelin (France)**

Michelin is a global leader in the tire industry. In 2000, due to commoditization pressures, the company launched Michelin Fleet Solutions (MFS), a comprehensive tire management solution offer targeted to large European transportation firms. MFS provided customers with three- to five-year agreements for their fleets of vehicles including several benefits such as improved cost control, fewer breakdowns, and less administration. Switching their business model from selling tires to selling kilometers represents a substantial strategic shift for the company. The formerly strongly product-driven firm in part became a provider of services and solutions, bearing potential for Michelin to differentiate from its competitors in the tire industry and stimulate long-lasting relationships with its customers.

Source: Ulaga, Dalsace, and Renault (2010).

---

## Global Competition

Improvements to communication and logistics technology and capabilities support transactions between producers and consumers at greater distances; in effect, they duplicate pre-industrial local bazaars on a global level. In such worldwide markets, facilitated through technological advancements, information about companies, products, and prices is publicly available and accessible to customers, which enhances market transparency and comparability—and thus global competition. Data availability also has considerably lowered customers' search costs and empowered them to compare companies and find the best value and most suitable relational partner. Considering this global-scale transparency and comparability of company information, managers must work harder to distill and communicate their value proposition clearly to stand out in the competitive landscape. In particular, increased global competition, higher customer churn rates (especially for commodities), and transparent prices across various markets all combine to require firms to concentrate on customer retention and loyalty. Sellers need to develop non–price-based strategies to make customers loyal and willing to pay premium prices—or at least not demand price cuts. The higher costs of acquiring, compared with retaining, customers also reinforce loyalty-building strategies, and relationship marketing programs are primary tools to support such goals. In B2B markets, initiatives such as total quality management (TQM) and closer relationships with suppliers in new product or service development teams also have increased firms' drive to build long-lasting bonds with partners (Sheth and Parvatiyar 1995).

---

**Example 1.4  Personal Computer Manufacturers**

Looking at the global market shares of PC vendors, U.S. manufacturers HP, Dell, and Apple are facing strong competition from Asian competitors Lenovo (China), Asus (Taiwan), and Acer (Taiwan). In 2013, Chinese PC vendor Lenovo (18.1% unit market share) surpassed HP (16.4%) as the top PC vendor worldwide for the first time and kept its leading position until 2017, when HP (22.5% versus 22.0% of Lenovo) took over again.

Sources: Gartner (2018); Gartner (2014b).

---

## Emerging Markets

In parallel with this global competition, sellers must serve markets and customers on a global scale to enhance their business performance. In 2014, the 500 firms listed by Standard & Poor's reported that one-third of their aggregate revenue came from selling in foreign markets (Ro 2015). Companies in mature, developed markets in particular are working to increase the proportions of their overall business that come from "emerging markets [that] evolve from the periphery to the core of marketing practice" (Sheth 2011, p. 166). Such markets, and the BRIC (Brazil, Russia, India, and China) nations in particular, are experiencing explosive growth. The four BRIC nations already account for 40% of the world's population (more than 2.8 billion people) and cover more than 25% of the planet (Global Sherpa 2018). And they continue to grow, in both population and per capita income, leading to vastly increased purchasing power for the consumers in these countries. By 2030, the four BRICs together may account for 36% of the world's gross domestic product (GDP) and 41% of the world's market capitalization (Moe, Maasry, and Tang 2010).

China is the biggest BRIC country, with staggering economic growth rates. Its 2010 GDP of $6 trillion and equity market capitalization of $5 trillion are estimated to grow substantially until 2030, to a GDP of $32 trillion and an equity market capitalization of $41 trillion, respectively. As a result, by 2030, China could surpass the United States (2010 GDP: $15 trillion, estimated 2030 GDP: $23 trillion; 2010 equity market capitalization: $14 trillion, estimated 2030 equity market capitalization $34 trillion) as the world's biggest economy and the largest individual equity market globally (Moe, Maasry, and Tang 2010). Already China leads the world in e-commerce revenues and smartphone penetration rates (Statista 2018a; Statista 2018b). Such trends suggest the massive opportunities in emerging markets for companies that adopt relationship marketing strategies. According to one meta-analysis of international relationship marketing research, these strategies are much more effective outside the United States (Samaha, Beck, and Palmatier 2014). In particular, customers in emerging markets appear substantially more receptive to companies' relationship marketing efforts, so the relationships are more effective for increasing business performance. Compared with the United States, they are 28% more effective in Brazil, 20% more in Russia, 71% more in India, and 100% more effective in China.

---

**Example 1.5 Daimler (Germany)**

For German automobile manufacturer Daimler, BRIC countries represent major growth markets for its truck business. In particular, Russia, India, and China exhibit rapidly growing demand for high-quality yet cost-effective trucks. According to company estimates, by 2020, these three emerging economies are expected to account for over 50% of the worldwide market for medium- and heavy-duty trucks. To penetrate the Russian, Indian, and Chinese markets, Daimler is using strategic partnerships, such as a joint venture with Chinese automobile company Foton.

Source: Daimler (2012).

## Aging Populations

In most developed countries, birth rates have been decreasing at the same time that advances in medical science have increased people's life expectancy. These trends lead to shrinking populations and aging societies, as reflected in countries' median ages. For example, Germany's median age is 46.8 years; Japan's is 46.9 years (CIA 2018). By 2030, the cohort of Japanese people younger than 50 years is expected to decrease by 26%. At around the same time, the adult population in the United States likely will reach the median age of 50 years. These middle-aged consumers in turn will impose their values and perspectives on the national psyche, as well as shift their purchasing and demands toward services and products that address older consumers. This group of "Silver Agers" or "Generation Gold" represents an attractive and potentially profitable segment for marketers, with strong purchasing power and a proneness to engage in loyal relationships. Compared with younger consumers (e.g., digital natives, Generations Y and Z), older generations (e.g., Generation X, baby boomers) are less familiar with digital technologies, tend to be more skeptical about using them (e.g., purchasing online, communicating with a chatbot), perceive them as more difficult to use, and express greater privacy concerns (Goldfarb and Tucker 2013). To win over such consumers, systematic relationship marketing efforts can build trust, signal expertise, and reduce privacy threats. For example, assigning a dedicated, human salesperson or service employee to communicate with and support older customers may be highly effective. Investing relationship marketing resources to appeal to older customers thus might be more effective than trust-building efforts for younger customers, who already feel comfortable with technology-mediated company interactions.

---

### Example 1.6 CareLinx (USA)

Aging populations unleash a lot of potential in the health care industry. CareLinx, a California-based startup, operates a platform to serve the $100 billion-plus in-home care service market. Through the platform, CareLinx connects people in search of in-home care with nursing assistants, medical assistants, or nurses. Circumventing traditional "middleman" agencies enables people seeking help with aging parents or disabled family members to save money and health care professionals to increase their earnings. Families paying invoices through the platform are charged a 15% service fee by CareLinx, covering the cost of time tracking, secure online payment processing, and payroll tax services. Plus, the firm offers a family adviser to support families as they navigate the process of hiring a private caregiver. To secure the quality of the health care service provision for both parties involved (i.e., patients and caregivers), the platform also runs background checks on caregivers and provides professional liability insurance (e.g., property damage and bodily injury).

Source: DesMarais (2014).

---

## Advertising Saturation

People's expectations of company communications also have been changing. In the past, marketing communication was equated with advertising; advertising basically meant mass communication. Marketers used television, radio, or print media to transmit their messages—typically focused on product and price—to a broad audience of consumers, ignoring their heterogeneity. Such communication is one-way, from the seller to the customer. The proliferation of online advertising channels (e.g., e-mail, display banners on webpages, Facebook, Google, mobile in-app) instead has facilitated two-way communications, such that firms can track customers' response to their marketing efforts (e.g., click-through rates). But it also had increased the clutter, such that an average U.S. consumer today may be exposed to 10,000 advertisements daily (Marshall 2015). Such advertising saturation can impede marketing effectiveness; for example, responses to traditional direct mail have plunged by 25% in the past decade, and even if it still outperforms e-mail (4.4% versus .12% average response rates), its cost effectiveness and return on investment remain poor (ROI = $7.00 for direct mail, $28.50 for e-mail) (Direct Marketing News 2012). As this example indicates, many advertising approaches simply fail to resonate with modern consumers, who are sophisticated, informed, and knowledgeable and demand that firms address their diverse, individual needs instead of forcing them to accept a one-size-fits-all solution. Communicating with customers as relational partners and identifying and speaking to their individual preferences is exactly where relationship marketing comes in. Using customized approaches to target individual customers with relevant content and value-added offerings is a purposeful strategy for benefitting from people's sense of advertising saturation.

## The Digital Age: The Mega-Trend Increasing the Importance of Relationship Marketing

A mega-trend, overriding and facilitating the developments we discussed in the previous section, can be captured by the **digital age**, defined as "the present time, when most information is in a digital form, especially when compared to the time when computers were not used" (Cambridge Dictionary 2018). At first glance, digitalization seemingly has led to systematic desocialization, as we shift from human-to-human social interactions to digital, electronic, and impersonal interactions, mediated by technology. Nevertheless—or perhaps more accurately, because of that shift—nurturing marketing relationships and managing customers is more critical than ever before.

### Evolution of the Digital Age

The digital age has advanced in parallel with technological developments, from Web 1.0 to Web 4.0. Table 1.2 details four major milestones and what they have implied for sellers, customers, and their relationships.

Table 1.2 Evolution of the Digital Age and Implications for Sellers and Customers

| Developmental Milestone (Era) | Major Technological Advancements | Implications for Sellers | Implications for Customers |
|---|---|---|---|
| Web 1.0 (1990s) | World Wide Web, e-commerce | Companies can communicate with and sell to customers through multiple offline, online, and mobile channels (e.g., offline stores, online web shops, telephone-based customer hotlines, apps). | Customers are connected to the Internet most of the time. They carry and regularly use various devices, such as their smartphones, which have become key companions in their daily lives. |
| Web 2.0 (early to mid-2000s) | Social media | Companies can use social media to place contents and interact with consumers and customers. However, firms have no control over content distributed by customers. | Customers can use social media to interact and communicate with other customers and with companies. Customers are empowered to spread their opinions to a large audience (i.e., shift in the balance of power between companies and customers). |
| Web 3.0 (late 2000s to mid-2010s) | Smartphones and mobile apps, Internet of Things (IoT), big data | Through mobile apps, sellers can stay "close" to their customers at all times and issue personalized offers that reflect what the customer is doing at any particular point in time. By leveraging the IoT, sellers can prompt consumers to (re)purchase additional products and services for their IoT-enabled objects (e.g., washing machines, cars). The vast amount of information collected on customers can help companies learn how best to serve them. Too often, companies lack the resources and competencies required for data storage and analysis, so they cannot effectively make use of their big data to improve their relationship marketing efforts. | Through constant uses of mobile apps, households filled with technology-enabled objects, and big data collection efforts, customers and their behaviors become much more transparent and traceable for companies. This outcome may allow customers to receive better (i.e., more customized, better fitting) communications and offers from firms, but it also may prompt customers' privacy concerns and sense of intrusion. |

| Web 4.0 (since mid-2010s) | Artificial intelligence, augmented reality | Companies can employ artificial intelligence to automate service delivery and thus substitute for frontline employees (e.g., self-service machines, service robots). Augmented-reality applications help marketers mitigate some of the sensory disadvantages that customers face online, such as by helping them visualize how specific product offerings will fit into their personal environment. | Customers can conveniently consult artificial intelligence applications on demand for assistance. Augmented-reality tools can facilitate customers' decision-making process, for example by letting them virtually "try out" products, which should promote their perceptions of control and ownership. |

Source: Adapted from Steinhoff et al. (2018).

*Web 1.0*

**Web 1.0** refers to the implementation and dissemination of the World Wide Web and the spread of e-commerce during the 1990s. In 1990, the U.S. National Science Foundation decided to make the Internet usable for commercial purposes, and Tim Berners-Lee laid the foundation for the World Wide Web. The Internet has been among the most significant developments in information technology, in line with the invention of letterpress printing in the 15th century; the German Federal Supreme Court has declared access to the Internet a central and inevitable part of people's daily lives (Bundesgerichtshof 2013). In addition, the number of Internet users rises every day. In 2017, 3.9 billion people, more than half the world's population, used the Internet; in North America and Europe, respectively, 88% (320.1 million people) and 80% (659.6 million people) of the populations function online (Internet World Stats 2018). Starting with desktop personal computers, Internet technology today has spread to a multitude of electronic devices, such as laptops, tablets, smartphones, smart televisions, electrical appliances, and wearables (i.e., the Internet of Things) (see the Web 3.0).

For companies, the spread of Internet technology also revolutionized the way of doing business, particularly by multiplying the channels they could use. Firms communicate with and sell to customers through various offline, online, and mobile channels, but global e-commerce sales of products and services purchased using the Internet have reached US$2.3 trillion, accounting for 10.1% of overall retail sales (Statista 2018c). By 2020, they likely will grow to US$3.88 trillion and account for 14.6% of total retail sales (eMarketer 2017a). Desktop personal computers and laptops still are popular routes for online shopping, but mobile devices are catching up quickly; in some emerging markets like China, mobile phone shopping even surpasses other channels (Statista 2018d; Statista 2018e). That is, mobile shopping accounts for more than 80% of overall online purchases in China (China Internet Watch 2017), driven largely by the vastly popular and incessantly growing mobile app WeChat, with its 800 million monthly active users, 34% of whom spend at least $72 per month by transacting through the app (eShop World 2018). Chinese consumers largely skipped several steps in the path that people in developed economies traditionally followed, from physical stores to personal computers to laptops to mobile devices (i.e., tablets, smartphones); they just started using their smartphones as shopping devices, because this channel became available at around the same time that their economy was developing to the point that consumers had substantial purchasing power (Marketing to China 2017).

---

**Example 1.7  Alibaba Group (China)**

With close to 500 million active users in 2017, the Alibaba Group claims about 80% of all online Chinese retail sales. During its annual Singles Day promotional event in November of 2017, the company generated US$25.3 billion in product sales, thereby largely outnumbering Cyber Monday online sales in the U.S. (i.e., US$3.45 billion). A portfolio of three e-commerce platforms where Alibaba acts as a middleman to bring together different types of buyers and sellers constitutes the group's core. Launched in 1999, Alibaba.com represents a business-to-business trading platform, facilitating international exchanges between buyers and sellers from a wide range of countries, such as China, India, Pakistan, the United States, and Thailand, with international buyers. Taobao.com in turn is a business-to-consumer or consumer-to-consumer portal where small business and individuals can act as online merchants. Opened in 2003, Taobao.com today is China's largest e-commerce website. Tmall.com was launched in 2008. It represents an online store offering a wide selection of branded products. As such, the website focuses on larger companies as merchants, including multinational brands.

Sources: Blystone (2015); Russell (2017); Statista (2018f).

---

Many customers remain connected to the Internet at virtually all times, carrying and regularly using devices such as their smartphones to manage their personal lives and nurture social relationships, as well as to conduct commercial relations as consumers. Thus companies can interact with customers not just in person, via mail, or by telephone but also through e-mail, apps, and social networks. Already constant companions in many people's lives, smartphones continue to expand, such that worldwide, the number of smartphone users is expected to increase from 2.1 billion in 2016 to around 2.5 billion in 2019 (+19%). More than 36% of the world's entire population is already utilizing smartphones (Statista 2018g). As we have noted, China leads the smartphone revolution, so more than half of its population is using smartphones in 2018 (Statista 2018h).

*Web 2.0*

From the early to mid-2000s, **Web 2.0**, or the social web, proceeded as an important developmental step in the rise of the World Wide Web. While Web 1.0 is often referred to as the "read-only web," Web 2.0 advanced to become a "read and write web," enabling bilateral communication. Hence, Web 2.0 refers to Internet-based, collaborative systems in which the majority of content is produced by users, and users can interact socially beyond local boundaries. Users consume content, but they also generate and exchange that content with other users. Facebook, Instagram, Pinterest, YouTube, Twitter, and Wikipedia are among the most popular social media services, used by 2.46 billion people in 2017 (Statista 2018i). Launched in 2006, Facebook leads the market, with more than 1.94 billion monthly active users around the world (Statista 2018j).

Social media in turn offers an effective tool for companies to market their products and manage their customer relationships. In the United States, 81% of the population has some social media profile (Statista 2018k), so U.S. retailers work to reach them through Facebook pages (operated by 94% of companies), Pinterest accounts (81%), and Twitter entries (79%) (Statista 2018l). Unlike more traditional forms of unidirectional, company-initiated communications, social media strongly encourages and enables bidirectional communication between companies and customers. Customers respond to company-initiated communications, offering instant feedback to firms; companies respond to customer-initiated communications (e.g., queries, complaints), offering customers insights into their performance and relationship marketing efforts.

---

**Example 1.8  Starbucks (USA)**

Starbucks' social media initiative, My Starbucks Idea (MSI), encouraged customers to submit brand- and product-related ideas, develop and discuss others' ideas, and enjoy a sense of an online community. Multiple platforms cross-promoted MSI, including the company website, Facebook, Twitter, Pinterest, and YouTube. During 2008–2012, more than 190,000 ideas were submitted, 300 of which were commercialized (e.g., Skinny Mocha, K-Cups, continuation of the keychain card). Cake pops resulted from customers' requests for small treats, with 5.8 million units sold each year. Ideas (and comments) are published online and voted on by other members of the Starbucks community, and a leaderboard feature encourages participation.

Sources: Geisel (2015); Tolido (2016); Tsardaloglou (2016).

---

On average, U.S. users spend 323 minutes each week on social media (Statista 2018m). Beyond interacting with family or friends, they engage in talking about companies, whether their interactions involve other customers or the firms themselves. By exponentially expanding the reach of word-of-mouth communications, social media have empowered customers to spread their positive (e.g., through fan communities) and negative (e.g., by initiating a "shit storm") opinions about a company to a vast and global audience.

## Web 3.0

Emerging in the late 2000s and mid-2010s, **Web 3.0**, or the semantic web, introduced smartphones and mobile apps, the Internet of Things (IoT), and big data. In this semantic web, computers can communicate with one another, as well as analyze and semantically connect data from diverse sources. Since the launch of the first iPhone in 2007, smartphones have become mass-market products. We already described their ubiquity (see the Web 1.0 section); in addition, the expansion of smartphone usage created the new market of mobile apps, which today account for 80% of Internet users' access time (Arora, Hofstede, and Mahajan 2017). In January 2017, Apple's App Store offered 2.2 million apps for download (Statista 2018n), and by 2021, worldwide app revenue is forecasted to reach $139 billion.

---

### Example 1.9  Airbnb (USA)

Airbnb launched its app in 2012. It is used by 50% of hosts, enabling instantaneous communication and increasing the speed of bookings (by 8 times). By 2014, Airbnb totaled 10 million guests (up from 4 million in 2012) and 550,000 listings worldwide and was valued at US$10 billion. Integration with users from Craigslist boosted visibility, and customer preference data helped effectively personalize content. These lodging options in turn were 30%–80% cheaper than hotels. Airbnb also leveraged social connections through Facebook Connect, allowing customers to connect with mutual friends who had stayed at specific rentals and search for hosts based on demographics (e.g., university affiliation).

Sources: Brown (2014); Tanasoiu (2017).

---

The IoT also extends Internet technology to physical objects that traditionally have not been connected, such as vehicles and home appliances, equipping them with software and sensors that enable the objects themselves to connect to the Internet, communicate, and exchange data. By 2020, the value of the IoT market is projected to surpass $7 trillion, and the number of IoT devices could reach 25 billion, facilitating both consumers' and businesses' daily operations (Brandt 2014; Spencer 2014).

Due to these advances, staggering amounts of digital data get generated every day, and these big data then can be collected with unprecedented volume, velocity, and variety. Internet users leave digital footprints, such that their diverse online behaviors can be tracked and aggregated to learn detailed information about each user. Today, the worldwide data volume is 16.1 zettabytes; by 2025, it will increase by a factor of 10–163 zettabytes (Statista 2018o). The challenge is that big data are so complex and unstructured that they are difficult to analyze manually using conventional methods.

For relationship marketers, each of these Web 3.0 features is relevant. For example, if they can communicate through mobile apps, they can stay "close" and available to their customers at all times and issue personalized offers that reflect what the customer is doing at any particular point in time. By leveraging the IoT, sellers can prompt consumers to repurchase household items, such as when an IoT-enabled washing machine sends them a message that it needs more detergent; they can also increase sales of services, such as when an IoT-enabled car tells its driver that its tires need realigning. The vast amount of information collected about customers also can help companies learn how to serve them, which in turn can produce productivity and profit gains of 5%–6% over competitors that fail to make use of such information (Biesdorf, Court, and Willmott 2013). Even as firms spend an estimated $36 billion annually to collect and analyze customer data though (Columbus 2014), they often lack the data storage and analysis resources and competencies needed to use big data to the benefit of their relationship marketing efforts. In response, the technology solutions market is exploding—between 2011 and 2017, the number of solution providers grew from just 150 to more than 7,000 (Brinker 2018). Famous names such as Adobe, Google, IBM, Microsoft, Oracle, Salesforce, and SAP offer a variety of software-enabled tools to help companies manage their big data and enhance their relationship marketing efforts.

For consumers, Web 3.0 has both positive and negative implications. In particular, in an environment characterized by nearly constant uses of mobile apps, households filled with technology-enabled objects, and big data collection efforts, customers and their behaviors are far more transparent and traceable by companies. Helpfully, customers may receive better (i.e., more customized, better fitting) communications and offers from firms, which would increase their perceptions of the value of the relationship. Unhelpfully, customers may experience privacy concerns when marketers intrude too much into their lives, leading them to terminate or limit the relationships, especially if the companies fail to offer transparent data policies or suffer data breaches (Martin, Borah, and Palmatier 2017).

## Web 4.0

Finally, **Web 4.0** adds artificial intelligence and augmented reality as major technological advances. Machines and devices equipped with artificial intelligence can mimic the cognitive functions typically associated with human minds, such as learning and problem solving. They perceive and interpret their environment using a net of semantic linkages, then take action accordingly. The benefits of such assistance have led people to adopt artificial intelligence into their daily lives already, in applications such as virtual personal assistants (e.g., Apple's Siri, Amazon's Alexa, Google Now, Microsoft's Cortana), video games (e.g., Warner's "Middle Earth: Shadow of Mordor"), smart cars (e.g., Google's self-driving car project, Tesla's autopilot feature), online customer support, music and movie recommendation services (e.g., Spotify, Netflix), and smart-home devices. By 2017, 60.5 million U.S. consumers had added Siri, Alexa, or another virtual assistant to their homes, representing an increase of 23.1% from the previous year (eMarketer 2017b). Augmented reality instead relies on interactive technological interfaces to modify physical environments, such as by superimposing multimodal digital elements to appeal to a range of human sensory inputs (Javornik 2016). Related efforts to enhance customer experiences are predicted to prompt investments of more than $2.5 billion by 2018 (ABI Research 2013).

---

**Example 1.10  IKEA (Sweden)**

For a long time, it has been hard to imagine how to buy furniture without going to a physical store to see and try different products. By means of augmented-reality technology, Swedish furniture company IKEA is trying to change this. In 2017, the firm introduced its IKEA Place app, empowering customers to virtually place furniture inside their homes. According to IKEA, the app, which has been developed in cooperation with Apple, automatically scales products in real-world settings with 98% accuracy. Customers using IKEA Place can also share photos and videos of their virtually placed furniture with family and friends.

Source: Recchia (2018).

---

For companies, the use of artificial intelligence technologies promises to overhaul their service provision methods. It can automate certain service delivery processes, which may reduce the number of frontline employees, or even eliminate the need for customer-facing staff altogether. Self-service machines, such as check-in terminals at airports, and service robots, such as customer hotline virtual assistants, already have replaced some human interactions. With augmented reality applications, marketers also can mitigate some of the sensory disadvantages that customers face online, such as by helping them visualize how specific product offerings will fit into their personal environment (Hilken et al. 2017).

For customers, artificial intelligence applications should make life more convenient. Even if no customer manager or service representative is available (e.g., late at night), customers can consult with automated, artificial intelligence systems and receive assistance on demand. However, problems may arise if these systems are not sufficiently advanced or technically mature. If artificial intelligence cannot solve the customer's problem, severe frustration is likely to result, possibly growing into a service failure that the firm must find a way to recover from quickly. With regard to augmented reality, the tools can facilitate customers' decision-making process by layering virtual images and content on depictions of a person, product, or background, which should promote their perceptions of control and ownership (Javornik 2016).

### Characteristics of Customer–Seller Relationships in the Digital Age

To understand how customer–seller relationships have evolved and continue to do so in the digital age, we provide a contrast of relationships prevalent in the digital age, which are largely mediated by technology, with relationships as they looked in the predigital age. Table 1.3 synthesizes six characteristics and their specifications for the digital and predigital ages, reflecting two ends of a relationship continuum. In practice, of course, many customer–seller relationships fall somewhere in between these extreme ends of the continuum and represent hybrid relationships relying on a combination of both online and offline interactions.

First, relationship distance varies in these two eras. In offline, predigital relationships, the partners had to be geographically close to interact, which enabled them to participate in rich, face-to-face communication that strongly nurtured relational ties. A customer needed to pay an actual visit to the local supermarket to get ingredients for lunch, but in so doing, this customer could get to know the staffer behind the deli counter and enjoy relationship benefits, such as receiving service before others. In contrast, geographic distance is a common feature of relationships in the digital age, because global customers obtain products and services from companies located around the world. Because they never even consider meeting face to face, their lean communication offers few relationship cues, and customers might never actually identify the employee providing them with the service (Benedicktus et al. 2010). Ordering groceries online and having them delivered thus is more impersonal, and these interactions inevitably are mediated by Internet technology.

Second, the channels through which relationships take place have grown considerably. In the past, companies had to take advantage of face-to-face encounters or communicate using mass-media marketing tools to reach consumers. In the digital age, customer–seller relationships span a vast omnichannel environment, comprising face-to-face, telephone, mail, websites, e-mail, social media, and mobile app channels. With an omnichannel perspective, digital-age firms seek to align and manage "the numerous available channels and customer touchpoints, in such a way that the customer experience across channels and the performance over channels is optimized" (Verhoef, Kannan, and Inman 2015, p. 176). In

Table 1.3 Relationship Differences: Digital Versus Predigital Ages

| Relational Characteristics | Digital Age | Predigital Age |
|---|---|---|
| Geographic distance | **Distant:** Online relational partners can be anywhere in the world, and communication is leaner with limited visual and nonverbal cues: "The online environment tends to eliminate cues that customers might otherwise use to assess the trustworthiness of a firm. The lack of tangible cues and personal interaction are typical of online shopping and represent a critical challenge for online retailers" (Benedicktus et al. 2010, p. 324). | **Close:** Offline relational partners are typically geographically close, which supports richer face-to-face communication, especially during the relationship formation stage: "Communication literature emphasizes the importance of nonverbal cues in driving the interaction between people and it would be reasonable to expect that greater 'richness' in communication would lead to better perceptions, disclosure and relationship formation" (Kotlyar and Ariely 2013, p. 549). |
| Channel sophistication | **Omnichannel:** Relational partners interact through a broad array of channels (e.g., face to face, phone, mail, website, e-mail, social media profiles, mobile apps). Companies need to manage these channels in concert to provide a seamless customer experience and provide customers with the opportunity to tailor their channel usage to their personal taste. | **Single or multichannel:** Relational exchanges between customers and sellers were typically limited to one or a few different channels (e.g., face-to-face, phone, mail). |
| Interaction constraints | **No time constraints:** Interactions between online relational partners are independent from store or office hours. For example, customers may purchase or communicate online 24/7; companies may offer instant responses by automating their interactive processes. | **Time constraints:** Offline relational partners are usually constrained to interacting during store or office hours, as purchasing and communicating typically requires service employees to be available (e.g., in the store, via phone). |

(Continued)

*Table 1.3* (Continued)

| Relational Characteristics | Digital Age | Predigital Age |
|---|---|---|
| Availability of alternatives | **High:** Online, relational partners encounter less dependence on each other. Through the Internet, competition has become global. Customers can easily access and compare information about competitive providers of a certain product or service. Companies can acquire customers worldwide as long as product or service delivery is feasible. | **Limited:** In offline settings, relational partners typically face geographic boundaries, thus limiting the availability of alternatives. A limited number of providers offer a certain product or service. Likewise, firms are typically tied to sourcing customers from a certain geographic area. |
| Anonymity | **High anonymity:** Online relational partners have limited information or certainty regarding the identity of potential online partners. | **Low anonymity:** Offline relational partners typically know the identity (e.g., name, job, education, social status) of potential partners. |
| Data richness | **High:** Usually, in online relationships, customer behavior is traced, collected, and linked by companies in their customer relationship management database. Firms may observe individual click behavior in the online shop, social media behavior, mobile app usage, and so on. | **Mixed:** In offline relationships, customer behavior is not traced automatically at an individual level unless customers are members of a loyalty program, for example. |

turn, customers expect synergy among offline, online, and mobile channels, so that they can achieve a seamless experience that also reflects their precise, individual preferences (Lemon and Verhoef 2016).

Third, the boundaries that limit predigital relationships largely disappear with the increasing availability of interaction channels. That is, in offline relationships, the partners can only interact during business hours, and customers have to wait until a service provider is available. The digital age eliminates these time-based constraints nearly completely. Customers can make purchases whenever they choose when they use online or mobile channels; their communications with firms also can be asynchronous, such that they do not have to wait for the service provider to be on the clock before they make a request. Rather than requiring the sellers and customers to come together at a specific place and time, digital-age interactions are 24/7. In turn, companies seek to foster strong relationships by contacting customers in various settings, apart from their personal interactions during store visits.

Fourth, the meaning and span of competition has changed. Customers in the predigital age purchased from those companies they could reach easily, whether because they were geographically proximal (e.g., neighborhood grocer) or because they offered a catalog channel (e.g., Sears). Thus companies competed specifically with other local sellers or catalog providers. But in the absence of geographic or time constraints, competition has become global, because customers just click to access information about thousands of sellers, located everywhere in the world, promising the same products or services. The substantially greater competition makes it much harder for any one firm to achieve customer loyalty, in which context relationship marketing and its potential benefits become especially important.

Fifth, digital-age relationships tend to feature more anonymity than predigital links. Getting to know the seller even represents a benefit of offline relationships, as our deli counter example suggests; in both B2C and B2B settings, relational partners typically know something about each other (e.g., name, job, education, social status). In addition, the physical servicescape can signal the seller's quality to customers. With their technology-mediated, distant character, digital-age relationships instead can remain largely anonymous (Kozlenkova et al. 2017). Each partner obtains relatively limited information about the other party, and even if information is provided during digital interactions, the credibility of the information is difficult to assess (as in catfishing scams). The anonymity provided by online settings also limits legal sanctions, so either or both parties might hide their traits or create fake identities to take opportunistic advantage of the other party in the relatively impersonal interactions.

Sixth and finally, digital age relationships might be anonymous, but they still produce a wealth of rich data, far more than in the past.

Shopkeepers in the predigital era might have manually collected information about customers' preferences and habits, but such labor- and time-intensive efforts necessarily were limited in scope. Sellers in online and mobile channels instead can leverage the required technology mediation to see where customers go online, with automated systems that track every piece of data that people's behavior produces, whether clicking on an online offering, commenting on a social media post, or logging in to a mobile app. If they then combine and aggregate these rich data, digital age firms can develop extensive, detailed, individual profiles of customers, to which they can apply tailored relationship marketing efforts and offers. As noted, though, privacy concerns cause digital-age customers to consider whether they are willing to give up their personal data to receive personalized offers (Martin and Murphy 2017).

### Using Relationship Marketing to Succeed in the Digital Age

As this comparison of customer–seller relationships in the digital versus predigital ages should make clear, relationship marketing has grown increasingly critical. The human need for relationships is universal, and psychological mechanisms that enable and promote the development of relationships will never disappear (Zhu et al. 2012). More specifically, online relationships appear equally intimate and emotionally rich as relational exchanges encountered offline (Mathwick 2002). As much as any time in human history, modern people seek out relationships to reduce their uncertainty and obtain benefits from trusted resources in exchanges governed by relational norms (Adjei, Noble, and Noble 2010; Palmatier, Dant, and Grewal 2007). In a sense then, the basic premise of relationship marketing is to put into action, strategically and systematically, Peter Drucker's recommendation that firms see the business "from the customer's point of view." We propose that relationship marketing can provide the most substantial and meaningful sustainable competitive advantages for sellers in the digital age.

First, the core competency underlying relationship marketing is seeing customers as equivalent, relational partners rather than just as receivers of marketing messages. In relationship marketing, bilateral communication between the seller and the customer is the norm, not the exception, unlike traditional marketing communication in which firms send communications one way, to customers as recipients. This natural state represents an ideal fit with customers' expectations of digital-age sellers. With their increased knowledge, self-confidence, and power, customers expect and feel entitled to interact with sellers and be treated equally by them. Relationship marketers also are well prepared to embrace the multitude of channels that support bidirectional exchanges. Omnichannel environments and the irrelevance of geographic distance create new relationship marketing opportunities for firms, especially those that might traditionally have relied on their brand, advertising, or promotional strategies (e.g., big consumer firms, software producers). Sellers in digital-age consumer markets can engage directly with end customers (e.g., through social media), without needing middlemen (e.g., retailers). Software firms that previously felt compelled to pursue constant innovation to attract customers can manage their relationships with business and consumer buyers more effectively, such as by marketing software-as-a-service (SaaS) offerings.

Second, relationship marketing allows for personalization and purposeful targeting, rather than one-size-fits-all approaches, and the digital age strongly distinguishes consumers, especially with regard to their technological aptitude and readiness to cope with technological advances. Notably, people born in the digital age, after 1980—who constitute Generation Y/millennials (born 1980–1999) and Generation Z (born 2000–2015)—are digital natives who interact with digital technologies in a natural, self-evident way. Generation Y has been digitally socialized since their teens; Generation Z started to learn to use touchscreens (i.e., smartphones, tablets) as toddlers. People born before 1980, such as the baby boomers (1945–1964) and Generation X (1965–1989), are digital immigrants who did not encounter digital technologies until their adulthood. Relationship marketing already anticipates such heterogeneity, including in the ways people are willing to rely on digital technologies, so firms can better cater to their individual customer preferences. For example, relationship marketing can suggest which options customers find valuable, which then should inform the design of different offline and online communication and purchase channels.

Third, to understand and serve customers, relationship marketers analyze customer data. Specifically, customer relationship management leverages IT to generate deep customer insights, such as reviewing customers' past behavior to predict their future actions or preferences. In the big data era, relationship marketing thus offers both conceptual and analytical means to transform big data into valuable, actionable insights, enhancing the personalization of their relationship marketing efforts. A firm's IT department and data warehouse can benefit from collaborating with relationship marketers, who can offer expert insights into how various data sources should be merged and structured to enable the collected big data to support customer managers' decision making.

Fourth, relationship marketing can build trust in technology-driven and technology-dependent settings. The scope and pace of technological developments in the digital age paired with lagging legal regulation evokes perceptions of increasing complexity and uncertainty, and interactions in technology-mediated settings often are marked by data privacy concerns (Martin and Murphy 2017). Relationship marketers should regard this situation as a great opportunity: They can build trust among these customers by underscoring the company's sincere interest in a long-term relationship rather than discrete transactions. Embodying expertise, communicating clearly with customers (e.g., transparent data privacy policies), and investing resources in the relationship all offer appropriate strategies for enhancing customers' trust and commitment toward a seller. Clearly, then, relationship marketing can contribute unique insights into how to gain and sustain customer trust in a complex, inscrutable digital world.

Fifth, relationship marketing leverages the hardwired human propensity to embrace reciprocity principles. Throughout human history and across cultures, feelings of gratitude and norms of reciprocity have driven human behavior (Emmons 2004; Gouldner 1960). Even online, customers seek communal and emotionally rich relations (Mathwick 2002). Hence, while the digital age might involve impersonal links, geographic distance, and anonymity, reciprocity remains a strong force, as long as it can be activated (Kozlenkova et al. 2017). That is, even on an e-commerce platform, and even when the reciprocal behaviors seem trivial (e.g., following back, clicking "like"), reciprocity improves relationships, compared with unilateral buyer–seller relationships (Kozlenkova et al. 2017), by increasing customers' psychological commitment and purchase behaviors, substantially and with lasting effects. One study even specifies that reciprocal relationships increase sales by $9.93 over unilateral forms: 60% more than buyer ($6.29) and three times more than seller ($3.31) unilateral relationships. Because relationship marketers are experts at tapping into this force, they can spur reciprocal relationships and thereby enhance the firm's performance.

## Summary

Relationships have defined business exchanges ever since Homeric Greece. In 1983, the term "relationship marketing" first appeared in marketing literature. In the past four decades, relationship marketing has emerged as a specific priority for marketing academics and managers, reflected by the explosion of research papers and popular business books. Marketing science and practice concur: Strong customer relationships are vital to company strategy and performance. Because relationship marketing entails identifying, developing, maintaining, and terminating relational exchanges, with the purpose of enhancing performance, it differs from other popular marketing strategies. Compared with branding, promotions, and other such strategic marketing approaches, relationship marketing focuses on customers and exhibits a long-term, relational orientation. The terminology emerging from this field in turn reveals its development and the evolution of its emphases, from customer loyalty to customer relationship management to loyalty programs to customer centricity to customer engagement to customer experience.

This importance of strong customer–seller relationships, relative to other marketing mix factors, also has been augmented by a confluence of trends in global business, including the transition to service-based economies, faster product commoditization, increases in worldwide competition, the enhanced relevance of emerging markets, aging populations, and advertising saturation. But perhaps the most notable development, for which relationship marketing strategies are uniquely well suited, is the digital age. The related advancements and alterations of customer–seller relationships prioritize relationship marketing as an important source of sustainable competitive advantages for firms.

This digital age mega-trend comprises four main eras: Web 1.0 that introduced the World Wide Web and e-commerce; Web 2.0 that brought us social media; Web 3.0 and the emergence of smartphones, mobile apps, the Internet of Things, and big data; and Web 4.0, which promises expanded uses of artificial intelligence and augmented reality. Relationships in this digital age can involve geographically distant relational partners, tend to rely on omnichannel interactions, offer a means to avoid time constraints, must compete with many more available alternatives, allow for a higher degree of anonymity, and take place in data-rich environments. In turn, relationship marketing offers a particularly meaningful strategy in the digital age, for five reasons. First, it requires companies to regard customers as equivalent partners. Second, it features customization and purposeful targeting rather than one-size-fits-all approaches to customers. Third, relationship marketing relies on customer data analyses to understand and better serve customers. Fourth, it offers a trust-building option in technology-driven and technology-mediated environments. Fifth, relationship marketing evokes reciprocity norms.

## Takeaways

- Relationships represent a source of sustainable competitive advantages for firms, along with brands and offerings.
- The shift toward service economies and advancements of the digital age have highlighted the importance of relationship-based sustainable competitive advantages.
- Relationship marketing is "the process of identifying, developing, maintaining, and terminating relational exchanges, with the purpose of enhancing performance."
- Relationship marketing focuses on customers and exhibits a long-term, relational orientation, unlike branding strategies that focus on brands or promotional marketing strategies that feature a short-term, transactional orientation.
- The terminology associated with relationship marketing—customer loyalty, customer relationship management, loyalty programs, customer

centricity, customer engagement, and customer experience—marks major developments in the field.

- A confluence of global trends foster the need for relationships: transitions to service-based economies, faster product commoditization, increased worldwide competition, emerging markets, aging populations, advertising saturation, and the digital age (mega-trend).
- The digital age thus far consists of four major steps: Web 1.0 (World Wide Web, e-commerce), Web 2.0 (social media), Web 3.0 (smartphones, mobile apps, Internet of Things, big data), and Web 4.0 (artificial intelligence, augmented reality).
- Compared with relationships in the predigital age, customer–seller relationships in the digital age feature geographically distant relational partners, omnichannel interactions, a lack of time constraints, competition due to many alternatives, a high degree of anonymity, and a data-rich environment
- Relationship marketing—which perceives customers as partners, seeks to provide customization, relies on data analysis to understand customers, provides trust signals in technology-mediated settings, and can evoke reciprocity principles—offers a particularly meaningful strategy for the digital age.

## References

ABI Research (2013), "Developers to Invest $2.5 Billion in Augmented Reality in 2018; Look for Enterprise to Drive Smart Glasses." Available at: www.abiresearch.com/press/developers-to-invest-25-billion-in-augmented-reali/ (accessed 26 March 2018).

Adjei, Mavis T., Stephanie M. Noble, and Charles H. Noble (2010), "The Influence of C2C Communications in Online Brand Communities on Customer Purchase Behavior." *Journal of the Academy of Marketing Science* 38 (5), 634–53.

Amazon (2018), "Get the Most Out of Cyber Monday Deals Week." Available at: www.amazon.com/primeinsider/tips/cyber-monday-deals.html?ref=insider_homepage (accessed 19 August 2018).

Arora, Sandeep, Frenkel T. Hofstede, and Vijay Mahajan (2017), "The Implications of Offering Free Versions for the Performance of Paid Mobile Apps." *Journal of Marketing* 81 (6), 62–78.

Barney, Jay B., and Delwyn N. Clark (2007), *Resource-Based Theory: Creating and Sustaining Competitive Advantage*. Oxford: Oxford University Press.

Barney, Jay B., and William S. Hesterly (2012), *Strategic Management and Competitive Advantage: Concepts and Cases*, 3rd edn. Englewood Cliffs: Prentice Hall.

Bartels, Robert (1962), *The Development of Marketing Thought*. Homewood: Richard D. Irwin.

Becker, Howard S. (1986), *Doing Things Together: Selected Papers*. Evanston: Northwestern University Press.

Benedicktus, Ray L., Michael K. Brady, Peter R. Darke, and Clay M. Voorhees (2010), "Conveying Trustworthiness to Online Consumers: Reactions to Consensus, Physical Store Presence, Brand Familiarity, and Generalized Suspicion." *Journal of Retailing* 86 (4), 322–35.

Berry, Leonard L. (1983), "Relationship Marketing." In *Emerging Perspectives on Services Marketing*, eds. Leonard L. Berry, G. L. Shostack, and G. D. Upah, 25–8. Chicago: American Marketing Association.

Berry, Leonard L. (1995), "Relationship Marketing of Services-Growing Interest, Emerging Perspectives." *Journal of the Academy of Marketing Science* 23 (4), 236–45.

Biesdorf, Stefan, David Court, and Paul Willmott (2013), "Big Data: What's Your Plan?" Available at: www.mckinsey.com/business-functions/business-technology/ourinsights/big-data-whats-your-plan (accessed 15 August 2018).

Binder, Christof, and Dominique M. Hanssens (2015), "Why Strong Customer Relationships Trump Powerful Brands." *Harvard Business Review Online*. Available at: https://hbr.org/2015/04/why-strong-customer-relationships-trump-powerful-brands (accessed 15 August, 2018).

Blystone, Dan (2015), "Understanding Alibaba's Business Model." Available at: www.investopedia.com/articles/investing/062315/understanding-alibabas-business-model.asp (accessed 19 August 2018).

Brandt, Mathias (2014), "Internet of Things wird bis 2020 alltäglich." Available at: https://de.statista.com/infografik/2937/mit-dem-internet-of-things-verbundenen-geraete/ (accessed 15 August 2018).

Brinker, Scott (2018), "Marketing Technology Landscape Supergraphic (2018): Martech 5000 (actually 6,829)." Available at: https://chiefmartec.com/2018/04/marketing-technology-landscape-supergraphic-2018/ (accessed 15 August 2018).

Brown, Morgan (2014), "Airbnb: The Growth Story You Didn't Know." Available at: https://growthhackers.com/growth-studies/airbnb (accessed 19 August 2018).

Bundesgerichtshof (2013), "Bundesgerichtshof erkennt Schadensersatz für den Ausfall eines Internetanschlusses zu." Press Release No. 14/2013, Available at: http://juris.bundesgerichtshof.de/cgi-bin/rechtsprechung/document.py?Gericht=bgh&Art=pm&pm_nummer=0014/13 (accessed 15 August 2018).

Cambridge Dictionary (2018), "Digital Age." Available at: https://dictionary.cambridge.org/de/worterbuch/englisch/digital-age (accessed 15 August 2018).

China Internet Watch (2017), "Mobile Share Exceeded 80% in China Online Shopping Market in Q2 2017." Available at: www.chinainternetwatch.com/22461/mobile-shopping-q2-2017/ (accessed 15 August 2018).

CIA (2018), "The World Factbook: Median Age." Available at: www.cia.gov/library/publications/the-world-factbook/fields/2177.html (accessed 15 August 2018).

Cialdini, Robert B., and Kelton V. L. Rhoads (2001), "Human Behavior and the Marketplace." *Journal of Marketing Research* 13 (3), 8–13.

Columbus, Louis (2014), "2014: The Year Big Data Adoption Goes Mainstream in the Enterprise." Available at www.forbes.com/sites/louiscolumbus/2014/01/12/2014-the-year-big-dataadoption-goes-mainstream-in-the-enterprise/#4cf471e44f7d (accessed 19 July 2018).

Dahl, Darren, Heather Honea, and Rajesh V. Manchanda (2003), "The Nature of Self-Reported Guilt in Consumption Contexts." *Marketing Letters* 14 (3), 159–71.

Dahl, Darren, Heather Honea, and Rajesh V. Manchanda (2005), "Three Rs of Interpersonal Consumer Guilt: Relationship, Reciprocity, Reparation." *Journal of Consumer Psychology* 15 (4), 307–15.

Daimler (2012), "Daimler Trucks—A True, Global Player'." Available at: https://media.daimler.com/marsMediaSite/en/instance/ko/Daimler-Trucks—A-true-Global-Player.xhtml?oid=9917306 (accessed 19 August 2018).

Day, George S. (2006), "Aligning the Organization With the Market." *MIT Sloan Management Review* 48 (1), 41–9.

DesMarais, Christina (2014), "The New Booming Market? Aging Baby Boomers." Available at: www.inc.com/christina-desmarais/6-companies-profiting-from-an-aging-population.html (accessed 19 August 2018).

Direct Marketing News (2012), "DMA: Direct Mail Response Rates Beat Digital." Available at: www.dmnews.com/channel-marketing/direct-mail/news/13059655/dma-direct-mail-response-rates-beat-digital (accessed 15 August 2018).

Doney, Patricia M., and Joseph P. Cannon (1997), "An Examination of the Nature of Trust in Buyer-Seller Relationships." *Journal of Marketing* 61 (2), 35–51.

Dowling, Grahame R., and Mark Uncles (1997), "Do Customer Loyalty Programs Really Work?" *Sloan Management Review* 38 (4), 71–82.

Dwyer, Robert F., and Sejo Oh (1987), "Output Sector Munificence Effects on the Internal Political Economy of Marketing Channels." *Journal of Marketing Research* 24 (4), 347–58.

Egan, John (2004), *Relationship Marketing: Exploring Relational Strategies in Marketing*, 2nd edn., 13. London: Financial Times/Prentice Hall.

eMarketer (2017a), "Worldwide Retail and Ecommerce Sales: eMarketer's Estimates for 2016–2021." Available at: www.emarketer.com/Report/Worldwide-Retail-Ecommerce-Sales-eMarketers-Estimates-20162021/2002090 (accessed 15 August 2018).

eMarketer (2017b), "Alexa, Say What?! Voice-Enabled Speaker Usage to Grow Nearly 130% this Year." Available at: www.emarketer.com/Article/Alexa-Say-What-Voice-Enabled-Speaker-Usage-Grow-Nearly-130-This-Year/1015812 (accessed 15 August 2018).

Emmons, Robert A. (2004), "The Psychology of Gratitude: An Introduction." In *The Psychology of Gratitude*, eds. Robert A. Emmons and Michael E. McCullough, 3–16. New York: Oxford University Press.

eShop World (2018), "WeChat—Everything Online Retailers Need to Know About China's Smartphone Revolution." Available at: www.eshopworld.com/news/wechat-smartphone-revolution/ (accessed 15 August 2018).

Fang, Eric, Robert W. Palmatier, and Jan-Benedict E. M. Steenkamp (2008), "Effect of Service Transition Strategies on Firm Value." *Journal of Marketing* 72 (September), 1–15.

Fruend, Melissa (2017), *2017 Colloquy Loyalty Census: An In-Depth Analysis of Where Loyalty Is Now . . . and Where It's Headed*. Cincinnati: Colloquy.

Gartner (2014a), "Gartner Says Customer Relationship Management Software Market Grew 13.7 Percent in 2013." Available at: www.gartner.com/newsroom/id/2730317 (accessed 15 August 2018).

Gartner (2014b), "Gartner Says Worldwide PC Shipments Declined 6.9 Percent in Fourth Quarter of 2013." Available at: www.gartner.com/newsroom/id/2647517 (accessed 19 August 2018).

Gartner (2018), "Gartner Says Worldwide PC Shipments Declined 2 Percent in 4Q17 and 2.8 Percent for the Year." Available at: www.gartner.com/en/newsroom/press-releases/2018-01-11-gartner-says-worldwide-pc-shipments-declined-2-percent-in-4q17-and-28-percent-for-the-year (accessed 19 August 2018).

Geisel, Tina (2015), "My Starbucks Idea: The Starbucks Crowdsourcing Success Story." Available at: http://smbp.uwaterloo.ca/2015/02/my-starbucks-idea-the-starbucks-crowdsourcing-success-story/ (accessed 19 August 2018).

Global Sherpa (2018), "BRIC Countries—Background, Key Facts, News and Original Articles." Available at: http://globalsherpa.org/bric-countries-brics/ (accessed 15 August 2018).

Goldfarb, Avi, and Catherine Tucker (2013), "Why Managing Customer Privacy Can Be an Opportunity." *MIT Sloan Management Review* 54 (3), 10–12.

Gordon, Nancy, and Kelly Hlavinka (2011), *Buried Treasure: The 2011 Forecast of U.S. Consumer Loyalty Program Points Value*. Cincinnati: Colloquy.

Gouldner, Alvin W. (1960), "The Norm of Reciprocity: A Preliminary Statement." *American Sociology Review* 25 (April), 161–78.

Gronroos, Christian (1997), "Value-Driven Relational Marketing: From Products to Resources and Competencies." *Journal of Marketing Management* 13 (4), 407–19.

Harker, Michael J. (1999), "Relationship Marketing Defined? An Examination of Current Relationship Marketing Definitions." *Marketing Intelligence & Planning* 17 (1), 13–20.

Harmeling, Colleen M., Jordan W. Moffett, Mark J. Arnold, and Brad D. Carlson. (2017), "Toward a Theory of Customer Engagement Marketing." *Journal of the Academy of Marketing Science* 45 (3), 312–35.

Henderson, Conor, Joshua T. Beck, and Robert W. Palmatier (2011), "Review of the Theoretical Underpinnings of Loyalty Programs." *Journal of Consumer Psychology* 21 (July), 256–76.

Hilken, Tim, Ko de Ruyter, Mathew Chylinski, Dominik Mahr, and Debbie I. Keeling (2017), "Augmenting the Eye of the Beholder: Exploring the Strategic Potential of Augmented Reality to Enhance Online Service Experiences." *Journal of the Academy of Marketing Science* 45 (6), 884–905.

Internet World Stats (2018), "Internet Usage Statistics, The Internet Big Picture, World Internet Users and 2018 Population Stats." Available at: www.internetworldstats.com/stats.htm (accessed 15 August 2018).

Jacoby, Jacob, and Robert W. Chestnut (1978), *Brand Loyalty*. New York: John Wiley & Sons.

Javornik, Ana (2016), "Augmented Reality: Research Agenda for Studying the Impact of Its Media Characteristics on Consumer Behaviour." *Journal of Retailing and Consumer Services* 30 (May), 252–61.

Keller, Kevin Lane (1993), "Conceptualizing, Measuring, and Managing Customer-Based Brand Equity." *Journal of Marketing* 57 (January), 1–22.

Kotlyar, Igor, and Dan Ariely (2013), "The Effect of Nonverbal Cues on Relationship Formation." *Computers in Human Behavior* 29 (May), 544–51.

Kozlenkova, Irina V., Robert W. Palmatier, Eric (Er) Fang, Bangming Xiao, and Minxue Huang (2017), "Online Relationship Formation." *Journal of Marketing* 81 (3), 21–40.

Lemon, Katherine N., and Peter C. Verhoef (2016), "Understanding Customer Experience Throughout the Customer Journey." *Journal of Marketing* 80 (6), 69–96.

Marketing to China (2017), "A Report on China's Mobile E-Commerce Market." Available at: www.marketingtochina.com/report-chinas-mobile-e-commerce-market/ (accessed 15 August 2018).

Marshall, Ron (2015), "How Many Ads Do You See in One Day?" Available at: www.redcrowmarketing.com/2015/09/10/many-ads-see-one-day/ (accessed 15 August 2018).

Martin, Kelly D., Abhishek Borah, and Robert W. Palmatier (2017), "Data Privacy: Effects on Customer and Firm Performance." *Journal of Marketing* 81 (January), 36–58.

Martin, Kelly D., and Patrick E. Murphy (2017), "The Role of Data Privacy in Marketing." *Journal of the Academy of Marketing Science* 45 (March), 135–55.

Mathwick, Charla (2002), "Understanding the Online Consumer: A Typology of Online Relational Norms and Behavior." *Journal of Interactive Marketing* 16 (Winter), 40–55.

McRae, Hamish (2015), "Facebook, Airbnb, Uber, and the Unstoppable Rise of the Content Non-Generators." Available at: www.independent.co.uk/news/business/comment/hamish-mcrae/facebook-airbnb-uber-and-the-unstoppable-rise-of-the-content-non-generators-10227207.html (accessed 19 August 2018).

Moe, Timothy, Caesar Maasry, and Richard Tang (2010), "EM Equity in Two Decades: A Changing Landscape." Goldman Sachs Global Economics Paper No: 204. Available at: www.contributors.ro/wp-content/uploads/2010/11/0809_Global_Econ_Paper_No__204_Final2.pdf (accessed 15 August 2018).

Morgan, Robert M., and Shelby D. Hunt (1994), "The Commitment-Trust Theory of Relationship Marketing." *Journal of Marketing* 58 (July), 20–38.

Newman, Tim (2016), "Brain's Empathy Center Identified." Available at: www.medicalnewstoday.com/articles/312349.php?utm_source=TrendMD&utm_medium=cpc&utm_campaign=Medical_News_Today_TrendMD_1 (accessed 15 August 2018).

O'Brien, Louise, and Charles Jones (1995), "Do Rewards Really Create Loyalty?" *Harvard Business Review* 73 (3), 75–82.

Oliver, Richard L. (1999), "Whence Consumer Loyalty?" *Journal of Marketing* 63 (Special Issue), 33–44.

Palmatier, Robert W. (2008), *Relationship Marketing*. Cambridge: Marketing Science Institute.

Palmatier, Robert W., Rajiv P. Dant, and Dhruv Grewal (2007), "A Comparative Longitudinal Analysis of Theoretical Perspectives of Interorganizational Relationship Performance." *Journal of Marketing* 71 (4), 172–94.

Palmatier, Robert W., Rajiv P. Dant, Dhruv Grewal, and Kenneth R. Evans (2006), "Factors Influencing the Effectiveness of Relationship Marketing: A Meta-Analysis." *Journal of Marketing* 70 (October), 136–53.

Palmatier, Robert W., Cheryl Burke Jarvis, Jennifer R. Bechkoff, and Frank R. Kardes (2009), "The Role of Customer Gratitude in Relationship Marketing." *Journal of Marketing* 73 (September), 1–18.

Palmatier, Robert W., Lisa K. Scheer, Mark B. Houston, Kenneth R. Evans, and Srinath Gopalakrishna (2007), "Use of Relationship Marketing Programs in Building Customer-Salesperson and Customer-Firm Relationships: Differential Influences on Financial Outcomes." *International Journal of Research in Marketing* 24 (September), 210–23.

Palmatier, Robert W., Lisa K. Scheer, and Jan Benedict Steenkamp (2007), "Customer Loyalty to Whom? Managing the Benefits and Risks of Salesperson-Owned Loyalty." *Journal of Marketing Research* 44 (May), 185–99.

Palmatier, Robert W., and Shrihari Sridhar (2017), *Marketing Strategy: Based on First Principles and Data Analytics*. London: Palgrave.

Parvatiyar, Atul, and Jagdish N. Sheth (2001), "Conceptual Framework of Customer Relationship Management." In *Customer Relationship Management: Emerging Concepts, Tools and Applications*, eds. Jagdish N. Sheth, Atul Parvatiyar, and G. Shainesh, 3–25. New Delhi: Tata/McGraw-Hill.

Payne, Adrian, and Pennie Frow (2005), "A Strategic Framework for Customer Relationship Management." *Journal of Marketing* 69 (October), 167–76.

PLMA (2017), "Private Label's Market Share Reaches All-Time Highs in 9 European Countries." Available at: www.plmainternational.com/d/2017/WPL17/Press/PressReleaseYB2017_en.pdf (accessed 15 August 2018).

Quelch, John A. (2007), "When Your Product Becomes a Commodity." *Harvard Business School Working Knowledge*. Available at: https://hbswk.hbs.edu/item/when-your-product-becomes-a-commodity (accessed 19 July, 2018).

Recchia, Chad (2018), "Augmented Reality Marketing: Three Companies that Have Done It Best." Available at: www.forbes.com/sites/

forbesagencycouncil/2018/03/01/augmented-reality-marketing-three-companies-that-have-done-it-best/#161fad4b2dc8 (accessed 19 August 2018).

Rindfleisch, Aric, and Christine Moorman (2003), "Interfirm Cooperation and Customer Orientation." *Journal of Marketing Research* 40 (11), 421–36.

Ro, Sam (2015), "Here's How Much Business S&P 500 Companies Do Outside of the US." Available at: www.businessinsider.com/foreign-revenues-by-region-2015-7?IR=T (accessed 15 August 2018).

Russell, Jon (2017), "Alibaba Smashes Its Single's Day Record Once Again as Sales Cross $25 Billion." Available at: https://techcrunch.com/2017/11/11/alibaba-smashes-its-singles-day-record/?guccounter=1 (accessed 19 August 2018).

Rust, Roland T., Katherine N. Lemon, and Valarie A. Zeithaml (2004), "Return on Marketing: Using Customer Equity to Focus Marketing Strategy." *Journal of Marketing* 68 (January), 109–27.

Samaha, Steve, Josh Beck, and Robert W. Palmatier (2014), "The Role of Culture in International Relationship Marketing." *Journal of Marketing* 78 (September), 78–98.

Sheth, Jagdish N. (2011), "Impact of Emerging Markets on Marketing: Rethinking Existing Perspectives and Practices." *Journal of Marketing* 75 (4), 166–82.

Sheth, Jagdish N., and Atul Parvatiyar (1995), "The Evolution of Relationship Marketing." *International Business Review* 4 (4), 397–418.

Sheth, Jagdish N., and Atul Parvatiyar (2000), *Handbook of Relationship Marketing*. Thousand Oaks: Sage Publications, Inc.

Sheth, Jagdish N., Rajendra S. Sisodia, and Arun Sharma (2000), "The Antecedents and Consequences of Customer-Centric Marketing." *Journal of the Academy of Marketing Science* 28 (1), 55–66.

Sivadas, Eugene, and Robert F. Dwyer (2000), "An Examination of Organizational Factors Influencing New Product Success in Internal and Alliance-Based Processes." *Journal of Marketing* 64 (January), 31–49.

Spencer, Leon (2014), "Internet of Things Market to Hit $7.1 Trillion by 2020: IDC." Available at: www.zdnet.com/article/internet-of-things-market-to-hit-7-1-trillion-by-2020-idc/ (accessed 15 August 2018).

Srivastava, Rajendra K., Tasadduq A. Shervani, and Liam Fahey (1998), "Market-Based Assets and Shareholder Value: A Framework for Analysis." *Journal of Marketing* 62 (January), 2–18.

Statista (2018a), "Ranking der Länder mit den höchsten Umsätzen im E-Commerce weltweit im Jahr 2018 (in Millionen Euro)." Available at: https://de.statista.com/statistik/daten/studie/485047/umfrage/umsaetze-im-e-commerce-nach-laendern-weltweit/ (accessed 15 August 2018).

Statista (2018b), "Smartphone Penetration Rate as Share of the Population in China From 2015 to 2022." Available at: www.statista.com/statistics/321482/smartphone-user-penetration-in-china/ (accessed 15 August 2018).

Statista (2018c), "Retail E-Commerce Sales Worldwide From 2014 to 2021 (in billion U.S. dollars)." Available at: www.statista.com/statistics/379046/worldwide-retail-e-commerce-sales/ (accessed 15 August 2018).

Statista (2018d), "Digital Shopping Device Usage and Frequency Worldwide in 2017." Available at: www.statista.com/statistics/692846/online-shopping-device-worldwide-frequency/ (accessed 15 August 2018).

Statista (2018e), "Devices Used for Digital Purchases According to Digital Buyers in France, Germany and the UK as of July 2013." Available at: www.statista.com/statistics/290190/digital-shopping-device-usage-in-france-germany-and-uk/ (accessed 15 August 2018).

Statista (2018f), "Number of Active Consumers Across Alibaba's Online Shopping Properties From 2nd Quarter 2012 to 3rd Quarter 2017 (in Millions)."

Available at: www.statista.com/statistics/226927/alibaba-cumulative-active-online-buyers-taobao-tmall/ (accessed 19 August 2018).

Statista (2018g), "Number of Smartphone Users Worldwide From 2014 to 2020 (in billions)." Available at: www.statista.com/statistics/330695/number-of-smartphone-users-worldwide/ (accessed 15 August 2018).

Statista (2018h), "Smartphone Penetration Rate as Share of the Population in China From 2015 to 2022." Available at: www.statista.com/statistics/321482/smartphone-user-penetration-in-china/ (accessed 15 August 2018).

Statista (2018i), "Number of Social Media Users Worldwide From 2010 to 2021 (in billions)." Available at: www.statista.com/statistics/278414/number-of-worldwide-social-network-users/ (accessed 15 August 2018).

Statista (2018j), "Percentage of U.S. Population Who Currently Use Any Social Media From 2008 to 2018." Available at: www.statista.com/statistics/273476/percentage-of-us-population-with-a-social-network-profile/ (accessed 15 August 2018).

Statista (2018k), "Facebook—Statistics & Facts." Available at: www.statista.com/topics/751/facebook/ (accessed 15 August 2018).

Statista (2018l), "Social Media and User-Generated Content Tools Used by Omnichannel Retailers in the United States as of 1st Quarter 2014." Available at: www.statista.com/statistics/308539/us-omnichannel-retailer-social-media-tools/ (accessed 15 August 2018).

Statista (2018m), "Weekly Social Networking Time Per User in the United States as of 2nd Quarter 2016, by Ethnicity (in minutes)." Available at: www.statista.com/statistics/248158/social-networking-time-per-us-user-by-ethnicity/ (accessed 15 August 2018).

Statista (2018n), "Anzahl der im Apple App Store verfügbaren Apps in ausgewählten Monaten von Juli 2008 bis Januar 2017." Available at: https://de.statista.com/statistik/daten/studie/20150/umfrage/anzahl-der-im-app-store-verfuegbaren-applikationen-fuer-das-apple-iphone/ (accessed 15 August 2018).

Statista (2018o), "Prognose zum Volumen der jährlich generierten digitalen Datenmenge weltweit in den Jahren 2016 und 2025 (in Zettabyte)." Available at: https://de.statista.com/statistik/daten/studie/267974/umfrage/prognose-zum-weltweit-generierten-datenvolumen/ (accessed 15 August 2018).

Steinhoff, Lena, Denni Arli, Scott Weaven, and Irina V. Kozlenkova (2018), "Online Relationship Marketing." Working Paper.

Tanasoiu, Felicia (2017), "Mobile App Success Story: How Airbnb Did It." Available at: https://appsamurai.com/mobile-app-success-story-how-airbnb-did-it/ (accessed 19 August 2018).

Tolido, Ron (2016), "TechnoVision 2016—No Work." Available at: www.capgemini.com/2016/01/technovision-2016-no-work/ (accessed 19 August 2018).

Trivers, Robert L. (1971), "The Evolution of Reciprocal Altruism." *Quarterly Review of Biology* 46 (1), 35–57.

Trivers, Robert L. (1985), *Social Evolution*. Menlo Park: Benjamin/Cummings.

Tsardaloglou, Iliana (2016), "Community Building in the Digital & Social Media." Available at: https://communitybuildingblog.wordpress.com/2016/05/23/my-starbucks-idea/ (accessed 19 August 2018).

Ulaga, Wolfgang, Frédéric Dalsace, and Chloé Renault (2010), "Michelin Fleet Solutions: From Selling Tires to Selling Kilometers." The Case Centre. Available at: https://www.thecasecentre.org/educators/ordering/selecting/featured-cases/michelinfleet (accessed 25 August 2018).

University of Virginia (2013), "Human Brains Are Hardwired for Empathy, Friendship." *ScienceDaily*. Available at: www.sciencedaily.com/releases/2013/08/130822085804.htm (accessed 18 July, 2018).

Vargo, Stephen L., and Robert F. Lusch (2004), "Evolving to a New Dominant Logic for Marketing." *Journal of Marketing* 68 (January), 1–17.

Verhoef, Peter C., P. K. Kannan, J. Jeffrey Inman (2015), "From Multi-Channel Retailing to Omni-Channel Retailing: Introduction to the Special Issue on Multi-Channel Retailing." *Journal of Retailing* 91 (2), 174–81.

Watson IV, Gregiry F., Joshue T. Beck, Conor M. Henderson, and Robert W. Palmatier (2015), "Building, Measuring, and Profiting From Customer Loyalty." *Journal of the Academy of Marketing Science* 43 (6), 790–825.

Wierenga, Berend, and Han Soethoudt (2010), "Sales Promotions and Channel Coordination." *Journal of the Academy of Marketing Science* 38 (3), 383–97.

Wilson, David T. (1995), "An Integrated Model of Buyer-Seller Relationships." *Journal of the Academy of Marketing Science* 23 (4), 335–45.

Zeithaml, Valarie A., A. Parasuraman, and Leonard L. Berry (1985), "Problems and Strategies in Services Marketing." *Journal of Marketing* 49 (Spring), 33–46.

Zhu, Rui, Utpal M. Dholakia, Xinlei (Jack) Chen, and René Algesheimer (2012), "Does Online Community Participation Foster Risky Financial Behavior?" *Journal of Marketing Research* 49 (3), 394–407.

# Part I

# Understanding Relationship Marketing

# 2 Relationship Marketing Theory

## Learning Objectives

- Retrace the historic development of relationship marketing theory and acknowledge the various research disciplines that have informed it from the 1950s to the 2010s.
- Recognize how evolutionary psychology serves as an overarching theory to understand and explain relationship marketing phenomena.
- Understand the key theoretical perspectives and constructs that inform interpersonal, interfirm, and online customer–company relationships.
- Build an integrative, comprehensive theoretical framework of relationship marketing by synthesizing key theories and constructs.

## Introduction

Because researchers from many different disciplines have studied the impact of relationships on human behavior, marketing has a rich theoretical landscape from which to draw to understand relationship marketing. Many of these different disciplines take central positions in the development of relationship marketing theory. This chapter organizes that resulting theory into three parts. The first part provides a temporal overview, briefly delineating diverse disciplines' contributions to relationship marketing theory as it has evolved over time. The second part presents key insights from evolutionary psychology as an overarching theoretical framework to understand the mechanics of marketing relationships. The third part synthesizes multiple theoretical perspectives and constructs to distill three key types of customer–company relationships, focused on (1) *interpersonal relationships* (either business-to-consumer [B2C] or business-to-business [B2B]), (2) *interfirm relationships* (B2B), and (3) *online relationships* (B2C or B2B) mediated by technology. The fourth part integrates these three types of marketing relationships to weave a comprehensive theoretical framework of relationship marketing.

## Overview of the Evolution of Relationship Marketing Theory

Over time, a variety of scientific disciplines has informed and contributed to the understanding of marketing relationships. This section briefly depicts the temporal evolution of relationship marketing theory. Overall, a review of the literature shows a broad pattern of more institutional, macro-level theories (e.g., economics, sociology) giving way to more individual, micro-level theoretical perspectives (e.g., social psychology, psychology) over time. Figure 2.1 provides a timeline of this evolution of relationship marketing theory.

### 1950s–1970s

The earliest research into marketing relationships sought to add sociological and psychological insights to the dominant *institutional economics perspective*, which predicts that rational economic actors are driven by value maximization and market efficiency goals. Yet because people are inevitably involved in marketing, an effective theory needs to include noneconomic factors, such as power structures, two-way exchanges of commitments, communication channels, and emotional reactions (Alderson 1958).

From sociology, for example, channel researchers introduced the *power–dependence framework of social exchange theory* to explain the emergence and critical role of middlemen in business exchanges and thus the complicated relationships among channel partners (Emerson 1962). These early relational exchange contributions assigned a central theoretical role to dependence, but it has since been recast in a supporting role. That is, dependence might have a positive effect on performance, because a dependent partner wants to maintain a relationship to achieve its goals rather than undertake the cost of finding another, replacement partner (El-Ansary 1975; Frazier 1983). Yet instead of a clear driver of relationship performance, dependence really might represent a contextual or background variable (Morgan and Hunt 1994; Palmatier, Dant, and Grewal 2007), such that it affects the development of the relationship. It is not necessarily an immediate "precursor" of relationship performance (Palmatier, Dant, and Grewal 2007, p. 183) but rather appears to affect performance indirectly, through relationship quality and cooperation.

Interdependence is a related but distinct concept. Interdependence among exchange partners certainly can enhance cooperation and performance, but asymmetric dependence (i.e., dependence imbalance) can generate conflict and undermine cooperation (Bucklin and Sengupta 1993, Gassenheimer, Davis, and Dahlstrom 1998; Hibbard, Kumar, and Stern 2001; Kumar, Scheer, and Steenkamp 1995a). It has substantial direct and indirect effects on performance, mediated by relationship-specific

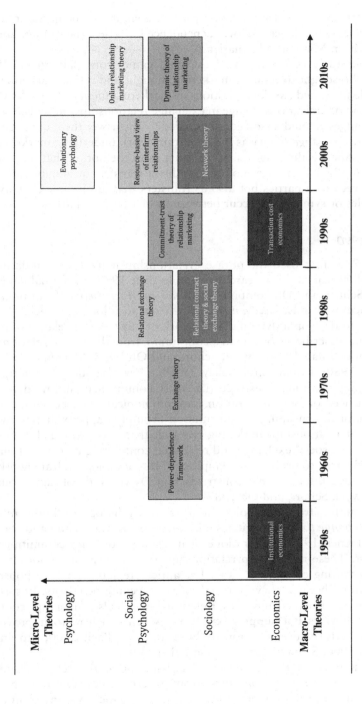

*Figure 2.1* Temporal Overview of the Evolution of Relationship Marketing Theory

investments and cooperation. Conceptually, then, it may be necessary to differentiate dependence and interdependence but assess them simultaneously (Scheer, Miao, and Palmatier 2015).

Another early contribution to the field came from Bagozzi (1975, p. 32), who sought to redirect marketing thought and refine marketing's focus. He identified two key questions of marketing theory: "(1) Why do people and organizations engage in exchange relationships? and (2) How are exchanges created, resolved, or avoided?" To answer these questions, he applied *exchange theory* as the core framework underlying marketing behavior. Specifically, Bagozzi (1975) puts forth the notion that marketing encompasses exchanges not only as direct transfers of tangible products between two parties but also as transfers that are indirect, involve intangibles or symbols, or occur between more than two parties.

### 1980s–1990s

Berry (1983) first used the phrase "relationship marketing," initiating the development of this research stream. In their 1987 conceptual paper, Dwyer, Schurr, and Oh combine *relational contract theory* (from political science) with *social exchange theory* (from sociology and social psychology) to develop a dynamic framework of buyer–seller relationships, which they describe according to a continuum, from discrete to relational transactions (Blau 1964; Dwyer, Schurr, and Oh 1987; Macaulay 1963; Macneil 1980; Thibaut and Kelley 1959). They also identify multiple instrumental relational constructs (i.e., trust, commitment, norms, dependence, justice, conflict, cooperation, and communication). The significant influence of this meaningful contribution prompted approximately two decades of relationship marketing research that was grounded almost exclusively in social exchange and relational contracting theory and that aimed primarily to propose and empirically test nomological frameworks that included the relational constructs that Dwyer and colleagues outlined (Dwyer, Schurr, and Oh 1987).

For example, from a sociology and social psychology tradition, *relational exchange theory* prioritizes relational norms (Kaufmann and Dant 1992; Macneil 1980), either alone or in conjunction with commitment and trust. These norms help relationship partners respond more effectively to shifting conditions, as well as anticipate actions and responses in the future, because they limit self-interest–seeking behaviors. In turn, exchange performance improves. Relational norms also encourage cooperative behaviors but suppress conflicts, which can lead to improved financial performance (Cannon, Achrol, and Gundlach 2000; Jap and Ganesan 2000; Siguaw, Simpson, and Baker 1998).

According to another empirically well-supported theoretical framework, *transaction cost economics* (from an economics tradition), people use guile to achieve their self-interests, so specific investments in an exchange must be monitored and safeguarded from partners' opportunistic behaviors (Rindfleisch and Heide 1997; Williamson 1985; Williamson 1975). When these relationship-specific investments increase, the partners must find a way to protect them. They might prefer to avoid monitoring and safeguarding costs, though, in which case they could seek to integrate vertically or else establish strong relational governance structures (i.e., build relationships). In a sense, relationship governance and vertical integration serve similar functions, at least from a transaction cost perspective: They suppress opportunistic behaviors and transaction costs (e.g., safeguarding and monitoring costs) while also promoting performance-enhancing investments. Empirical evidence affirms that good relationships among partners support performance, because they lead to increased investments, lower transaction costs, and reduced opportunistic behaviors (Gassenheimer, Davis, and Dahlstrom 1998; Heide and John 1990; John 1984; Wathne and Heide 2000; Weiss and Anderson 1992).

By linking social exchange theory with insights from marriage and organizational behavior research (gathered from sociology and social psychology research), Morgan and Hunt came up with the *commitment–trust theory* of relationship marketing, a theory that remains one of the strongest influences on relationship marketing thought. Focused on the key constructs of commitment and trust, these authors posit that the "presence of relationship commitment and trust is central to successful relationship marketing, not power" (Morgan and Hunt 1994, p. 22). This framework has earned strong empirical support, providing a default theoretical basis for most subsequent relationship marketing research (Morgan and Hunt 1994; Palmatier et al. 2006). With its emphasis on these two relational constructs, Morgan and Hunt's commitment–trust theory of relationship marketing effectively limits the scope established by Dwyer, Schurr, and Oh's conceptual framework, yet it ignores dynamic relationship effects (Dwyer, Schurr, and Oh 1987; Morgan and Hunt 1994).

## 2000s

Across these previous perspectives, both relational governance constructs (i.e., commitment, trust) and relationship-specific investments (i.e., communication, training) have emerged as clear precursors of relationship performance (Palmatier, Dant, and Grewal 2007), whereas dependence and relational norms appear to function mainly as antecedents of commitment, trust, and relationship-specific investments. Such combinations of multiple theoretical perspectives, into a parsimonious, unifying theoretical framework, prompts a *resource-based view of interfirm relationships* (Dyer and Singh 1998; Jap 1999; Palmatier, Dant, and Grewal 2007). In management literature, proponents of this view assert that resources or assets that are valuable, rare, and difficult to duplicate increase sustainable competitive advantages and promote superior firm performance (Wernerfelt 1984). Of the key precursors of performance, trust and commitment might strengthen the relational bonds needed to support good exchanges, but relationship investments improve other performance-enhancing aspects too. Thus, a relationship marketing approach can increase the joint knowledge of the partners and their informal communication, which may improve the effectiveness and efficiency of the relational exchange while *also* increasing trust and commitment.

With regard to interfirm relationships, a network perspective also has emerged as insightful. That is, *network theory* from sociology helps describe how the structural characteristics of an interaction among multiple entities (e.g., individuals, firms) define the overall network. This perspective implies that it is not just relationship quality (e.g., trust, commitment) but also relationship breadth (network density) and relationship composition (network diversity/attractiveness) that determine the performance of an exchange (Borgatti and Foster 2003; Houston et al. 2004; Palmatier 2008; Van Den Bulte and Wuyts 2007).

Finally, exchanges often involve interpersonal relationships, so researchers have sought to explain the observed behaviors within those links by adopting an *evolutionary psychology* view, stemming from both biology and psychology research. In this "quasi-Darwinian" perspective, the relationships that survive in the long run are those that benefit through a process of selection (Eyuboglu and Buja 2007; Palmatier et al. 2009). Furthermore, this theory relies on the individual partners' ingrained emotional processes (e.g., gift–gratitude, anger–punishment, guilt–reciprocation) to explain why they might cooperate, or not, with marketers' efforts. Such drivers also might influence the effectiveness of relationship marketing (Cialdini and Rhoads 2001; Dahl, Honea, and Manchanda 2005; Morales 2005; Palmatier et al. 2009).

## 2010s

In an effort to integrate, expand, and update Dwyer and colleagues' three-decades-old theory, modern researchers have extended static relationship marketing theories to propose a *dynamic theory of relationship marketing*, such that they investigate how relationships develop (Harmeling et al. 2015; Palmatier et al. 2013; Zhang et al. 2016). Few people would argue that relationships change over time, yet most academic research and managerial tactics rely on a static perspective when they seek to evaluate customer–seller relationships. Relationship marketing researchers assume relationships operate according to a *life cycle* process, during which they begin, develop, grow, and ultimately dissolve by migrating through path-dependent stages, such as exploratory, growth, maturity, and decline stages. Recent research contributes to the development of a dynamic theory of relationship marketing by detailing the time-varying trajectories of relationship commitment, delineating positive (exploration, endowment, recovery) and negative (neglect, betrayal) relationship migration mechanisms, or accounting for the dynamic effects of transformational relationship events (Harmeling et al. 2015; Palmatier et al. 2013; Zhang et al. 2016).

The digital age in particular is substantially changing the way companies and customers interact. Both transactions and communications in the modern era tend to be mediated by Internet technology and take place in a non–face-to-face (i.e., human-to-technology) environment (Steinhoff et al. 2018). Current relationship marketing research is thus working to develop on an *online relationship marketing theory*, leveraging insights from both psychology and communication science. Many relationship marketing researchers appreciate the insights of flow theory (Csikszentmihalyi 1975), which advances understanding of people's immersion and engagement in online activities; media richness theory (Daft and Lengel 1986), which helps explain the effectiveness of diverse communication channels in relational settings; and parasocial interaction theory (Giles 2002; Horton and Wohl 1956), which can describe the relational mechanisms that arise between media users (e.g., online customers) and media personae (e.g., firms encountered in online channels).

## Twin Pillars of Relationship Marketing Effectiveness: The Evolutionary Psychology of Gratitude and Unfairness

If we seek to move beyond the specifics of customer–company relationships, as detailed by these various theoretical approaches, and instead comprehend the overall functioning of relationships, we need to turn to gratitude and unfairness. Relationship marketing effectiveness largely can be explained by these evolutionary psychological mechanisms. The psychological traits that have allowed humans to feel gratitude but also perceive unfairness likely developed as evolutionary survival mechanisms over our ancestral hunter–gatherer past. In recognition of these inherent traits, evolutionary psychology combines modern psychology with evolutionary biology and uses the logic of natural selection to explain the development of human mental processes and behaviors (Saad 2011). A key assumption is that organisms always seek to ensure their survival and pass their genes on to future generations (Colarelli and Dettmann 2003).

Survival has long depended on an individual member's adherence to group norms. Members of a group—whether of cells, animals, or humans—are more likely to survive if they team up and cooperate with other cooperative members, as long as the group is able to protect each member from the selfish behaviors of noncooperating others (Ridley 1985). Rewarding group members who cooperate and punishing group members who fail to adhere to cooperative norms is crucial. The process of natural selection thus led to psychological systems that allowed groups to reap the mutual benefits of reciprocal relations while simultaneously protecting them from cheaters or selfish individuals who do not reciprocate sufficiently (Trivers 1971).

Gratitude and unfairness can be thought of as two opposite sides of the same coin, because they serve to either reward adherence to group norms (i.e., gratitude) or mitigate deviance from such norms through punishment (i.e., perceived unfairness). Both mechanisms are universal, hereditary, and deeply ingrained in human beings and serve to reinforce cooperation within groups. People are hardwired to experience gratitude and unfairness, across all ages and cultures, so these mechanisms also represent indispensable traits in relationship marketing, through their powerful ability to reinforce relationship reciprocity and cooperation through gratitude or else destroy relationships through punishment. Because they can promote or impede relationships, gratitude and unfairness represent the *twin pillars of relationship marketing.* To increase relationship marketing success, managers need a clear understanding of both these underlying psychological mechanisms, as well as their behavioral consequences, then should use these insights to design, implement, and adapt their relationship marketing strategies. Gratitude evokes a compelling urge to reciprocate beneficial acts, and the very act of repayment itself generates positive feelings of pleasure. A failure to reciprocate instead creates uncomfortable feelings of guilt. In this sense, gratitude is the catalyst for a cycle of reciprocation, which leads directly to relationship formation and growth. Unfairness perceptions instead tend to be more critical in stages dedicated to maintaining relationships and preventing relationship destruction (or, even worse, retaliatory behaviors). Unfairness is "relationship poison" and can completely ruin good relationships or prompt customers to find ways to punish firms that treat them unfairly (Samaha, Palmatier, and Dant 2011). We review these critical pairs—gratitude and reciprocity and unfairness and punishment—in detail next.

### Understanding Gratitude and Reciprocity

Evolutionary psychologists argue that feelings of gratitude, pleasure from reciprocating, and guilt for failing to reciprocate are well-developed, genetic "systems" that encourage reciprocal, cooperative behaviors (Becker 1986; Trivers 1985). Reciprocating behaviors get reinforced over time by culturally relevant social norms, which span all societies. The emotions and resultant behaviors are so ubiquitous that clinical psychologists use a person's failure to feel gratitude as an indication of psychosis (Buck 2004).

Because people are hardwired to feel gratitude, they instinctively repay others who provide them some benefit, through a sophisticated emotional carrot-and-stick system. A salesperson takes a client to lunch, so the client feels gratitude and acts on the psychological drive to reciprocate, perhaps by providing helpful information or placing an additional order (Palmatier et al. 2009). If the client succumbs to this urge to reciprocate, he or she is rewarded with a sense of pleasure. If the client fails to reciprocate, he or she starts to feel guilt. From an evolutionary psychology perspective, the emotion of guilt developed, at least partly, to motivate cheaters to compensate for their misdeeds and behave reciprocally in the future and thus prevent the rupture of reciprocal relationships (Trivers 1971). Similarly, feelings of gratitude that prompt giving and reciprocity are an adaptive mechanism that evolved as a result of the survival benefits associated with food sharing, coalition formation, or predator avoidance (Saad and Gill 2000).

Over time, gratitude serves as a catalyst in the process of relationship development (Palmatier et al. 2009). The close link between emotional gratitude and reciprocal behaviors then encourages a strengthening cycle, in which partners switch off being in each other's debt. This back-and-forth provides an ongoing bond, linking them and enhancing their relationship. Gratitude thus represents the emotional core of successful relationship marketing efforts by providing an "imperative force" to repay any benefits received. Most effective relationship marketing programs tap into this force. Even Adam Smith acknowledged that "The sentiment which most immediately and directly prompts us to reward, is gratitude" (Smith 1759, p. II.I.4). Similarly, movements of individuals from one band to another in hunter–gatherer relationships (e.g., relationship termination) occurred in response to a lack of reciprocity or perceived cheating (Lee and DeVore 1968). Thus, gratitude is essential for creating an ongoing cycle of relationship continuity.

### Understanding Unfairness and Punishment

From an evolutionary psychology standpoint, reactions to unfair treatment also are strongly ingrained in people's psychological makeup; children as young as five years of age have an innate, well-developed sense of "fairness" that causes them to respond angrily to any perceived violations. Such negative emotions often compel people to take on costs associated with inflicting punishment, despite receiving no net economic benefit in the present, near short term, or long term from this costly action (Bowles, Fehr, and Gintis 2003). Such punitive behaviors, without benefit to the actors, likely evolved in humans because they benefitted the group as a whole; punishments force members to embrace group norms rather than behave in a self-interested manner (Wasieleski and Hayibor 2009). Motivating adherence to group norms through punishment positively affects a group's ability to survive and propagate. Research also suggests that strong negative behaviors, like punishment, could have had a positive influence in terms of increasing the group size, which would reduce the chances of group extinction (Bowles, Fehr, and Gintis 2003). The notion of punishment for unfair acts takes negative reciprocity to a higher level, because people are willing to sacrifice resources and incur costs to inflict punishment, even if such sacrifices do not result in any future economic benefit.

People also seek explanations for negative events, more than for positive events, and unfairness provides a clear indication of a negative motive or intent by the other party (Folkes 1988). Some conflict is inevitable in relationships, so customers rarely hold a partner accountable for "expected" negative interactions. But the presence of unfairness implies an underlying negative motive that prompts customers to perceive that conflict is not just expected or unavoidable but rather is the direct result of the seller's actions. That is, in the presence of unfairness perceptions, customers assign more accountability and responsibility for problems to the seller, with a higher degree of intentionality. When those problems arise, customers react more emotionally and often punitively. Typical disagreements and conflict have little effect on customer performance when perceived unfairness is low; they exert massively negative effects when accompanied by high unfairness perceptions (Samaha, Palmatier, and Dant 2011). For example, "lost customer" analyses often show that customers leave because the emotional push of perceptions of unfairness motivate them to expend substantial effort and cost to switch to another firm.

---

### Example 2.1 Netflix (USA)

In 2011, Netflix surprised its customers with a substantial price increase. The firm announced that its extremely popular $9.99 all-inclusive streaming and DVD rental plan would be abolished and replaced by three separate plans: just streaming for $7.99, or just one-at-a-time DVD rental for $7.99, or a combination of both streaming and DVD rental for $15.98. Thus overnight, Netflix confronted its customers with a 60% price hike. Netflix users were not just furious at what they perceived to be the company's unfair greed but also shocked that one of their favorite firms could do something like this to them, in a seeming cloak-and-dagger operation with no up-front warning. Customers' reactions were clear and blatant: Within just a few days, the blog post announcing the price change had prompted more than 8,800 pages of comments, and vast numbers of users publicly abandoned the company.

Source: Gilbert (2011).

---

Unfortunately, companies often seem to be the ones exposing themselves to these toxic effects, because they generate and even encourage customers' perceptions of unfairness. Loyalty or rewards programs are notable culprits, because bystanders—those customers not targeted by the loyalty program—detest the unfair treatment they receive compared with other customers (Steinhoff and Palmatier 2016). The hotel scene from *Up in the Air* portrayed the situation dramatically: George Clooney, as a premium customer, provokes the resentment of a long line of waiting customers when he skips ahead to be served instantly. Bystander effects occur directly, through explicit observation; then they continue to exert indirect effects, through customers' word-of-mouth communication and social media. When customers believe the ratio of benefits to costs they receive is somehow worse than others', their anger leads them to a desire to punish the firm in a way that will help restore their perceived balance. In an airline study, bystanders' perceptions of unfairness when they watched other customers receive priority boarding were so high that the resulting effects on their loyalty and annual sales were nearly 10 times greater than the parallel effect of gratitude in increasing the target customers' loyalty and annual sales (Steinhoff and Palmatier 2016).

## A Typology of Marketing Relationships

In summary, researchers from many different theoretical perspectives and disciplines have provided insight into how and why relationship marketing works and suggested various focal constructs as critical for understanding relationship performance. As becomes evident from our overview of the evolution of relationship marketing theory, different theoretical lenses often have different relationship foci. Researchers use more micro-level theories (e.g., evolutionary psychology) to understand the core of interpersonal relationships; they turn to macro-level theories (e.g., network theory) to theorize about interfirm relationships. The many conceptual differences across these two contexts (Iacobucci and Ostrom 1996; Reynolds and Beatty 1999) have prompted a distinction in relationship marketing research, between relationships that involve two firms (interfirm) and those that include two individuals (interpersonal) (Palmatier et al. 2007; Palmatier, Scheer, and Steenkamp 2007). Specifically, different types of relationship marketing activities are more effective at building interpersonal rather than interfirm relationships; all else being equal, interpersonal relationships also exert stronger effects on customer behaviors and financial performance than do interfirm relationships.

In addition to distinguishing theoretically between interpersonal and interfirm relationships, we need to account for changes to relationship marketing in the digital age. Accordingly, in this section, we distill the various theoretical lenses to derive theoretically distinct models of relationship marketing for three major types of relationships: (1) interpersonal (e.g., individual customer-to-salesperson), (2) interfirm (e.g., network of individual customer-to-salesperson, individual customer-to-seller firm, and customer firm-to-seller firm), and (3) online (e.g., individual/firm customer-to-technology). Although distinct, these relationships also build on one another. For each relationship type, we discuss the key theories and focal constructs critical for understanding relationship performance.

## Interpersonal Relationships

**Interpersonal relationships** involve exchange dyads of two individuals, one representing the customer side (i.e., individual customer) and the other representing the company side (i.e., individual salesperson). Theorizing about the effectiveness of interpersonal relationships has identified four key drivers of relationship performance; two theories provide a rich foundation for identifying and understanding these mechanisms. Specifically, social exchange theory cites the pivotal role of customer commitment and trust in relationships. Evolutionary psychology adds customer gratitude and reciprocity norms, which accurately capture and predict relationship marketing performance. Figure 2.2 depicts a theoretical model of interpersonal relationships that encompasses commitment, trust, gratitude, and reciprocity norms as key catalysts of relationship performance.

## Customer Commitment and Trust

According to *social exchange theory*, relationships arise following subjective cost–benefit analyses, such that participants attempt to maximize benefits and minimize costs (Thibaut and Kelley 1959). When the net

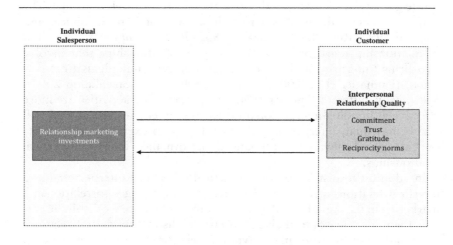

*Figure 2.2* Theoretical Model of Interpersonal Relationships

benefit of a relationship exceeds the (anticipated) net benefits of comparable alternatives, a customer maintains that relationship. If the costs of a relationship instead exceed its benefits, the customer withdraws and likely seeks alternatives that offer more favorable cost–benefit balances.

Social exchange theory also predicts influences of commitment and trust (Blau 1964; Thibaut and Kelley 1959), because mutual trust and commitment provide the essence for distinguishing social relationships among exchange partners from purely transactional interactions (Cook and Emerson 1978; McDonald 1981). As introduced previously, Morgan and Hunt's commitment–trust theory of relationship marketing empirically delineates these key roles as ways to explain how relationships determine performance (Morgan and Hunt 1994). Because **commitment** pertains to "an enduring desire to maintain a valued relationship," (Moorman, Zaltman, and Deshpande 1992, p. 316) committed relationship partners devote extra effort to maintaining and strengthening relational bonds, which then enhance the parties' cooperation, financial performance, and so forth (Kumar, Hibbard, and Stern 1994; Morgan and Hunt 1994; Palmatier et al. 2009). Because **trust** involves "confidence in an exchange partner's reliability and integrity," (Morgan and Hunt 1994, p. 23) it has positive direct effects on relationship outcomes, whether in the form of interpersonal trust or global trust in the company as a whole (Doney and Cannon 1997; Ganesan 1994; Garbarino and Johnson 1999; Moorman, Zaltman, and Deshpande 1992; Morgan and Hunt 1994; Sirdeshmukh, Singh, and Sabol 2002). As a precursor to commitment, trust also indirectly enhances performance (Ambler, Styles, and Xiucum 1999; Crosby, Evans, and Cowles 1990; Hibbard et al. 2001; Mohr and Spekman 1994; Palmatier et al. 2009). Since 1994, this theory has provided a default theoretical basis for most relationship research.

## Customer Gratitude and Reciprocity Norms

Focusing just on how commitment and trust determine relationship performance may not be sufficient, though, for both theoretical and empirical reasons. First, with its primarily cognitive explanation of human relationships, social exchange theory cannot capture the psychological mechanisms that take place in emotionally charged interpersonal dyads. Even though social exchange theory cites reciprocity norms, along with gratitude, as key drivers of relationships, such norms tend to be ignored in relationship marketing models (Gouldner 1960). Second, in an empirical sense, a meta-analysis that reviewed 111 independent samples, covering 38,000 relationships, provides support for critical roles of commitment and trust but also reveals a persistent, positive, direct effect of relationship marketing investments on objective performance, beyond any indirect effect mediated by trust or commitment (Palmatier et al. 2006). Thus, other performance-enhancing mediators can contribute to the effort to explain the positive financial effect of relationship marketing.

As we briefly described previously, *evolutionary psychology* argues that gratitude and the resulting need for reciprocity, among other human psychological traits, represent adaptations that result from natural selection processes (Saad 2011), such that they are genetically and socially hardwired and pervasive throughout all human societies (Becker 1986; Trivers 1985; Trivers 1971). Similar to an evolutionary perspective on adaptations of physiological mechanisms (e.g., heart, lungs, and immune system) to fulfill different functions and ensure survival, psychological mechanisms reflect adaptations that developed to increase survival likelihood (Colarelli and Dettmann 2003). These fundamental social and moral components ensure the functioning of stable social systems (Emmons and McCullough 2004; Gouldner 1960; Ostrom and Walker 2003). Not surprisingly, then, gratitude and reciprocity, which are dynamically and innately linked, foster interpersonal relationship performance (Bagozzi 1995).

Defined as "feelings of gratefulness, thankfulness, or appreciation for a benefit received" (Palmatier et al. 2009, p. 3), **gratitude** represents the "emotional core" of reciprocity, inseparable from it, that catalyzes psychological pressure to return a favor (Emmons 2004). These **reciprocity norms** summarize those normative pressures to behave in similar fashion toward an initiator of the favor or provider of benefits (Emmons and McCullough 2003; Morales 2005; Palmatier et al. 2009). The act of reciprocating can generate pleasure; a failure to behave reciprocally can generate guilt (Becker 1986; Buck 2004; Dahl, Honea, and Manchanda 2005). Grateful people acknowledge how others contribute to their well-being, such as when grateful customers reward firms that provide them with benefits by complying with the firm's subsequent requests (e.g., for information, for higher prices) (Goei and Boster 2005; Morales 2005; Watkins et al. 2003). If they feel obligated to salespeople, customers likely make purchases. Thus, when firms' relationship marketing investments foster feelings of gratitude, consumers engage in behaviors that benefit firm performance (Dahl, Honea, and Manchanda 2005; Palmatier et al. 2009).

In a way, gratitude as a short-term emotion functions like a starting mechanism, prompting prosocial reciprocal behaviors that persist as long as the emotion lasts. In the short run, customers display reciprocal purchase behaviors and thus satisfy their psychological obligation, as induced by the gratitude stemming from relationship marketing efforts. Then its longer-term effects emerge from gratitude's creation of reciprocity norms, leading to the development of a relationship (Bartlett and DeSteno 2006). The ongoing cycles of gratitude, reciprocation, and self-reinforcing reciprocal behaviors secure the continuation of a relationship (Schwartz 1967). Gratitude thus promotes the development of norms of reciprocity over time and initiates reciprocation cycles, fostering long-term, positive customer behaviors (Palmatier et al. 2009).

---

**Example 2.2  Airbnb (USA)**

Airbnb has managed to build a community of hosts and guests based on mutual trust, gratitude, and reciprocity cycles. As Chip Conley, Airbnb's head of global hospitality and strategy, indicates, "What's interesting is that in the hotel business about 10–15 percent of hotel guests will fill out an online survey after they've stayed in a hotel. At Airbnb, 70–75 percent of our hosts and guests review each other after a stay" (O'Dell 2016). In contrast with often-generic hotel experiences, hosts at Airbnb go out of their way to provide their guests with localized and personalized experiences, stimulating a sense of gratitude, which those guests reciprocate by providing a favorable review to the host. The interpersonal style of the host–guest relationships is a powerful initiator of cycles of gratitude and reciprocity.

Source: O'Dell (2016).

---

But gratitude, as an emotional concept, also cannot be separated from cognitive constructs: Emotional gratitude increases cognitive judgments of trust (Dunn and Schweitzer 2005), which enhance commitment, and together, they promote relational performance outcomes (Palmatier et al. 2009). That is, gratitude has another, indirect effect on relationship performance, by moving through trust and commitment. In evolutionary psychology terms, gratitude and reciprocity operate at the lowest level of awareness (i.e., ingrained emotions and psychological pressures); in social exchange theory frameworks, commitment and trust allude to higher-level cognitive processing. Integrating gratitude and reciprocity norms as mediators in interpersonal relationship marketing paradigms thus provides a more "micro-level" theoretical explanation of the association between relationship marketing investments and outcomes, not limited to cognitive assessments of commitment and trust (Palmatier et al. 2009). Overall, these four elements (gratitude, reciprocity norms, commitment, trust) capture most of the effects of interpersonal relationship marketing, which is why such strong empirical support exists for the influence of interpersonal relationships on customers' decision making.

## Interfirm Relationships

With these theoretical foundations, any theory of interfirm relationship marketing also must account for the groups of employees who participate on both sides of an exchange dyad. **Interfirm relationships** involve multiple interactions among many people at multiple levels in the organization—in effect, a network of multilevel relationships. Individual consumers might develop relationships with individual salespeople (interpersonal) or with the selling firm as a whole (individual-to-firm); a group of buyers employed by a customer firm might develop relationships with a group of salespeople employed by the seller firm (interfirm). Each tie is also an interpersonal dyad, so a good theory of interfirm relationships must encompass theoretical models of interpersonal relationships based on commitment, trust, gratitude, and reciprocity norms, together with the unique, multilevel nature of firm-to-firm relations. A fully specified model would account for each level and identify the conditions in which each one exerts a stronger influence over exchange outcomes.

From sociology, *network theory* fits these requirements by providing a parsimonious theoretical framework that describes the impact of structural elements of interactions among multiple social entities (e.g., individuals, firms) in an overall multilevel network (Wasserman and Faust 1994; Rainie and Wellman 2012; Van Den Bulte and Wuyts 2007). A network perspective predicts that relationship quality (i.e., commitment, trust, gratitude, and reciprocity norms), relationship breadth (i.e., network density), and relationship composition (i.e., network diversity/attractiveness) all determine exchange performance in interfirm relationships (Borgatti and Foster 2003; Houston et al. 2004; Palmatier 2008; Van Den Bulte and Wuyts 2007). Their ultimate outcomes result from both interpersonal-level decisions (dyadic trust, commitment, gratitude, and reciprocity norms) and group-level decisions (group-level relationship quality, breadth, and composition). Figure 2.3 accordingly contains our theoretical model of interfirm relationships, which contains three interfirm-specific mechanisms that drive performance: relationship quality, breadth, and composition.

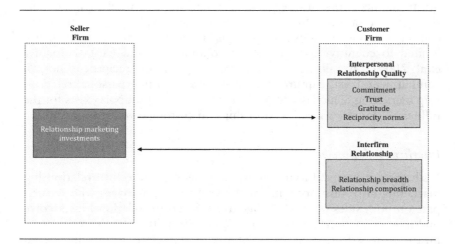

*Figure 2.3* Theoretical Model of Interfirm Relationships

## Relationship Quality

The composite **relationship quality** construct parallels the concept of tie strength in network theory (relational bonds between actors) (Granovetter 1973). It captures diverse elements required to establish a high-caliber relational bond, including commitment, trust, gratitude, and reciprocity norms (Crosby, Evans, and Cowles 1990; Kumar, Scheer, and Steenkamp 1995b). Each related construct actually captures unique aspects of relational bonds that positively influence specific exchange outcomes; only in aggregate do they reflect the overall quality or caliber of the bond. In detail, though, commitment refers to exchange partners' desire to maintain valued relationships and thus their relational motivation. Because it reflects an evaluation of a partner's reliability and integrity, trust generates confidence in that partner's actions and supports cooperation. Feelings of gratitude foster immediate, continuous reciprocal behaviors. Reciprocity also has pervasive impacts on exchange behaviors, which take a little longer to develop. Overall, relationship quality benefits relationship performance (Palmatier 2008).

## Relationship Breadth

**Relationship breadth** reflects the number of bonds with an exchange partner; when interorganizational relationships include more interpersonal ties, they likely uncover key information and profit-enhancing opportunities while avoiding any disruption to individual bonds (e.g., reorganizations, turnover). Such broad links mean that the relationship can avoid long-lasting impacts from the departure of key personnel, for example (Bendapudi and Leone 2002). A replacement boundary spanner quickly becomes socialized into the existing relational norms by those who remain with the firm, through a process of "norm persistence" (Jacobs and Campbell 1961). Relationship breadth also reflects concepts such as network density (i.e., level of interconnectedness among network members) and degree of centrality (i.e., number of direct ties between a specific member and other network members) (Houston et al. 2004), which themselves enhance cooperation, knowledge transfer, communication efficiency, and product development performance (Rowley 1997; Tsai 2001; Walker, Kogut, and Shan 1997). When a seller and customer share more interpersonal ties, they enjoy better access to information and sales opportunities and less disruption due to turnover, which improves exchange performance (Palmatier 2008).

## Relationship Composition

The **relationship composition** construct implies decision-making capability; a diverse, authoritative contact portfolio increases a seller's ability to effect change in customer organizations. More diversity and authority allow the seller to confirm information across various perspectives and gain access to critical decision makers (Katrichis 1998). Imagine a new product-approval process, for example. It likely includes the customer's engineering, manufacturing, quality, and purchasing departments. If the salesperson only enjoys a strong relationship with a vice president of purchasing, that does little to determine how long the product will sit ignored on the quality technician's bench. Even high-quality relationships with multiple contacts (breadth) in the customer firm might suffer limitations if they do not include key decision makers or only involve people in similar positions. Of course, relationship breadth and composition could correlate; all else being equal, sellers with more contacts have more diverse contacts. However, they can diverge, too, such as when sellers have several but mostly homogeneous contacts or just a few very different contacts. Relationship composition thus captures a portfolio's overall ability to influence decisions, with the recognition that different customer firm departments make key decisions, not just those with the most authority. As Arora and Allenby (1999, p. 476) show empirically, "instead of exclusively focusing on the group members with a higher overall influence, it may be more beneficial to communicate to members who have lower overall influence but higher influence on specific aspects of the decision."

We accordingly can align relationship composition with the network concepts of diversity and attractiveness, reflecting the unique knowledge, skills, and capabilities owned by network partners (Anderson, Hakansson, and Johanson 1994; Wasserman and Faust 1994). More diverse network partners provide greater information value and complementarity, stronger network performance, and efficiency (Baum, Calabrese, and Silverman 2000; Burt 1992). The underlying logic by which relationship composition should exert a positive effect on performance thus is consistent with sales research that determines that a seller with a well-structured customer contact portfolio has greater access to valuable and nonredundant information, can identify and overcome barriers, and enjoys increased performance (Bonoma and Johnston 1978; Rackham 1996).

In our proposed model, we integrate social network theory to develop an interfirm-specific relationship marketing theoretical framework, in which two relational drivers, relationship breadth and composition, in addition to relationship quality, determine the impact of interfirm relationships on performance. This direct representation of the three key mechanisms that mediate the effects of relationship marketing investments on seller outcomes in interfirm relationships captures the different aspects of interfirm relationships. Together, the three mechanisms reinforce one another and optimize relationship value, such that relationship quality has direct effects on the seller's outcomes but also conceptually meaningful, leveraging effects through its interaction with relationship breadth and composition.

### Implications of Multilevel Interfirm Relationships

In interfirm relational settings, the relationships that develop and operate simultaneously at multiple levels also may simultaneously and differentially affect customer behaviors and performance outcomes. Relationships that function at multiple levels operate in multiple ways (Iacobucci and Ostrom 1996). For example, "the processes by which trust develops appear to differ when the target is an organization . . . as opposed to an individual salesperson" (Doney and Cannon 1997, p. 45). In particular, relationships with individuals (e.g., salespeople) tend to have a greater direct effect on relational behaviors and subsequent financial outcomes than relationships with firms or groups. These individual-level relationships also exert indirect impacts on outcomes, through the customer's relationship with the firm for which the salesperson acts as a representative. In turn, firm-level relationships exert stronger effects on behavior and performance when the firm's employees, policies, and procedures appear consistent, because consistent groups get treated like individual entities (Palmatier et al. 2007; Palmatier, Scheer, and Steenkamp 2007).

The level of loyalty also varies across individual- and firm-level relationships. Loyalty in salesperson–customer relationships often is transient, such that it disappears if the salesperson leaves to join a competitive firm (Reichheld and Teal 1996). Empirical evidence reveals that "salesperson-owned loyalty, [and] the customer's intention to perform behaviors that signal motivation to maintain a relationship specifically with the focal salesperson" can drive performance but would be lost to the selling firm as soon as the salesperson leaves (Palmatier, Scheer, and Steenkamp 2007, p. 186). Individual-level relationships have stronger impacts on outcomes, but they also are more susceptible to disruption due to turnover (Bendapudi and Leone 2002)—a serious concern for some firms. An estimated 30% of American Express customers would follow their relationship manager to a new firm, for example (Tax and Brown 1998).

Loyalty to the firm often is inextricable from loyalty to the salesperson. In a sense, customer loyalty consists of three elements. First, a customer who expresses an intention to behave in ways that help maintain the relationship with the focal salesperson is displaying *salesperson-owned loyalty*. Second, loyalty to a seller, independent of the salesperson, arises in response to elements that the organization controls, including other employees, which we refer to as *seller-owned loyalty*. Third, *synergistic loyalty* is engendered by neither the seller alone nor the salesperson individually; it emerges from customer benefits generated by the seller–salesperson association. Thus, relationship managers must be constantly aware of where the relationship gets generated and what actions to take to manage it.

With a consideration of the joint impact of trust at these three levels, research has shown that interfirm relationships between parent companies, interpersonal trust among the parent firm's representatives, and the parent firms' trust in their own representatives (i.e., agency trust) all exert unique influences on resource investments and the performance of the venture (Fang et al. 2008). When the different levels of trust interact, they also can increase coordination and suppress reactionary responses. Thus, relationships of different entities, composed of numerous constituents, warrant a more nuanced view that includes relational ties among multiple constituents.

### Online Relationships

In the digital age, many relationships, both interpersonal and interfirm, have evolved—at least to a certain extent—into online relationships. By 2020, customers are predicted to manage 85% of their relationships with firms without any human interaction (Gartner 2011). In offline settings, customer–company relationships rely on face-to-face (e.g., customer shopping at a retailer's location) or non–face-to-face verbal (e.g., phone) or written (e.g., mail) interactions. In recent years, communication between firms and their customers has changed dramatically, especially as firms add new, online communication channels and customers develop new expectations. In online contexts, face-to-face interactions may disappear completely, and the exchanges are indirect and mediated by Internet technologies. At the extreme, no human-to-human interaction takes place; instead, the chain of relational exchanges involves human-to-technology-to-human interactions. Thus, we define **online relationships** as relational exchanges that are mediated by technology (e.g., Internet, computer) and take place in a non–face-to-face (individual/firm customer-to-technology) environment.

The digital age in turn has shaped the development of relationship marketing theory by extending interpersonal and interfirm relationships to online contexts. With a rich theoretical foundation derived from interpersonal and interfirm relationships, recent online relationship marketing theory integrates several additional theories and constructs that are increasingly relevant in the digital age: flow, media richness, and parasocial interaction. In Figure 2.4, we offer a theoretical model of online relationships in which technology mediates the interactions (purchase transactions, communications) of any exchange.

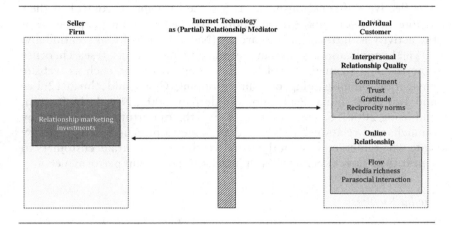

*Figure 2.4* Theoretical Model of Online Relationships

---

**Example 2.3  Amazon (USA)**

Until the recent opening of several offline bookstores and the Amazon Go supermarket, the e-commerce giant Amazon has been doing business with customers online exclusively. With its easy-to-understand user interface and easy-to-use self-help options, Amazon has limited the need for (human) customer service and typically can transact and communicate with customers without any human interaction between the customer and Amazon employees. If human intervention is needed, Amazon allows customers to access a service manager by phone, e-mail, or live chat. In a vast understatement, creating and nurturing technology-mediated relationships online with customers has seemed to work out pretty well for the company: It enjoys 95% annual customer retention rates, and 75% of those customers come back weekly.

Sources: ChannelReply (2018); BI Intelligence (2016); Danziger (2018).

---

*Flow*

The psychological *flow theory*, developed by Csikszentmihalyi, refers to "the holistic experience that people feel when they act with total involvement" (Csikszentmihalyi 1975, p. 36). **Flow** is a psychological state in which customers exhibit a high level of involvement and immersion in an activity, accompanied by feelings of fun and enjoyment (Csikszentmihalyi 1975). When in a state of flow, people typically reveal (1) an intense focus on the present moment, (2) merged action and awareness, (3) loss of reflective self-consciousness, (4) a sense of being in control of their actions, (5) distortion of the temporal experience, and (6) experience of the activity as intrinsically rewarding (Nakamura and Csikszentmihalyi 2011). In applications to human–technology interactions, researchers use flow theory to explain people's online usage behavior, such as website navigation, online gaming, or online shopping (Chang and Zhu 2012; Lee and Tsai 2010; Luna, Peracchio, and de Juan 2002; Novak, Hoffmann, and Yung 2000). Sellers can make use of the opportunities provided by omnichannel relationships in the digital age to put customers in a flow state when interacting with the firm, which may encourage customers to repeat their flow experiences and increase relationship performance.

*Media Richness*

Originating in communication science, *media richness theory* seeks to explain the communication effectiveness of different communication channels (Daft and Lengel 1986). It also has been extended to detail communication issues in new media contexts (e.g., online shopping, e-mail, mobile messaging, videoconferencing) (Kaplan and Haenlein 2010; Kim, Suh, and Lee 2013). Communication channels differ in the degree of information and cues provided, or **media richness**, defined as the ability "to change understanding within a time interval" (Daft and Lengel 1986, p. 560). Richer channels can convey information faster and with fewer misunderstandings than leaner channels, due to their capacity for immediate feedback (i.e., synchronicity), multiple cues (e.g., verbal, visual), and natural language, all of which help foster mutual understanding. Popular communication channels can be ranked in the following order of decreasing richness: (1) face to face, (2) video, (3) telephone, (4) radio, and (5) e-mail or mail (Daft and Lengel 1986; Reinartz, Thomas, and Kumar 2005).

In an online context, firms interact with customers through multiple channels, encompassing a plethora of communication media with varying degrees of richness (Verhoef, Kannan, and Inman 2015). Media richness theory proposes that, depending on their level of richness, some media channels are better suited than others for communicating various messages. Richer channels can handle complex messages (i.e., with multiple, possibly conflicting interpretations), whereas leaner channels can accommodate simple messages more efficiently (Cable and Yu 2006). Compared with leaner channels, richer channels have greater direct effects on relationship performance, work more effectively for building relationships during the onboarding stage, can communicate more complex messages, and tend to have more persistent (carryover) effects that can span multiple periods (Samaha et al. 2018). In turn, richer channels also lead to diminishing returns at a faster rate than leaner channels, but with higher communication costs (time, effort, cognitive bandwidth, social engagement).

### Parasocial Interaction

With a basis in communication science but also spurring significant interest among psychologists, *parasocial interaction theory* provides rich insights into the interactions and relationships of media users and personas (Giles 2002; Horton and Wohl 1956). This theory focuses on the phenomenon by which media users perceive parasocial interactions with media entities as close, reciprocal relationships. The initial focus of this research stream was on media personas represented in mass media, such as talk show hosts, celebrities, or movie characters. But researchers also have extended it to individual and institutional characters that media users encounter in Internet-mediated channels (e.g., social media) (Ballantine and Martin 2005; Labrecque 2014).

In online relationship marketing environments, **parasocial interaction** describes a customer's communication and identification with a nonhuman, technological entity (e.g., website, embodied virtual agent) that acts in place of a seller's human representatives. Customers may regard these parasocial, nonhuman interactions with a firm as just as authentic, relevant, and intimate as social, human interactions in offline contexts (McKenna, Green, and Gleason 2002). In turn, parasocial interactions can be expected to enhance favorable customer behaviors and overall relationship performance.

## An Integrative Theoretical Framework of Relationship Marketing

Relationship marketing theory has evolved to explain key mechanisms in and the performance of interpersonal, interfirm, and online relationships between companies and customers. Taken together, these three perspectives provide an integrative framework of how marketing relationships work, synthesizing existing interpersonal, interfirm, and online relationship marketing theory. Table 2.1 recapitulates the key theories and constructs that have contributed to the development of a comprehensive relationship marketing theory that encompasses the interpersonal, interfirm, and online relational contexts.

Interpersonal relationship marketing theory clarifies the core psychology that informs customer–company relationships. Specifically, social exchange theory and evolutionary psychology inform a microlevel perspective of human-to-human relationships, in which two individual exchange partners engage in relational interactions. Relationship marketing research has theoretically and empirically established that a salesperson's relationship marketing investments enhance company

Table 2.1 Overview of Key Constructs and Theories for Different Types of Marketing Relationships

| Relationship Type Construct | Construct Definition | Relevant Theory and Discipline | Key Contribution | Representative Relationship Marketing Research |
|---|---|---|---|---|
| **Interpersonal Relationships** | | | | |
| Commitment | "An enduring desire to maintain a valued relationship" (Moorman, Zaltman, and Deshpandé 1992, p. 316) | Commitment–trust theory of relationship marketing; social exchange theory (sociology and social psychology) | Together with trust, mutual commitment among exchange partners is the major differentiator of social from purely exchange relationships. Commitment positively affects cooperation, financial performance, and other positive outcomes and thus represents one of the key mediators of the impact of relationship marketing investments on performance. | Anderson and Weitz 1992; De Wulf, Odekerken-Schröder, and Iacobucci 2001; Jap and Ganesan 2000; Kumar, Hibbard, and Stern 1994; Moorman, Zaltman, and Deshpandé 1992; Morgan and Hunt 1994 |
| Trust | "Confidence in an exchange partner's reliability and integrity" (Morgan and Hunt 1994, p. 23) | Commitment–trust theory of relationship marketing; social exchange theory (sociology and social psychology) | Together with commitment, mutual trust among exchange partners is the major differentiator of social from purely exchange relationships. Trust exerts both positive direct and indirect effects (through commitment) on relationship outcomes; it represents the second key mediator of the impact of relationship marketing investments on performance. | De Wulf, Odekerken-Schröder, and Iacobucci 2001; Doney and Cannon 1997; Hibbard et al. 2001; Moorman, Zaltman, and Deshpandé 1992; Morgan and Hunt 1994; Sirdeshmukh, Singh, and Sabol 2002 |
| Gratitude | "Feelings of gratefulness, thankfulness, or appreciation for a benefit received" (Palmatier et al. 2009, S. 3) | Evolutionary psychology (psychology) | Customer gratitude represents one of the missing mediators that can explain marketing's performance impact. Hardwired into people, gratitude offers a micro-level explanation for relationship performance, in that it initiates long-lasting cycles of reciprocation. | Morales 2005; Palmatier et al. 2009; Steinhoff and Palmatier 2016 |

| | | | |
|---|---|---|---|
| Reciprocity norms | Pressures to repay or reciprocate benefits received | Evolutionary psychology (psychology) | Reciprocity norms are the other mediator missing from previous models of relationship marketing effectiveness. As psychological pressures stemming from experienced feelings of gratitude, reciprocity norms secure relational longevity in both the short and long run. | Bagozzi 1995; Dahl, Honea, and Manchanda 2005; Palmatier et al. 2009 |

*Interfirm Relationships*

| | | | |
|---|---|---|---|
| Relationship quality | Composite construct capturing the diverse interaction characteristics required to create a high-caliber relational bond, such as commitment, trust, gratitude, reciprocity norms, and exchange efficiency | Network theory (sociology) | Relationship quality parallels the concept of tie strength in network theory and reflects the overall quality or caliber of the bond, which enhances relationship performance. | Crosby, Evans, and Cowles 1990; Houston et al. 2004; Kumar, Scheer, and Steenkamp 1995b; Palmatier 2008; Van Den Bulte and Wuyts 2007 |
| Relationship breadth | Number of relational bonds with an exchange partner | Network theory (sociology) | Relationship breadth mirrors the network concepts of network density (i.e., level of interconnectedness among network members) and degree centrality (i.e., number of direct ties between a specific member and other network members). Network interconnections with many interpersonal ties can uncover key information, find profit-enhancing opportunities, and withstand disruptions to individual bonds (e.g., reorganizations, turnover). | Houston et al. 2004; Palmatier 2008; Van Den Bulte and Wuyts 2007 |

*(Continued)*

*Table 2.1* (Continued)

| Relationship Type Construct | Construct Definition | Relevant Theory and Discipline | Key Contribution | Representative Relationship Marketing Research |
|---|---|---|---|---|
| Relationship composition | Decision-making capability of relational contacts | Network theory (sociology) | Relationship composition matches the network concepts of diversity and attractiveness, which entail the extent of unique knowledge, skills, and capabilities owned by network partners. Diverse network partners increase information value and complementarity, as well as overall relationship performance and efficiency. | Houston et al. 2004; Palmatier 2008; Van Den Bulte and Wuyts 2007 |
| **Online Relationships** | | | | |
| Flow | "The holistic experience that people feel when they act with total involvement" (Csikszentmihalyi 1975, p. 36) | Flow theory (psychology) | In the digital age, companies can use technology to put customers into a state of complete involvement and immersion in an activity, accompanied by feelings of fun and enjoyment. Flow theory predicts the antecedents and consequences of such customer flow states. | Csikszentmihalyi 1975; Rheinberg et al. 2003 |
| Media richness | The ability "to change understanding within a time interval" (Daft and Lengel 1986, p. 560) | Media richness theory (communication science) | In the digital age, firms interact with customers through multiple channels and a plethora of communication media with varying degrees of richness. Media richness theory predicts the differential effects of richer and leaner channels for diverse interaction purposes, which may enhance the effectiveness of companies' omnichannel strategies. | Daft and Lengel 1986 |

| Parasocial interaction | A customer's communication and identification with a nonhuman, technological entity (e.g., website, embodied virtual agent) that acts in place of a seller's human representatives | Parasocial interaction theory (communication science) | In the digital age, customers often interact with a parasocial, nonhuman technological entity (e.g., website, embodied virtual agent) that acts in place of a seller's human representatives. Customers may regard these parasocial, nonhuman interactions as equally authentic, relevant, and intimate as social, human interactions in offline contexts. Parasocial interaction theory indicates how social emotions, cognitions, conations, and behaviors evolve between a customer and a firm's parasocial representative. | Giles 2002; Horton and Wohl 1956; Rubin, Perse, and Powell 1985 |

performance if they spark commitment, trust, gratitude, and reciprocity norms with the customer. A customer's perceptions of trust and commitment toward the relational partner capture the cognitive evaluations of the relational tie. A customer's feelings of gratitude toward a relational partner represent a powerful emotion that carries the relationship forward. Over time, gratitude propels reciprocal behaviors and consolidates and strengthens the relationship. Thus customers' commitment, trust, gratitude, and reciprocity norms together constitute the key mediating mechanisms that drive relationship marketing performance in interpersonal relationships.

Interfirm relationship marketing theory extends this view by going beyond relational dyads to encompass a whole network of interpersonal, individual-to-firm, and interfirm relationships present in a typical interfirm relationship between seller and buyer companies. Sociological network theory contributes to an understanding of what constitutes a strong relational network between two firm exchange partners. Interpersonal relationships between individual members of both firms represent the foundation of this network. The strength of these interpersonal ties can be captured by relationship quality, a composite assessment of the commitment, trust, gratitude, and reciprocity norms that representatives of the customer firm experience in their relationships with representatives of the seller firm. From these interpersonal relationships, more abstract, holistic relations evolve between an individual customer and the seller firm as a whole, as well as between the two company entities. Beyond the relationship quality of each interpersonal relationship, customers assess their interpersonal ties in aggregate, such that the breadth and composition of the overall interfirm relationship affect relationship evaluations and performance. In particular, more interpersonal relational bonds in a networked interfirm relationship enhance relationship performance. Likewise, an interfirm relationship composed of interpersonal ties with diverse, unique, decision-making capabilities increases overall relationship effectiveness and efficiency. A seller's relationship marketing investments to enhance quality, breadth, and composition, as judged by the customer, thus augment performance outcomes from the interfirm relationship.

Then online relationship marketing theory broadens knowledge even further, by accommodating the developments of the digital age and clarifying relationships in which interactions between exchange partners are partially or fully mediated by Internet technology. The basic mechanisms pertaining to interpersonal (i.e., commitment, trust, gratitude, and reciprocity norms) and interfirm (i.e., relationship quality, relationship breadth, and relationship composition) relationships apply to online relationships, but the actual interactions between exchange partners have changed substantially. Specifically, human-to-human (i.e., face-to-face, oral, or written) communications between relational partners increasingly have been substituted by human-to-technology interactions, with Internet technology acting as a communication medium. Such developments have produced leaner but also more manifold (i.e., omnichannel) communications. Theories seeking to explain human interaction with technology, such as flow, media richness, or parasocial interaction theories, are key for comprehending online relationships. The related constructs subsume existing relationship marketing theory and extend it to account for the developments of the digital age. The more effective companies' relationship marketing investments are in inducing favorable perceptions of flow, media richness, and parasocial interactions, the higher their overall relationship performance.

Thus the impact of firms' relationship marketing investments on relationship and, eventually, company performance is mediated by a series of mechanisms (i.e., customer commitment, customer trust, customer gratitude, customer reciprocity norms, relationship breadth, relationship composition, flow, media richness, and parasocial interaction). Each mechanism contributes individually to a specific facet or type of relationship (i.e., interpersonal, interfirm, online). Jointly, the mechanisms provide a comprehensive theory of relationship marketing effectiveness.

## Summary

Relationships and their impact on human behavior are frequently researched topics in various disciplines. Thus marketing enjoys a rich theoretical landscape from which to gather insights to understand relationship marketing. Over more than six decades of relationship marketing research, concepts from diverse domains (e.g., economics, sociology, social psychology, psychology) have informed relationship marketing theory. A temporal overview suggests a broad pattern, proceeding from the application of institutional, macro-level theories (e.g., economics, sociology) to individual, micro-level theoretical perspectives (e.g., social psychology, psychology).

To distill the essence of the basic functioning of relationships, evolutionary psychology in particular proves fruitful. By combining modern psychology with evolutionary biology, evolutionary psychology indicates that relationship marketing effectiveness can be explained parsimoniously through the mechanisms of gratitude and fairness—two universal, hereditary, and deeply ingrained notions in human beings that reinforce cooperation within groups to ensure their survival. These characteristics make gratitude and (un)fairness indispensable to relationship marketing theory, because they either reinforce relationship reciprocity and cooperation through gratitude or destroy relationships through punishment in response to perceived unfairness. Whether promoting or impeding relationships, gratitude and unfairness represent the twin pillars of relationship marketing.

In addition, relationships can be classified into three main types: (1) interpersonal (e.g., individual customer-to-salesperson), (2) interfirm (e.g., network of individual customer-to-salesperson, individual customer-to-seller firm, and firm customer-to-seller firm), and (3) online (e.g., individual/firm customer-to-technology-to-salesperson/seller firm). Each relationship type features its own key theories and focal constructs, critical for understanding relationship performance. Interpersonal relationship marketing theory is informed by social exchange theory and evolutionary psychology, which together establish customer commitment, trust, gratitude, and reciprocity norms as core mechanisms mediating the impact of relationship marketing investments on performance outcomes. Building on those ideas, interfirm relationship marketing theory also uses network theory to underscore the key roles of relationship quality, breadth, and composition for explaining relationship marketing performance. In the next step, online relationship marketing theory introduces Internet technology as a communication transmitter. Flow, media richness, and parasocial interaction represent key constructs determining online relationship marketing effectiveness.

Customer–seller relationships in the digital age often are hybrid constellations, encompassing interpersonal, interfirm, and online elements. Integrating these three relationship types, which systematically build on one another, produces a more comprehensive relationship marketing theory. The mechanisms pertaining to interpersonal relationships (i.e., customer commitment, trust, gratitude, reciprocity norms) represent the core of any relationship type, but interfirm relationship marketing theory also extends to broader networks of interpersonal, individual-to-firm, and interfirm ties. This portfolio of individual relationships can be evaluated by assessing relationship quality, relationship breadth, and relationship composition. In online relationships, the theoretical framework used to explain interpersonal and interfirm relationships can be expanded to encompass relationships in which interactions between exchange partners are partially or fully mediated by Internet technology, suggesting a key role of customer-perceived flow, media richness, and parasocial interaction.

## Takeaways

- For more than six decades of relationship marketing research, insights from diverse domains such as economics, sociology, social psychology, and psychology have informed theory building.
- Over time, relationship marketing theory has shifted from more institutional, macro-level theories (e.g., economics, sociology) to more individual, micro-level theoretical perspectives (e.g., social psychology, psychology).
- Evolutionary psychology parsimoniously identifies the psychological mechanisms of gratitude and unfairness as the twin pillars of relationship marketing.

- Both gratitude and unfairness are universal, hereditary, and hard-wired into human beings. Gratitude reinforces relationships through reciprocity; unfairness impedes relationships through punishment.
- Three types of marketing relationships are interpersonal, interfirm, and online relationships. Each type features its own characteristics, key theories, and constructs.
- Interpersonal relationship marketing theory is based on social exchange theory and evolutionary psychology; it identifies customer commitment, trust, gratitude, and reciprocity norms as key mechanisms of relationship performance.
- Interfirm relationship marketing theory draws on network theory to establish relationship quality, breadth, and composition as the key drivers of relationship performance.
- Online relationship marketing theory distills flow, media richness, and parasocial interaction as major antecedents to relationship performance in online contexts.
- An integrative theory of relationship marketing combines interpersonal, interfirm, and online perspectives and their respective theories and constructs to illuminate relationship marketing effectiveness in the digital age.

## References

Alderson, Wroe (1958), "The Analytical Framework for Marketing." In *Proceedings: Conference of Marketing Teachers from Far Western States*, ed. Delbert Duncan, 15–28. Berkeley: University of California Press.

Ambler, Tim, Chris Styles, and Wang Xiucum (1999), "The Effect of Channel Relationships and Guanxi on the Performance of Inter-Province Export Ventures in the People's Republic of China." *International Journal of Research in Marketing* 16 (February), 75–87.

Anderson, Erin, and Baron A. Weitz (1992), "The Use of Pledges to Build and Sustain Commitment in Distribution Channels." *Journal of Marketing Research* 29 (February), 18–34.

Anderson, James C., Hakan Hakansson, and Jan Johanson (1994), "Dyadic Business Relationships Within a Business Network Context." *Journal of Marketing* 58 (October), 1–15.

Arora, Neeraj, and Greg M. Allenby (1999), "Measuring the Influence of Individual Preference Structures in Group Decision Making." *Journal of Marketing Research* 36 (November), 476–87.

Bagozzi, Richard P. (1975), "Marketing as Exchange." *Journal of Marketing* 39 (October), 32–9.

Bagozzi, Richard P. (1995), "Reflections on Relationship Marketing in Consumer Markets." *Journal of the Academy of Marketing Science* 23 (4), 272–7.

Ballantine, Paul W., and Brett A. S. Martin (2005), "Forming Parasocial Relationships in Online Communities." In *Advances in Consumer Research*, eds. G. Menon and A. R. Rao, 197–201. Duluth: Association for Consumer Research.

Bartlett, Monica Y., and David DeSteno (2006), "Gratitude and Prosocial Behavior." *Psychological Science* 17 (April), 319–25.

Baum, Joel A. C., Tony C. Calabrese, and Brian S. Silverman (2000), "Don't Go It Alone: Alliance Network Composition and Startups' Performance in Canadian Biotechnology." *Strategic Management Journal* 21 (March), 267–94.

Becker, Lawrence C. (1986), *Reciprocity*. New York: Routledge & Kegan Paul.

Bendapudi, Neeli, and Robert P. Leone (2002), "Managing Business-to-Business Customer Relationships Following Key Contact Employee Turnover in a Vendor Firm." *Journal of Marketing* 66 (April), 83–101.

Berry, Leonard L. (1983), "Relationship Marketing." In *Emerging Perspectives on Services Marketing*, eds. Leonard L. Berry, G. L. Shostack, and G. D. Upah, 25–8. Chicago: American Marketing Association.

BI Intelligence (2016), "Amazon's Customer Loyalty Eats into Competitors." Available at: www.businessinsider.de/amazons-customer-loyalty-eats-into-competitors-2016-11?r=US&IR=T (accessed 15 August 2018).

Blau, Peter (1964), *Exchange and Power in Social Life*. New York: John Wiley & Sons.

Bonoma, Thomas V., and Wesley J. Johnston (1978), "The Social Psychology of Industrial Buying and Selling." *Industrial Marketing Management* 7 (August), 213–24.

Borgatti, Stephen P., and Pacey C. Foster (2003), "The Network Paradigm in Organizational Research: A Review and Topology." *Journal of Management* 29 (6), 991–1013.

Bowles, Samuel, Ernst Fehr, and Herbert Gintis (2003), *Strong Reciprocity May Evolve With or Without Group Selection*. Unpublished Manuscript. Center for Empirical Economics, University of Zurich.

Buck, Ross (2004), "The Gratitude of Exchange and the Gratitude of Caring: A Developmental-Interactionist Perspective of Moral Emotion." In *The Psychology of Gratitude*, eds. Robert A. Emmons and Michael E. McCullough, 100–22. New York: Oxford University Press.

Bucklin, Louis P., and Sanjit Sengupta (1993), "Organizing Successful Co-Marketing Alliances." *Journal of Marketing* 57 (April), 32–46.

Burt, Ronald S. (1992), *Structural Holes: The Social Structure of Competition*. Cambridge, MA: Harvard University Press.

Cable, Daniel M., and Kang Y. T. Yu (2006), "Managing Job Seekers' Organizational Image Beliefs: The Role of Media Richness and Media Credibility." *Journal of Applied Psychology* 91 (4), 828–40.

Cannon, Joseph P., Ravi S. Achrol, and Gregory T. Gundlach (2000), "Contracts, Norms, and Plural Form Governance." *Journal of the Academy Marketing Science* 28 (Spring), 180–94.

Chang, Ya P., and Dong H. Zhu (2012), "The Role of Perceived Social Capital and Flow Experience in Building Users' Continuance Intention to Social Networking Sites in China." *Computers in Human Behavior* 28 (3), 995–1001.

ChannelReply (2018), "What Amazon Teaches Us About CRM Strategy." Available at: www.channelreply.com/blog/view/amazon-crm-strategy (accessed 15 August 2018).

Cialdini, Robert B., and Kelton V. L. Rhoads (2001), "Human Behavior and the Marketplace." *Marketing Research* 13 (3), 8–13.

Colarelli, Stephen M., and Joseph R. Dettmann (2003), "Intuitive Evolutionary Perspectives in Marketing Practices." *Psychology & Marketing* 20 (9), 837–65.

Cook, Karen S., and Richard M. Emerson (1978), "Power. Equity and Commitment in Exchange Networks." *American Sociological Review* 43 (October), 721–39.

Crosby, Lawrence A., Kenneth R. Evans, and Deborah Cowles (1990), "Relationship Quality in Services Selling: An Interpersonal Influence Perspective." *Journal of Marketing* 54 (July), 68–81.

Csikszentmihalyi, Mihali (1975), *Beyond Boredom and Anxiety: Experiencing Flow in Work and Play*. San Francisco: Jossey-Bass Publishers.

Daft, Richard L., and Robert H. Lengel (1986), "Organizational Information Requirements, Media Richness and Structural Design." *Management Science* 32 (5), 554–71.

Dahl, Darren W., Heather Honea, and Rajesh V. Manchanda (2005), "Three Rs of Interpersonal Consumer Guilt: Relationship, Reciprocity, Reparation." *Journal of Consumer Psychology* 15 (4), 307–15.

Danziger, Pamela N. (2018), "Amazon's Customer Loyalty Is Astounding." Available at: www.forbes.com/sites/pamdanziger/2018/01/10/amazons-customer-loyalty-is-astounding/2/#1e60b4384162 (accessed 15 August 2018).

De Wulf, Kristof, Gaby Odekerken-Schröder, and Dawn Iacobucci (2001), "Investments in Consumer Relationships: A Cross-Country and Cross-Industry Exploration." *Journal of Marketing* 65 (October), 33–50.

Doney, Patricia M., and Joseph P. Cannon (1997), "An Examination of the Nature of Trust in Buyer-Seller Relationships." *Journal of Marketing* 61 (April), 35–51.

Dunn, Jennifer R., and Maurice E. Schweitzer (2005), "Feeling and Believing: The Influence of Emotion on Trust." *Journal of Personality & Social Psychology* 88 (5), 736–48.

Dwyer, Robert F., Paul H. Schurr, and Sejo Oh (1987), "Developing Buyer-Seller Relationships." *Journal of Marketing* 51 (April), 11–27.

Dyer, Jeffrey H., and Harbir Singh (1998), "The Relational View: Cooperative Strategy and Sources of Interorganizational Competitive Advantage." *Academy of Management Review* 23 (4), 660–79.

El-Ansary, Adel I. (1975), "Determinants of Power-Dependence in Distribution Channel." *Journal of Retailing* 51 (Summer), 59–94.

Emerson, Richard M. (1962), "Power-Dependence Relations." *American Sociological Review* 27 (February), 31–41.

Emmons, Robert A., and Michael E. McCullough (2003), "Counting Blessings Versus Burdens: An Experimental Investigation of Gratitude and Subjective Well-Being in Daily Life." *Journal of Personality and Social Psychology* 84 (2), 377–89.

Emmons, Robert A., and Michael E. McCullough (2004), "The Psychology of Gratitude: An Introduction." In *The Psychology of Gratitude*, eds. Robert A. Emmons and Michael E. McCullough, 3–16. New York: Oxford University Press.

Eyuboglu, Nermin, and Andreas Buja (2007), "Quasi-Darwinian Selection in Marketing Relationships." *Journal of Marketing* 71 (October), 48–62.

Fang, Eric, Robert W. Palmatier, Lisa K. Scheer, and Ning Li (2008), "Trust at Different Organizational Levels." *Journal of Marketing* 72 (March), 80–98.

Folkes, Valerie S. (1988), "Recent Attribution Research in Consumer Behavior: A Review and New Directions." *Journal of Consumer Research* 14 (March), 548–65.

Frazier, Gary L. (1983), "On the Measurement of Interfirm Power in Channels of Distribution." *Journal of Marketing Research* 20 (May), 158–66.

Ganesan, Shankar (1994), "Determinants of Long-Term Orientation in Buyer-Seller Relationships." *Journal of Marketing* 58 (April), 1–19.

Garbarino, Ellen, and Mark S. Johnson (1999), "The Different Roles of Satisfaction, Trust, and Commitment in Customer Relationships." *Journal of Marketing* 63 (April), 70–87.

Gartner (2011), "Gartner Customer 360 Summit 2011." Available at: www.gartner.com/imagesrv/summits/docs/na/customer-360/C360_2011_brochure_FINAL.pdf (accessed 19 August 2018).

Gassenheimer, Jule B., J. Charlene Davis, and Robert Dahlstrom (1998), "Is Dependent What We Want to Be? Effects of Incongruency." *Journal of Retailing* 74 (2), 247–71.

Gilbert, Jason O. (2011), "'How Could Netflix Do This To Me?': Netflix Users Lash Out." Available at: www.huffingtonpost.com/2011/07/14/how-could-netflix-do-this-to-me_n_897763.html (accessed 15 August 2018).

Giles, David C. (2002), "Parasocial Interaction: A Review of the Literature and a Model for Future Research." *Media Psychology* 4 (3), 279–305.

Goei, Ryan, and Franklin J. Boster (2005), "The Roles of Obligation and Gratitude in Explaining the Effect of Favors on Compliance." *Communication Monographs* 72 (September), 284–300.

Gouldner, Alvin W. (1960), "The Norm of Reciprocity: A Preliminary Statement." *American Sociology Review* 25 (April), 161–78.

Granovetter, Mark (1973), "The Strength of Weak Ties: A Network Theory Revisited." *Sociological Theory* 1 (1983), 201–33.

Harmeling, Colleen M., Robert W. Palmatier, Mark B. Houston, Mark J. Arnold, and Stephen A. Samaha (2015), "Transformational Relationship Events." *Journal of Marketing* 79 (September), 39–62.

Heide, Jan B., and George John (1990), "Alliances in Industrial Purchasing: The Determinants of Joint Action in Buyer-Supplier Relationships." *Journal of Marketing Research* 27 (February), 24–36.

Hibbard, Jonathan D., Frederic F. Brunel, Rajiv P. Dant, and Dawn Iacobucci (2001), "Does Relationship Marketing Age Well?" *Business Strategy Review* 12 (4), 29–35.

Hibbard, Jonathan D., Nirmalya Kumar, and Louis W. Stern (2001), "Examining the Impact of Destructive Acts in Marketing Channels Relationship." *Journal of Marketing Research* 38 (February), 25–61.

Horton, Donald, and Richard Wohl (1956), "Mass Communication and Para-social Interaction: Observation on Intimacy at a Distance." *Psychiatry* 19, 215–29.

Houston, Mark B., Michael D. Hutt, Christine Moorman, Peter H. Reingen, Aric Rindfleisch, Vanitha Swaminathan, and Beth A. Walker (2004), "A Network Perspective on Marketing Strategy." In *Assessing Marketing Strategy Performance*, eds. Christine Moorman and Donald R. Lehman, 247–68. Cambridge, MA: Marketing Science Institute.

Iacobucci, Dawn, and Amy Ostrom (1996), "Commercial and Interpersonal Relationships; Using the Structure of Interpersonal Relationships to Understand Individual-to-individual, Individual-to-firm, and Firm-to-firm Relationships in Commerce." *International Journal of Research in Marketing* 13 (1), 53–72.

Jacobs, Robert C., and Donald T. Campbell (1961), "The Perpetuation of an Arbitrary Tradition Through Several Generations of a Laboratory Microculture." *Journal of Abnormal and Social Psychology* 62 (3), 649–58.

Jap, Sandy D. (1999), "Pie-Expansion Efforts: Collaboration Processes in Buyer-Supplier Relationships." *Journal of Marketing Research* 36 (November), 461–75.

Jap, Sandy D., and Shankar Ganesan (2000), "Control Mechanisms and the Relationship Life Cycle: Implications for Safeguarding Specific Investments and Developing Commitment." *Journal of Marketing Research* 37 (May), 227–45.

John, George (1984), "An Empirical Investigation of Some Antecedents of Opportunism in a Marketing Channel." *Journal of Marketing Research* 21 (August), 278–89.

Kaplan, Andreas M., and Michael Haenlein (2010), "Users of the World, Unite! The Challenges and Opportunities of Social Media." *Business Horizons* 53 (1), 59–68.

Katrichis, Jerome M. (1998), "Exploring Departmental Level Interaction Patterns in Organizational Purchasing Decisions." *Industrial Marketing Management* 27 (March), 135–46.

Kaufmann, Patrick J., and Rajiv P. Dant (1992), "The Dimensions of Commercial Exchange." *Marketing Letters* 3 (April), 171–85.

Kim, Hongki, Kil-Soo Suh, and Un-Kon Lee (2013), "Effects of Collaborative Online Shopping on Shopping Experience Through Social and Relational Perspectives." *Information & Management* 50 (4), 169–80.

Kumar, Nirmalya, Jonathan D. Hibbard, and Leonard D. Stern (1994), *The Nature and Consequences of Marketing Channel Intermediary Commitment.* Cambridge, MA: Marketing Science Institute.

Kumar, Nirmalya, Lisa K. Scheer, and Jan-Benedict E. M. Steenkamp (1995a), "The Effects of Perceived Interdependence on Dealer Attitudes." *Journal of Marketing Research* 32 (August), 348–56.

Kumar, Nirmalya, Lisa K. Scheer, and Jan-Benedict E. M. Steenkamp (1995b), "The Effects of Supplier Fairness on Vulnerable Resellers." *Journal of Marketing Research* 32 (February), 54–65.

Labrecque, Lauren I. (2014), "Fostering Consumer–Brand Relationships in Social Media Environments: The Role of Parasocial Interaction." *Journal of Interactive Marketing* 28 (2), 134–48.

Lee, Ming-Chi, and Tzung-Ru Tsai (2010), "What Drives People to Continue to Play Online Games? An Extension of Technology Model and Theory of Planned Behavior." *International Journal of Human–Computer Interaction* 26 (6), 601–20.

Lee, Richard, and Irven DeVore (1968), *Man the Hunter.* Chicago: Aldine.

Luna, David, Laura A. Peracchio, and María D. de Juan (2002), "Cross-cultural and Cognitive Aspects of Web Site Navigation." *Journal of the Academy of Marketing Science* 30 (4), 397–410.

Macaulay, Stewart (1963), "Non-Contractual Relations in Business." *American Sociological Review* 28 (1), 55–67.

Macneil, Ian (1980), *The New Social Contract: An Inquiry into Modern Contractual Relations.* New Haven: Yale University Press.

McDonald, Gerald W. (1981), "Structural Exchange and Marital Interaction." *Journal of Marriage and the Family* (November), 825–39.

McKenna, Katelyn Y. A., Amie S. Green, and Marci E. J. Gleason (2002), "Relationship Formation on the Internet: What's the Big Attraction?" *Journal of Social Issues* 58 (1), 9–31.

Mohr, Jakki J., and Robert Spekman (1994), "Characteristics of Partnership Success: Partnership Attributes, Communication Behavior, and Conflict Resolution Techniques." *Strategic Management Journal* 15 (2), 135–52.

Moorman, Christine, Gerald Zaltman, and Rohit Deshpandé (1992), "Relationships Between Providers and Users of Market Research: The Dynamics of Trust Within and Between Organizations." *Journal of Marketing Research* 29 (August), 314–29.

Morales, Andrea C. (2005), "Giving Firms an 'E' for Effort: Consumer Responses to High-Effort Firms." *Journal of Consumer Research* 31 (March), 806–12.

Morgan, Robert M., and Shelby D. Hunt (1994), "The Commitment-Trust Theory of Relationship Marketing." *Journal of Marketing* 58 (July), 20–38.

Nakamura, Jeanne, and Mihaly Csikszentmihalyi (2011), "Flow Theory and Research." In *Handbook of Positive Psychology,* 2nd ed., eds. C. R. Snyder and Shane J. Lopez, 195–206. Oxford: Oxford University Press.

Novak, Thomas P., Donna L. Hoffmann, and Yiu-Fai Yung (2000), "Measuring the Customer Experience in Online Environments: A Structural Modeling Approach." *Marketing Science* 19 (1), 22–42.

O'Dell, Carla (2016), "How Airbnb Builds Trust, Engagement, and Community Through Peer-to-Peer Ratings." Available at: www.apqc.org/blog/

how-airbnb-builds-trust-engagement-and-community-through-peer-peer-ratings (accessed 15 August 2018).

Ostrom, Elinor, and James Walker, eds. (2003), *Trust and Reciprocity: Interdisciplinary Lessons From Experimental Research*. New York: Russell Sage Foundation.

Palmatier, Robert W. (2008), "Interfirm Relational Drivers of Customer Value." *Journal of Marketing* 72 (July), 76–89.

Palmatier, Robert W., Rajiv P. Dant, and Dhruv Grewal (2007), "A Comparative Longitudinal Analysis of Theoretical Perspectives of Interorganizational Relationship Performance." *Journal of Marketing* 71 (October), 172–94.

Palmatier, Robert W., Rajiv P. Dant, Dhruv Grewal, and Kenneth R. Evans (2006), "Factors Influencing the Effectiveness of Relationship Marketing: A Meta-Analysis." *Journal of Marketing* 70 (October), 136–53.

Palmatier, Robert W., Mark B. Houston, Rajiv P. Dant, and Dhruv Grewal (2013), "Relationship Velocity: Toward a Theory of Relationship Dynamics." *Journal of Marketing* 77 (January), 13–30.

Palmatier, Robert W., Cheryl Burke Jarvis, Jennifer R. Bechkoff, and Frank R. Kardes (2009), "The Role of Customer Gratitude in Relationship Marketing." *Journal of Marketing* 73 (September), 1–18.

Palmatier, Robert W., Lisa K. Scheer, Mark B. Houston, Kenneth R. Evans, and Srinath Gopalakrishna (2007), "Use of Relationship Marketing Programs in Building Customer-Salesperson and Customer-Firm Relationships: Differential Influences on Financial Outcomes." *International Journal of Research in Marketing* 24 (September), 210–23.

Palmatier, Robert W., Lisa K. Scheer, and Jan Benedict Steenkamp (2007), "Customer Loyalty to Whom? Managing the Benefits and Risks of Salesperson-Owned Loyalty." *Journal of Marketing Research* 44 (May), 185–99.

Rackham, Neil (1996), *The SPIN Selling Fieldbook*. New York: McGraw-Hill Professional Publishing.

Rainie, Lee, and Barry Wellman (2012), *Networked: The New Social Operating System*. Cambridge, MA: MIT Press.

Reichheld, Fredrick F., and Thomas Teal (1996), *The Loyalty Effect*. Boston: Harvard Business School Press.

Reinartz, Werner, Jacquelyn S. Thomas, and V. Kumar (2005), "Balancing Acquisition and Retention Resources to Maximize Customer Profitability." *Journal of Marketing* 69 (1), 63–79.

Reynolds, Kristy E., and Sharon E. Beatty (1999), "Customer Benefits and Company Consequences of Customer-Salesperson Relationships in Retailing." *Journal of Retailing* 75 (1), 11–32.

Rheinberg, Falko, Regina Vollmeyer, and Stefan Engeser (2003), "Die Erfassung des Flow-Erlebens [The Assessment of Flow Experience]." In *Diagnostik von Selbstkonzept, Lernmotivation und Selbstregulation* [Diagnosis of Motivation and Self-Concept], eds. Joachim Stiensmeier-Pelster and Falko Rheinberg. Göttingen: Hogrefe.

Ridley, Mark (1985), *The Problems of Evolution*. Oxford: Oxford University Press.

Rindfleisch, Aric, and Jan B. Heide (1997), "Transaction Cost Analysis: Past, Present, and Future Applications." *Journal of Marketing* 61 (October), 30–54.

Rowley, Timothy J. (1997), "Moving Beyond Dyadic Ties: A Network Theory of Stakeholder Influences." *Academy of Management Review* 22 (4), 887–910.

Rubin, Alan M., Elizabeth M. Perse, and Robert A. Powell (1985), "Loneliness, Parasocial Interaction, and Local Television News Viewing." *Human Communication Research* 12 (2), 155–80.

Saad, Gad (2011), "The Missing Link: The Biological Roots of the Business Sciences." In *Evolutionary Psychology in the Business Sciences*, ed. Gad Saad, 1–16. Berlin: Springer.

Saad, Gad, and Tripat Gill (2000), "Applications of Evolutionary Psychology in Marketing." *Psychology & Marketing* 17 (12), 1005–34.

Samaha, Stephen, Jordan Moffett, Irina Kozlenkova, and Robert W. Palmatier (2018), "Multichannel Communication Strategies." Working Paper.

Samaha, Stephen A., Robert W. Palmatier, and Rajiv P. Dant (2011), "Poisoning Relationships: Perceived Unfairness in Channels of Distribution." *Journal of Marketing* 75 (May), 99–117.

Scheer, Lisa K., C. Fred Miao, and Robert W. Palmatier (2015), "Dependence and Interdependence in Marketing Relationships: Meta-Analytic Insights." *Journal of the Academy of Marketing Science* 43 (November), 694–712.

Schwartz, Barry (1967), "The Social Psychology of the Gift." *The American Journal of Sociology* 73 (July), 1–11.

Siguaw, Judy A., Penny M. Simpson, and Thomas L. Baker (1998), "Effects of Supplier Market Orientation on Distributor Market Orientation and the Channel Relationship: The Distributor Perspective." *Journal of Marketing* 62 (July), 99–111.

Sirdeshmukh, Deepak, Jagdip Singh, and Barry Sabol (2002), "Consumer Trust, Value, and Loyalty in Relational Exchanges." *Journal of Marketing* 66 (January), 15–37.

Smith, Adam (1759), *The Theory of Moral Sentiments*. London: A. Millar.

Steinhoff, Lena, Denni Arli, Scott Weaven, and Irina V. Kozlenkova (2018), "Online Relationship Marketing." Working Paper.

Steinhoff, Lena, and Robert W. Palmatier (2016), "Understanding Loyalty Program Effectiveness: Managing Target and Bystander Effects." *Journal of the Academy of Marketing Science* 44 (January), 88–107.

Tax, Stephen S., and Stephen W. Brown (1998), "Recovering and Learning From Service Failure." *Sloan Management Review* 40 (1), 75–88.

Thibaut, John W., and Harold H. Kelley (1959), *The Social Psychology of Groups*. New York: John Wiley & Sons. Inc.

Trivers, Robert (1971), "The Evolution of Reciprocal Altruism." *Quarterly Review of Biology* 46 (March), 35–57.

Trivers, Robert (1985), *Social Evolution*. Menlo Park: The Benjamin/Cummins Publishing Company, Inc.

Tsai, Wenpin (2001), "Knowledge Transfer in Interorganizational Networks: Effects of Network Position and Absorptive Capacity on Business Unit Innovation and Performance." *Academy of Management Journal* 44 (October), 996–1001.

Van Den Bulte, Christophe, and Stefan Wuyts (2007), *Social Networks and Marketing*. Cambridge, MA: Marketing Science Institute.

Verhoef, Peter C., P. K. Kannan, and J. Jeffrey Inman (2015), "From Multi-Channel Retailing to Omni-Channel Retailing: Introduction to the Special Issue on Multi-Channel Retailing." *Journal of Retailing* 91 (2), 174–81.

Walker, Gordon, Bruce Kogut, and Weijan Shan (1997), "Social Capital, Structural Holes and the Formation of Industry Networks." *Organization Science* 8 (March–April), 109–25.

Wasieleski, David M., and Sefa Hayibor (2009), "Evolutionary Psychology and Business Ethics Research." *Business Ethics Quarterly* 19 (4), 587–616.

Wasserman, Stanley, and Katherine Faust (1994), *Social Network Analysis: Methods and Applications*. Cambridge: Cambridge University Press.

Wathne, Kenneth H., and Jan B. Heide (2000), "Opportunism in Interfirm Relationships: Forms, Outcomes, and Solutions." *Journal of Marketing* 64 (October), 36–51.

Watkins, Philip C., Kathrane Woodward, Tamara Stone, and Russell L. Kolts (2003), "Gratitude and Happiness: Development of a Measure of Gratitude, and Relationships With Subjective Well-Being." *Social Behavior & Personality: An International Journal* 31, 431–51.

Weiss, Allan M., and Erin Anderson (1992), "Converting From Independent to Employee Salesforce: The Role of Perceived Switching Costs." *Journal of Marketing Research* 29 (February), 101–15.

Wernerfelt, Birger (1984), "A Resource-Based View of the Firm." *Strategic Management Journal* 5 (2), 171–80.

Williamson, Oliver E. (1975), *Markets and Hierarchies: Analysis and Antitrust Implications.* New York: The Free Press.

Williamson, Oliver E. (1985), *The Economic Institute of Capitalism: Firms, Markets, Relational Contracting.* New York: The Free Press.

Zhang, Jonathan Z., George F. Watson IV, Robert W. Palmatier, and Rajiv P. Dant (2016), "Dynamic Relationship Marketing." *Journal of Marketing* 80 (September), 53–75.

# 3   Relationship Marketing Framework

## Learning Objectives

- Understand the three causal stages of the relationship marketing framework: seller relationship marketing investments → customer relational mechanisms → seller relationship marketing performance outcomes.
- Identify financial, social, and structural relationship marketing investments as three generic relationship marketing strategies available to companies and consider their differential effectiveness.
- Classify emotional, cognitive, conative, and behavioral relational mechanisms among customers and understand their causal order.
- Recognize the various financial and nonfinancial performance ramifications spurred by effective relationship marketing investments.

## Introduction

In a way, relationship marketing efforts are like any other marketing tactics. Managers devote substantial time and money to them, with the assumption that doing so ultimately will improve company performance. Yet similar to resources assigned to advertising, public relations, or celebrity endorsements, it is difficult to specify the returns on investments in relationship marketing, in terms of their actual financial and nonfinancial impacts or the precise routes through which they improve performance. To address this challenge, this chapter synthesizes extant knowledge and seeks to derive an overall causal framework of relationship marketing's performance impacts. Relationship marketing investments do not affect financial performance directly but rather gear relational mechanisms among customers, which then generate improvements in the company's performance outcomes. That is, the performance impact of relationship marketing investments occurs through the stimulation of positive emotions, cognitions, conations, and behaviors among customers (i.e., gratitude, commitment, trust, reciprocity norms, relationship breadth, relationship composition, media richness, parasocial interaction, relationship velocity, experience, flow, loyalty, and engagement). Negative emotions such as customer unfairness instead need to be avoided. These mechanisms in turn represent the most common explanations for how relationships influence firms' performance and mediate the impact of relationship marketing investments on performance outcomes. Figure 3.1 depicts this three-stage causal model: seller relationship marketing investments → customer relational mechanisms → seller relationship marketing performance outcomes. We discuss each of these causally linked stages in turn.

## Seller Relationship Marketing Investments

Relationship marketing investments consist of dedicated relationship marketing strategies or programs, designed and implemented to build, grow, and maintain strong customer–company relational bonds by stimulating favorable relational mechanisms among customers. Different types of relationship marketing investments have differential effects on customers and varying levels of return (Berry 1995; Bolton, Smith, and Wagner 2003; Cannon, Achrol, and Gundlach 2000; Palmatier, Gopalakrishna, and Houston 2006; Palmatier et al. 2007). Disentangling and categorizing different **seller relationship marketing investments** often relies on a classification of relationship marketing programs according to their financial, social, or structural focus. Some components may overlap within a specific program (e.g., loyalty programs often involve both financial and social components), but distinguishing financial, social, and structural relationship marketing investments provides an effective, parsimonious grouping (Palmatier, Gopalakrishna, and Houston 2006; Palmatier et al. 2007). Within each category, customer responses to the seller's investments are similar; across categories, the effectiveness of investments in strengthening relational ties varies.

### Financial Relationship Marketing Investments

Financial programs appeal to relationship marketers because they are so easy to implement. Furthermore, for virtually every firm, investing in customer relationships demands some **financial relationship marketing investment** to encourage customer loyalty by providing them with discounts, giveaways, free shipping, extended payment terms, and so on. These investments are very common, especially among retail, travel, financial services, and consumer product companies, whose customer service employees can easily issue a financial incentive (e.g., free sample). Building a broader interpersonal relationship or developing a structural program requires more time and effort, but these forms of financial investments are relatively simple to apply. For example, loyalty rewards programs often issue discounts or special benefits to regular customers who earn points by buying more.

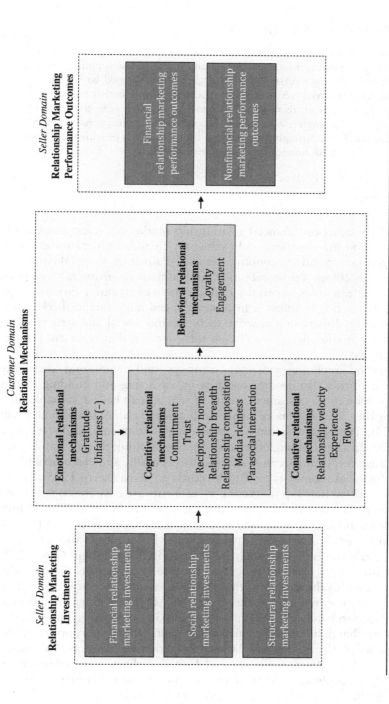

*Figure 3.1* A Framework of Relationship Marketing's Impact on Seller Performance Outcomes

---

**Example 3.1  Amazon (USA)**

Amazon Business is a business-to-business (B2B) e-commerce platform that allows registered businesses to sell and buy business supplies. Businesses, institutions, enterprises, or other organizations located within the United States that have been assigned a tax identification number may apply for a business account. Business sellers provide exclusive items to business buyers; these customers also receive discounted prices and tiered quantity discounts. Thus, through the platform, business sellers provide their business customers with financial and relational incentives.

Source: Johnson (2016).

---

The returns on financial relationship marketing investments tend to depend on the situation, and exclusively financial programs usually fail to generate positive economic returns (Palmatier, Gopalakrishna, and Houston 2006). Yet despite their simplicity, such efforts take on important strategic roles, especially in response to competitive threats. To protect its existing business, a firm might spend more financial relationship marketing dollars in a reactive tactic (unlike social and structural relationship marketing, as we discuss subsequently, that represent proactive weapons).

Beyond retaining existing customers and countering competitive threats, firms also need to compete by attracting and building relationships with more customers, many of whom may be less valuable, in the hope they will grow more loyal or valuable over time (Johnson and Selnes 2004). Financial relationship marketing investments might encourage such transitions, though they also "may well flunk the profitability test" because competitors can match incentives easily, and customers focused on financial incentives tend to be costly to serve (Berry 1995). Because financial relationship marketing investments are easy for competitors to copy, the advantages derived from them tend to be unsustainable unless they are underlaid by unique sources (e.g., low cost structure) (Day and Wensley 1988). Customers attracted solely by incentives also tend to seek out deals and ultimately may be less profitable (Cao and Gruca 2005). Yet financially oriented programs provide good returns in some situations, and loyalty programs that feature economic incentives can increase both customer retention and share growth (Bolton, Kannan, and Bramlett 2000; Marchand et al. 2016; Verhoef 2003). Some firms ignore the conditions that define whether such investments will be appropriate and thus misallocate their financial relationship marketing resources. Others, such as Best Buy, Hertz, Citibank, and United Airlines, have reviewed their investments closely and are actively reducing their investments in financially focused relationship marketing programs.

## Social Relationship Marketing Investments

When customers receive special treatment, it implies the firm has made **social relationship marketing investments** in its effort to personalize the customer relationship and convey that particular customer's special status. The resulting bonds are difficult to duplicate; they also prompt customers to reciprocate with repeat sales, recommendations, or continued loyalty (Blau 1964; De Wulf, Odekerken-Schröder, and Iacobucci 2001).

---

**Example 3.2 Nordstrom (USA)**

For its Level 4 loyalty program members, Nordstrom regularly hosts exclusive VIP shopping events, such as the private fall fashion shopping day. Selected stores get closed down to the general public. Eligible customers are invited to bring a friend and enjoy drinks, appetizers, and other special amenities while shopping, stimulating their sense of being special and important to the company.

Sources: Nordstrom (2018); Leigh (2005).

---

Specifically, social programs create interpersonal feelings of gratitude and indebtedness that evoke the need to reciprocate, such that they often generate immediate returns (Cialdini 2001) but also indirectly enhance relationship quality, which can evoke favorable seller financial outcomes. Likewise, status rankings in loyalty programs directly strengthen the customer–firm relational tie. Overall then, social relationship marketing programs should improve customer–seller relationships (Bolton, Smith, and Wagner 2003; Hennig-Thurau, Gwinner, and Gremler 2002), and research shows that in the short term, they exert direct, strong (approximately 180%) impacts on profit—much greater than the impact of financial or structural investments (Palmatier, Gopalakrishna, and Houston 2006). Yet social programs rely on interpersonal interactions, such that customers might attribute all the benefits they receive to the salesperson rather than the selling firm, increasing the risk that the firm would lose the customer if the salesperson were to leave (Bendapudi and Leone 2002). Even with this cautionary note, which suggests the need for the selling firm to maintain direct communication with customers, most examples indicate that the effects of social programs are virtually immune to contextual influences.

## Structural Relationship Marketing Investments

**Structural relationship marketing investments** support the provision of benefits that customers cannot or would not obtain on their own, such as an electronic order-processing interface or customized packaging in

B2B relationships. These investments increase customer efficiency and productivity, so they can produce significant, if hard-to-quantify, benefits. Most programs demand considerable effort to establish. But they also offer unique benefits, so they create sustainable competitive advantages. The close bond between customers and sellers discourages customers from switching, as does their desire to retain the structural benefits. Customers even might increase their purchases from the seller to take full advantage of the value-enhancing structural offers (Berry 1995).

---

**Example 3.3 Wöhler (Germany)**

The medium-sized B2B company Wöhler supplies measuring and cleaning instruments, production machinery, and technical brushes. Through its Power Partner program, it hosts exclusive seminars, webinars, and on-site training to help customers enhance their know-how and extract more value from Wöhler's products.

Source: Wöhler (2018).

---

The influence of structural relationship marketing investments on profit tends to depend on interaction frequency in the relationship. That is, customers with an average interaction frequency (i.e., a few times per week) might produce break-even revenues, but frequent interactions could lead to returns on structural relationship marketing investments that reach 120% (Palmatier, Gopalakrishna, and Houston 2006). Clearly, sellers should prioritize those frequent customers who can benefit the most from customized structural solutions. However, they should not ignore customers who allow the firm to break even on its investment, because the structural linkages that result from these investments likely improve profits in the long term. Even infrequent customers might pursue increasing interactions if they want to take advantage of the value of structural interfaces. Furthermore, the links that emerge from structural relationship marketing investments typically focus on the selling firm, not interpersonal relationship quality with salespeople (Palmatier et al. 2007), though they also do not undermine the relationship with the salesperson.

## Customer Relational Mechanisms

Through their relationship marketing investments, seller firms seek to stimulate relational mechanisms in customers. As outlined in Chapter 2, relationship marketing theory pertaining to interpersonal, interfirm, and online relationships suggests a battery of processes at play—often simultaneously—when a customer evaluates a relational partner's actions. In particular, **customer relational mechanisms** capture the customer's emotions, cognitions, conations, and behaviors stemming from his or her interactions with the seller; they mediate or transmit the effect of relationship marketing investments on performance. Emotions, cognitions, and conations represent the three components of the human mind that together form attitudes and drive behaviors. Thus relational mechanisms reflect the incremental, typically intangible value that a firm receives from its relational bonds with a customer. In the following, we classify relational mechanisms according to their emotional, cognitive, conative, or behavioral core and delineate the causal sequence among these constructs. Table 3.1 provides a summary of the constructs, definitions, example measurement items, and representative research for customer relational mechanisms, as well as the other building blocks of the causal relationship marketing framework.

### Emotional Relational Mechanisms

*Emotional relational mechanisms* reflect a customer's feelings toward the seller firm. Compared with cognitions, emotions are relatively shorter-term, more affective, and less rational. Representing the customer's spontaneous, short-term reaction to the seller's actions, emotions influence and represent important precursors of cognitive judgments, conative motivations, and behaviors (Forgas and George 2001; Palmatier et al. 2009). Research also has identified customer gratitude and unfairness as the twin pillars of relationship marketing effectiveness.

Specifically, customer **gratitude**, or emotional appreciation in response to received benefits, is a key emotional mechanism ignited by the seller's relationship marketing efforts, especially on an interpersonal level, with both short- and long-term positive effects on firm performance (Morales 2005; Palmatier et al. 2009). Gratitude experienced by customers enhances relationship marketing performance in three ways (Palmatier et al. 2009). First, in the short run, customers engage in positive, gratitude-based reciprocal behaviors to satisfy their feelings of obligation in response to relationship marketing–induced feelings of gratitude. Second, in the short and long runs, gratitude enhances customer-perceived trust, which in turn fosters customer commitment and thus relational performance. Third, in the long run, gratitude initiates cycles of reciprocation that reflect persistent reciprocity norms, which also promote the long-term development and prosperity of relationships.

As a counterpart, customer **unfairness**, defined as customers' perception of the degree to which the ratio of their received outcomes relative to inputs, compared with the corresponding input–outcome ratios of other customers, seems unacceptable or inequitable, represents a serious threat to relationship performance (Steinhoff and Palmatier 2016). When customers feel treated unfairly by the seller, for example by observing other

*Table 3.1* Relationship Marketing Framework: Overview of Key Constructs and Example Measures

| Stage of Framework Construct | Construct Definition | Representative Measurement Items | Key Findings | Representative Relationship Marketing Research |
|---|---|---|---|---|
| **Seller Relationship Marketing Investments** | | | | |
| Financial relationship marketing investments | "Provision of direct economic benefits in exchange for past or future customer loyalty, includes special discounts, free products to generate incremental sales, and other incentives that easily may be converted to cost savings (e.g., free shipping; extended payment terms)" (Palmatier et al. 2007, pp. 212–13) | "This customer often gets free products and services." "This customer frequently gets special pricing or discounts." "This customer receives special financial benefits and incentives." | Financial programs generally fail to provide short-term returns on their investment. | Palmatier, Gopalakrishna, and Houston 2006; Palmatier et al. 2007 |
| Social relationship marketing investments | "Efforts to personalize the relationship and convey special status, entails social engagements such as meals and sporting events and therefore may vary from ad hoc, low cost interactions to expensive, formal recognitions" (Palmatier et al. 2007, p. 212) | "This customer often receives special treatment or status." "This customer is often provided meals, entertainment, or gifts by me or my firm." "This customer often receives special reports and/or information." | Social programs have the highest payoff in terms of short-term returns on investment. | Palmatier, Gopalakrishna, and Houston 2006; Palmatier et al. 2007 |

| | | | | |
|---|---|---|---|---|
| Structural relationship marketing investments | "Offer tangible, value-added benefits that are difficult for customers to supply themselves, may include electronic order-processing interfaces, customized packaging, or other custom procedural changes" (Palmatier et al. 2007, p. 212) | "This customer often receives special value-added benefits (inventory control, expediting, etc.)." "Special structural changes (electronic data interchanges, packaging, etc.) have been instituted for this customer." "Our policies and procedures are often adapted for this customer." "Dedicated personnel are assigned to this customer beyond what is typical for our firm." | Structural programs break even with regard to short-term returns on investment. | Palmatier, Gopalakrishna, and Houston 2006; Palmatier et al. 2007 |

*Customer Relational Mechanisms*

*Emotional*

| | | | | |
|---|---|---|---|---|
| Gratitude | "Feelings of gratefulness, thankfulness, or appreciation for a benefit received" (Palmatier et al. 2009, p. 3) | "I feel [My firm feels] grateful to this salesperson [selling firm]." "I feel [My firm feels] thankful to this salesperson [selling firm]." "I feel [My firm feels] obligated to this salesperson [selling firm]." | Relationship marketing investments increase customer gratitude. The effect is particularly strong if the benefits provided are based on the seller's free will and benevolent motives, incur some kind of risk for the seller, and the customer needs the benefit. Customer gratitude both directly and indirectly (through trust and commitment) enhances customer loyalty. | Morales 2005; Palmatier et al. 2009; Steinhoff and Palmatier 2016 |

(Continued)

Table 3.1 (Continued)

| Stage of Framework Construct | Construct Definition | Representative Measurement Items | Key Findings | Representative Relationship Marketing Research |
|---|---|---|---|---|
| Unfairness | "A customer's view of the degree to which the ratio of his or her received outcomes relative to inputs, compared with the corresponding input–outcome ratios of other customers, seems unacceptable or inequitable" (Steinhoff and Palmatier 2016, p. 92) | "The way this salesperson [selling firm] treats me [my firm] is unfair." "The way this salesperson [selling firm] treats me [my firm] is unjustified." "Given my [my firm's] behavior as a customer, this salesperson [selling firm] treats me unfairly." "Given what this salesperson [selling firm] earns from his/her [its] sales to me [my firm], he/she [it] treats me unfairly." | Treating customers as bystanders may create unfairness perceptions. Perceived unfairness has strong negative effects on customer loyalty and relationship performance. It also aggravates the negative effects of conflict and opportunism. Typical disagreements and conflict have little effect on customer performance when perceived unfairness is low; they exert massively negative effects on relationship performance when accompanied by high unfairness perceptions. | Henderson, Beck, and Palmatier 2011; Samaha, Palmatier, and Dant 2011; Steinhoff and Palmatier 2016 |

*Cognitive*

| | | | | |
|---|---|---|---|---|
| Commitment | "An enduring desire to maintain a valued relationship" (Moorman, Zaltman, and Deshpandé 1992, p. 316) | "I am [My firm is] willing 'to go the extra mile' to work with this salesperson [selling firm]." "I feel [My firm feels] committed to the relationship with this salesperson [selling firm]." "I [My firm] would work hard to maintain my [our] relationship with this salesperson [selling firm]." | Commitment positively affects loyalty, cooperation, financial performance, and other positive outcomes and thus represents one of the key mediators of the impact of relationship marketing investments on performance. | Anderson and Weitz 1992; De Wulf, Odekerken-Schröder, and Iacobucci 2001; Jap and Ganesan 2000; Kumar, Hibbard, and Stern 1994; Moorman, Zaltman, and Deshpandé 1992; Morgan and Hunt 1994 |
| Trust | "Confidence in an exchange partner's reliability and integrity" (Morgan and Hunt 1994, p. 23) | "This salesperson [selling firm] gives me a feeling [us feelings] of trust." "This salesperson [selling firm] is always honest." "This salesperson [Selling firm] is trustworthy." | Trust exerts both positive direct and indirect (through commitment) effects on relationship outcomes; it represents the second key mediator of the impact of relationship marketing investments on performance. | De Wulf, Odekerken-Schröder, and Iacobucci 2001; Doney and Cannon 1997; Hibbard et al. 2001; Moorman, Zaltman, and Deshpandé 1992; Morgan and Hunt 1994; Sirdeshmukh, Singh, and Sabol 2002 |

*(Continued)*

*Table 3.1* (Continued)

| Stage of Framework Construct | Construct Definition | Representative Measurement Items | Key Findings | Representative Relationship Marketing Research |
|---|---|---|---|---|
| Reciprocity norms | Internalized patterns of behaviors and feelings that regulate the balance of obligations between exchange partners | "I [My firm] would help this salesperson [selling firm] if there was a need or problem in the future." "In the long term, the benefits this salesperson [selling firm] and I [my firm] receive from each other will balance out." "Buying from this salesperson makes [selling firm makes] me [us] feel good." "I [My firm] would expect this salesperson [selling firm] to help me [us] in the future." | Feelings of gratitude ignite reciprocity norms, which stimulate customer loyalty. | Bagozzi 1995; Dahl, Honea, and Manchanda 2005; Palmatier et al. 2009 |
| Relationship breadth | Number of relational ties with an exchange partner | "How many different relationship ties are there among employees at [selling firm] and your firm?" (number) | Relationship breadth increases customer value. It especially benefits sellers whose customers exhibit high employee turnover rates. | Houston et al. 2004; Palmatier 2008; Van Den Bulte and Wuyts 2007 |
| Relationship composition | Decision-making capability of the relational contacts at an exchange partner | "[Selling firm] knows the key decision makers at our firm." "[Selling firm] has relationships with the important gatekeepers at our firm." "[Selling firm] deals with the important decision makers in our company." "[Selling firm] has contacts with what percent of the key decision makers at your firm?" (percentage) "[Selling firm] has contacts in how many different functional departments in your firm?" (number). | Relationship composition increases the value of a customer. Relationships with key decision makers generate the highest returns among customers that are more difficult to access. | Houston et al. 2004; Palmatier 2008; Van Den Bulte and Wuyts 2007 |

| Construct | Definition | Measurement items | Rationale | References |
|---|---|---|---|---|
| Media richness | Ability "to change understanding within a time interval" (Daft and Lengel 1986, p. 560) | "The selling firm's communication medium gives and receives timely feedback." "The selling firm's communication medium transmits a variety of different cues beyond the spoken message (nonverbal cues)." "The selling firm's communication medium tailors messages to my [my firm's] own or other personal characteristics." "The selling firm's communication medium uses rich and varied language." | Richer channels have greater direct effects on relationship performance, work more effectively for building relationships during the onboarding stage, communicate complex messages better, and tend to have more persistent (carryover) effects that can span multiple periods, compared with leaner channels. In turn, richer channels lead to diminishing returns at a faster rate than leaner channels. | Daft and Lengel 1986 |
| Parasocial interaction | A customer's communication and identification with a nonhuman, technological entity (e.g., website, embodied virtual agent) that acts in place of a seller's human representatives | "The selling firm's embodied virtual agent shows me what the selling firm is like." "The selling firm's embodied virtual agent makes it easier for me to interact with the firm." "I feel sorry for the selling firm's embodied virtual agent when it makes a mistake." "When I am interacting with the selling firm's embodied virtual agent, I feel as if I am part of the firm." | Empirical evidence is scarce, but positive parasocial interactions likely enhance favorable customer behaviors and thus overall relationship performance. | Giles 2002; Horton and Wohl 1956; Rubin, Perse, and Powell 1985 |

(Continued)

Table 3.1 (Continued)

| Stage of Framework Construct | Construct Definition | Representative Measurement Items | Key Findings | Representative Relationship Marketing Research |
|---|---|---|---|---|
| | | "The selling firm's embodied virtual agent makes me feel comfortable, as if I am with friends." | | |
| | | "I see the selling firm's embodied virtual agent as a natural, down-to-earth person." | | |
| | | "I like hearing the voice of the selling firm's embodied virtual agent in my home." | | |
| | | "The selling firm's embodied virtual agent keeps me company." | | |
| | | "I look forward to interacting with the selling firm's embodied virtual agent." | | |
| | | "When the selling firm's embodied virtual agent communicates with me, it seems to understand the kinds of things I want to know or do." | | |
| | | "I miss interacting with the selling firm's embodied virtual agent when I did not interact with it for a while." | | |
| | | "I think the selling firm's embodied virtual agent is like an old friend." | | |
| | | "I am not as satisfied when I get my information from a medium different than the selling firm's embodied virtual agent." | | |

*Conative*

| | | | |
|---|---|---|---|
| Relationship velocity | "The rate and direction of changes in relational constructs" (Palmatier et al. 2013, p. 14) | "My [My firm's] relationship with this salesperson [selling firm] is improving." "My [Our firm's] relationship with this salesperson [selling firm] is getting worse over time." (reversed) "My [My firm's] relationship with this salesperson [selling firm] is on a positive trajectory." | Commitment velocity has a strong impact on relationship performance (i.e., sales growth), beyond static measures of commitment. The initial level of commitment only partially affects performance; commitment velocity consistently enhances sales growth. | Harmeling et al. 2015; Palmatier et al. 2013 |
| Experience | "A multidimensional construct focusing on a customer's cognitive, emotional, behavioral, sensorial, and social responses to a firm's offerings during the customer's entire journey" (Lemon and Verhoef 2016, p. 71) | Klaus and Maklan (2013) and Klaus (2015) suggest a 19-item scale encompassing four components: peace of mind, moments of truth, outcome focus, and product experience. Assessments of the facets of reliability, assurance, tangibles, empathy, and responsiveness, as employed to measure service quality (Parasuraman, Zeithaml, and Berry 1988), also may inform customer experience measurement. | Research on the antecedents and consequences of the customer experience is still scarce. It entails both short-term (e.g., conversion rates, market share) and long-term (e.g., loyalty, engagement, retention, customer lifetime value) performance outcomes. | Klaus and Maklan 2012; Lemon and Verhoef 2016; Neslin et al. 2006; Parasuraman, Zeithaml, and Berry 1988; Pucinelli et al. 2009 |

*(Continued)*

Table 3.1 (Continued)

| Stage of Framework Construct | Construct Definition | Representative Measurement Items | Key Findings | Representative Relationship Marketing Research |
|---|---|---|---|---|
| Flow | "The holistic experience that people feel when they act with total involvement" (Csikszentmihalyi 1975, p. 36) | "When interacting with this selling firm, I feel just the right amount of challenge."<br>"When interacting with this selling firm, my thoughts/activities run fluidly and smoothly."<br>"When interacting with this selling firm, I don't notice time passing."<br>"When interacting with this selling firm, I have no difficulty concentrating."<br>"When interacting with this selling firm, my mind is completely clear."<br>"When interacting with this selling firm, I am totally absorbed in what I am doing."<br>"When interacting with this selling firm, the right thoughts/movements occur of their own accord."<br>"When interacting with this selling firm, I know what I have to do each step of the way."<br>"When interacting with this selling firm, I feel that I have everything under control."<br>"When interacting with this selling firm, I am completely lost in thought." | Performance-enhancing effects of flow states emerge from people's online usage behavior, such as website navigation, online gaming, or online shopping. | Csikszentmihalyi 1975; Rheinberg et al. 2003 |

| Behavioral | | | | |
|---|---|---|---|---|
| Loyalty | "A collection of attitudes aligned with a series of purchase behaviors that systematically favor one entity over competing entities" (Watson et al. 2015) | *Attitudinal loyalty*<br>"I prefer [My firm prefers] this salesperson [selling firm] over competitors."<br>"I enjoy [My firm enjoys] doing business with this salesperson [selling firm]."<br>"I consider [My firm considers] this salesperson [selling firm] my first preference."<br>"I have [My firm has] a positive attitude toward this salesperson [selling firm]."<br>"I really like [My firm really likes] this salesperson [selling firm]."<br><br>*Behavioral loyalty*<br>"I often buy [My firm often buys] products/services from this salesperson [selling firm]."<br>"I only buy [My firm only buys] products/services from this salesperson [selling firm]."<br>"The last time I [my firm] purchased a product/service, I [my firm] bought from this salesperson [selling firm]."<br>"I frequently buy [My firm frequently buys] from this salesperson [selling firm]."<br>"I buy [My firm buys] most from this salesperson [selling firm]." | Relationship marketing investments and emotional and cognitive mechanisms foster customer loyalty. In turn, customer loyalty enhances customer engagement behaviors (e.g., word-of-mouth), as well as objective performance. | Dick and Basu 1994; Oliver 1999; Watson et al. 2015 |

(Continued)

*Table 3.1* (Continued)

| Stage of Framework Construct | Construct Definition | Representative Measurement Items | Key Findings | Representative Relationship Marketing Research |
|---|---|---|---|---|
| Engagement | "A customer's voluntary resource contribution to a firm's marketing function, going beyond financial patronage" (Harmeling et al. 2017, p. 316) | *Purchases*<br>"I [My firm] will continue buying the products/ services of this selling firm in the near future."<br>"My [Our] purchases with this selling firm make me [us] content."<br>"I do [My firm does] not get my [its] money's worth when I [we] purchase from this selling firm."<br>"Owning the products/services of this selling firm makes me [my firm] happy."<br><br>*References*<br>"I promote [my firm promotes] the selling firm because of the monetary referral benefits provided by the selling firm."<br>"In addition to the value derived from the product, the monetary referral incentives also encourage me [my firm] to refer this selling firm to my friends and relatives [colleagues/ other firms]."<br>"I enjoy [My firm enjoys] referring this selling firm to my friends and relatives [colleagues/ other firms] because of the monetary referral incentives."<br>"Given that I use [my firm uses] this selling firm, I refer [my firm refers] my friends and relatives [colleagues/other firms] to this selling firm because of the monetary referral incentives." | Customer engagement positively influences firm performance. The performance-enhancing effect is stronger for B2B (versus B2C) and for service (versus manufacturing) firms. | Harmeling et al. 2017; Kumar and Pansari 2016; Kumar 2013; Kumar et al. 2010; Pansari and Kumar 2017 |

*Influence*

"I do [My firm does] not actively discuss this selling firm on any media."

"I love [My firm loves] talking about my [our] experience with the selling firm."

"I discuss [My firm discusses] the benefits that I [we] get from this selling firm with others."

"I am [My firm is] a part of this selling firm and mention [mentions] it in my [its] conversations."

*Knowledge*

"I provide [My firm provides] feedback about my [our] experiences with the firm to the selling firm."

"I provide [my firm provides] suggestions for improving the performance of the selling firm."

"I provide [My firm provides] suggestions/ feedbacks about the new products/services of the selling firm."

"I provide [My firm provides] feedback/ suggestions for developing new products/ services for this selling firm."

*Seller Relationship Marketing Performance Outcomes*

| | | | |
|---|---|---|---|
| *Financial* | | | |
| Sales-based | Performance measures related to revenue enhancements | Annual sales growth<br>Sales diversity<br>Sales volatility<br>Share of wallet<br>Number of new customers generated<br>Retention rate<br>Churn rate | Relationship marketing investments enhance relational mediators and thus sales-based firm performance. | Palmatier et al. 2006 |

(Continued)

Table 3.1 (Continued)

| Stage of Framework Construct | Construct Definition | Representative Measurement Items | Key Findings | Representative Relationship Marketing Research |
|---|---|---|---|---|
| Profitability-based | Performance measures related to profit enhancements, driven by revenue enhancements or cost reductions | Customer lifetime value (CLV)<br>Customer referral value (CRV)<br>Customer influencer value (CIV)<br>Customer knowledge value (CKV)<br>Customer engagement value (CEV = CLV + CRV + CIV + CKV)<br>Return on investment (ROI) | Research on antecedents of CLV indicates that relationship marketing initiatives (e.g., direct mail, reward programs) positively affect customer loyalty and overall CLV. Customer cognitions (e.g., perceptions of quality, price, convenience, and preferential treatment) also drive CLV. Overall, customer loyalty enhances CLV, and different facets of customer engagement increase CRV, CIV, and CKV. | Kumar 2017; Kumar and Reinartz 2016; Palmatier et al. 2006; Rust, Lemon, and Zeithaml 2004; Venkatesan and Kumar 2004 |
| *Nonfinancial* | | | | |
| Knowledge advantages | Performance measures related to enhanced market knowledge that are difficult to capture in (short-term) financial terms | Number of patents<br>Time to market<br>Number of innovations<br>New product success rate | Empirical insights on relationship marketing's impact on the seller's knowledge advantages are scarce due to measurement challenges. Yet it is reasonable to assume that customers' cooperative loyalty and engagement behaviors offer superior knowledge for the seller. | Palmatier et al. 2006 |

customers receiving better treatment than themselves, they often react punitively, such as by decreasing their loyalty or even leaving the firm. Typical disagreements and conflict have little effect on customer performance when perceived unfairness is low; they exert massively negative effects on relationship performance when accompanied by high unfairness perceptions (Samaha, Palmatier, and Dant 2011).

### Cognitive Relational Mechanisms

Customers' *cognitive relational mechanisms* capture their more rational evaluations of the seller, based on knowledge, learning, memory, or judgment. Cognitions are affected by emotions and in turn determine conations and then behavioral responses. Extant relationship marketing research has theorized about and empirically substantiated various cognitive relational mechanisms that capture the essence of relationships and are key to understanding relationship marketing's performance impact.

Broadly, a composite **relationship quality** construct should provide a sense of the overall caliber of a relationship (Crosby, Evans, and Cowles 1990; De Wulf, Odekerken-Schröder, and Iacobucci 2001). It comprises various dimensions, each of which might capture a unique facet of that relational bond. According to De Wulf, Odekerken-Schröder, and Iacobucci (2001, p. 36), the composite construct is preferable though "because, even though . . . various forms of attitude may be conceptually distinct, consumers have difficulty making fine distinctions between them and tend to lump them together." In support of their assertion, a meta-analysis reveals that no single relational mediator captures the full essence or depth of a customer–company relationship (Hennig-Thurau, Gwinner, and Gremler 2002; Johnson 1999; Palmatier et al. 2006). Instead, the aggregated relationship quality measure predicts a seller's performance better than any single relational measure (Palmatier et al. 2006).

The key components of this composite construct include customer commitment, trust, and reciprocity norms. Customer **commitment**, the desire to maintain a valued relationship, and customer **trust**, the confidence in the reliability and integrity of the relational partner, are the most often studied cognitive constructs (Moorman, Zaltman, and Deshpande 1992; Morgan and Hunt 1994). Whether these constructs function individually or combine to represent a global measure of relationship quality remains a topic of some debate (Crosby, Evans, and Cowles 1990; De Wulf, Odekerken-Schröder, and Iacobucci 2001; Gundlach, Achrol, and Mentzer 1995; Morgan and Hunt 1994; Sirdeshmukh, Singh, and Sabol 2002), as is the question of whether commitment or trust is dominant. Consider several well-known claims in this topic area for example:

- Doney and Cannon (1997, p. 35) note the "central role in the developing of marketing theory" that trust has achieved.

- Berry (1996, p. 42) calls trust "the single most powerful relationship marketing tool available to a company," especially service firms.
- Spekman (1988, p. 79) refers to trust as the "cornerstone" of long-term relationships.
- Gundlach, Achrol, and Mentzer (1995, p. 78) instead cite commitment as the "essential ingredient for successful long-term relationships."
- Finally, Morgan and Hunt (1994, p. 23) confirm that "commitment among exchange partners as key to achieving valuable outcomes."

Customer **reciprocity norms** are perceived psychological pressures to return a benefit received, spurred by feelings of gratitude toward the seller (Bagozzi 1995; Palmatier et al. 2009). These norms propel the relational bond forward by initiating ongoing cycles of reciprocation and self-reinforcing loyal behaviors, such that they ensure relationship continuation (Palmatier et al. 2009; Schwartz 1967).

Because interfirm relationships often encompass relational bonds among multiple persons on both sides of the exchange dyad, additional aspects of interfirm relationships also must be considered to capture interfirm relational mechanisms. In this context, **relationship breadth** (i.e., number of relational ties with exchange partner) and **relationship composition** (i.e., decision-making capability of the relational contacts) capture important performance-enhancing information, because an interfirm relationship built on the basis of many interpersonal relationships with important decision makers is more valuable than an interfirm relationship based on only one interpersonal tie with a low-level contact.

In online relationships, communication channels that mediate interactions between customers and sellers can be distinguished according to their level of **media richness**, defined as the ability "to change understanding within a time interval" (Daft and Lengel 1986, p. 560). Richer channels convey information faster and with fewer misunderstandings than leaner channels, due to their capacity for immediate feedback (i.e., synchronicity), multiple cues (e.g., verbal, visual), and natural language, all of which help foster mutual understanding. Compared with leaner channels, richer channels have greater direct effects on relationship performance, work more effectively for building relationships during the onboarding stage, can communicate more complex messages, and tend to have more persistent (carryover) effects that even can span multiple periods (Samaha et al. 2018). In turn, though, richer channels lead to diminishing returns at a faster rate than leaner channels.

Also in online relationship marketing environments, **parasocial interaction** describes a customer's communication and identification with a nonhuman, technological entity (e.g., website, embodied virtual agent) that acts in place of the seller's human representatives. If customers regard these parasocial, nonhuman interactions with a firm as equally authentic, relevant, and intimate as human interactions in offline contexts

(McKenna, Green, and Gleason 2002), they likely enhance favorable customer behaviors and thus overall relationship performance.

### Conative Relational Mechanisms

Some relationship marketing researchers also employ *conative constructs* to capture customers' relational processes. For example, relationship velocity captures the dynamic evolution of relationships, and in the digital age, when omnichannel relationships have taken on a more prominent role, customer experience and flow also are pertinent.

**Relationship velocity** captures the rate and direction of change in relational constructs, thereby indicating relationships' dynamics and trajectories (Palmatier et al. 2013). Commitment velocity has been established as an empirically meaningful construct, with a strong impact on relationship performance (i.e., sales growth), beyond static measures of commitment levels. The initial level of commitment only partially affects performance, but commitment velocity consistently enhances sales growth. That is, the direction and rate of change in relational constructs such as customer commitment provide crucial information for explaining and predicting relational outcomes. Evaluating relationship velocity in turn provides critical insights into the future of the relationship and its eventual impact on performance.

With the advent of multiple new channels through which customers can purchase and engage with the firm and technology-mediated interfaces between customers and companies, a customer's journey with a company also has become much more complex, such that "customers now interact with firms through myriad touchpoints in multiple channels and media, resulting in more complex customer journeys. Firms are confronted with accelerating media and channel fragmentation, and omnichannel management has become the new norm" (Lemon and Verhoef 2016, p. 69). Accordingly, it has become ever-more important to confirm that all these diverse touchpoints act in concert to provide a comprehensive, seamless customer experience. Recent research defines the customer **experience** as "a multidimensional construct focusing on a customer's cognitive, emotional, behavioral, sensorial, and social responses to a firm's offerings during the customer's entire journey" (Lemon and Verhoef 2016, p. 71). The customer journey captures the dynamic, iterative experience with a company over time and across touchpoints, encompassing three main stages: prepurchase, purchase, and postpurchase (Howard and Sheth 1969; Lemon and Verhoef 2016; Neslin et al. 2006; Pucinelli et al. 2009). In all three stages of this complex customer journey, customers interact with the company and other stakeholders at various touchpoints. This complete set of customer experiences over time then mediates the impact of relationship marketing investments on firm performance. The customer experience construct thus offers a comprehensive evaluation of the company's relationship marketing activities, and empirical studies suggest an important role of this customer experience in driving customer behaviors and then company performance (Lemon and Verhoef 2016; Novak, Hoffman, and Yung 2000).

---

**Example 3.4  Disney (USA)**

Disney has always enjoyed a strong reputation based on its expertise in delivering inspiring, delightful customer experiences. To create personal connections with Disney World visitors and immerse them more fully into the world of Disney, the company offers surprising moments of personalization, often relying on technology to deliver them. For example, the MyMagic+ tool helps both streamline and elevate guests' park and hotel experiences. The vacation planning system allows visitors to access information and perks, such as advance ride booking and restaurant reservations, before they even arrive for their stays. It also supports a seamless customer experience. The MagicBand, worn around guests' wrists, acts as a room key, park ticket, and even optional payment method. Then the MyMagic+ system sends personalized messages, via a mobile app and again at specific touchpoints throughout the park and resorts. Members might see their name appear on a screen as they walk by (alongside the caption "It's a small world"); a photo taken of them on a ride might unexpectedly appear on the app (along with an option to buy a copy, of course).

Source: Gilliland (2017).

---

**Flow** refers to a psychological state in which customers exhibit a high level of involvement and immersion in an activity, accompanied by feelings of fun and enjoyment (Csikszentmihalyi 1975). Sellers can leverage the opportunities provided by omnichannel relationships in the digital age to put customers in a flow state. Because this state is so enjoyable, customers then likely seek to repeat their experiences, which leads to enhanced relationship performance. The performance-enhancing effects of flow states have been confirmed in relation to people's online usage behavior, such as website navigation, online gaming, and online shopping (Chang and Zhu 2012; Lee and Tsai 2010; Luna, Peracchio, and de Juan 2002).

### Behavioral Relational Mechanisms

The relational emotions, cognitions, and conations that customers perceive toward a seller are antecedents of their behavioral manifestations. Customers' *behavioral relational mechanisms*, as induced by the emotional, cognitive, and conative processes spurred by the company's relationship marketing investments, consist of two main categories: customer loyalty and customer engagement.

First, customer **loyalty** is "a collection of attitudes aligned with a series of purchase behaviors that systematically favor one entity over competing entities" (Watson IV et al. 2015, p. 803). Customers who display loyalty to a seller engage in a limited search for alternatives, rebuy without soliciting competitive bids, or disclose competitive quotes so the favored company can have a final opportunity to win the business (i.e., last look). Increased customer loyalty represents one of the most anticipated outcomes of relationship marketing efforts, but loyalty also can be defined and measured in a plethora of ways (Jacoby and Chestnut 1978; Oliver 1999; Watson IV et al. 2015). Some studies focus on behavioral intentions (e.g., repurchase intentions, expectation of continuity)—measures that often suffer unduly from situational influences (Dick and Basu 1994; Jacoby and Chestnut 1978). For example, customers with weak relational bonds and little ultimate or true loyalty may report a high expectation of relationship continuity simply because of high switching costs, a lack of time to evaluate alternatives, or plain habit or laziness (Oliver 1999). Even customers with strong relational bonds could lack total control over purchases or be forced to end a relationship prematurely because of unforeseen conditions. Thus, in some situations, behavioral intentions have limited explanatory power for the seller's actual financial outcomes. In contrast, relationship-induced loyalty focuses on customer behaviors caused by emotional and cognitive relational mechanisms or bonds, not transaction inertia. For example, customers' commitment, trust, gratitude, relationship quality, or experience with a firm positively influence their overall attitude and thus loyalty, because they perceive less risk in dealing with trusted partners, act on relationally generated belonging, and minimize search costs by buying from valued sellers (Doney and Cannon 1997; Garbarino and Johnson 1999; Hewett, Money, and Sharma 2002; Macintosh and Lockshin 1997). Loyal customers also exhibit empathic behaviors and are both more forgiving of service failures and more understanding of the challenges and pressures a seller might face.

Second, favorable emotions, cognitions, and conations toward the seller drive customers' voluntary, requested or unrequested engagement, beyond purchase (Barksdale, Johnson, and Suh 1997; Brodie et al. 2011; Harmeling et al. 2017; Hennig-Thurau, Gwinner, and Gremler 2002; van Doorn et al. 2010; Verhoef, Franses, and Hoekstra 2002). Customer **engagement** captures "a customer's voluntary resource contribution to a firm's marketing function, going beyond financial patronage," and it subsumes a multitude of customer behaviors beyond purchase that still are beneficial to the company (Harmeling et al. 2017, p. 316). A prominent type of engagement behavior is providing word-of-mouth or referrals. In the digital age, the reduced cost and increased availability and use of online referrals make such behavior even more significant. When they offer referrals, customers speak positively about a company to another potential customer (inside or outside their own firm). Trust and commitment positively affect such word-of-mouth behaviors (Barksdale, Johnson, and Suh 1997; Hennig-Thurau, Gwinner, and Gremler 2002; Verhoef, Franses, and Hoekstra 2002). For the seller, customers engaging in word-of-mouth communications represent good news in several respects, because referrals initiate two performance-enhancing relational pathways. On the one hand, word-of-mouth consolidates the relationship *with the focal referring customer* by further increasing that customer's loyalty (Garnefeld et al. 2013). On the other hand, referrals can affect financial performance outcomes by generating business *with new customers*. Beyond word-of-mouth behaviors, customer engagement also encompasses cooperative behaviors toward the seller, whether that means the customer shares and discloses information to the firm, provides helpful feedback, or proposes ideas for new products or services. Committed customers, by definition, want to maintain valued relationships, so they cooperate with companies even in the absence of a quid pro quo benefit to strengthen and maintain their important customer–company bond (Morgan and Hunt 1994). As research shows, commitment, trust, and relationship quality between exchange partners are critical for cooperation and engagement (Anderson and Narus 1990; Bettencourt 1997; Hewett and Bearden 2001; Palmatier et al. 2006).

---

**Example 3.5  Nike (USA)**

The Nike+ website provides a platform for customer engagement. Specifically, runners can upload data about their recent runs and see the history of their runs on maps. They can share this information with friends, get advice from peers, and post information about upcoming events. Nike thus has given its customers a reason to want to come back to the website every day and engage—with the firm, with the community of Nike+ users, with their friends, and so forth. This win–win relational instrument provides added value to both customers and the firm. Customers receive support for their fitness goals and can interact with friends and like-minded peers; Nike gets valuable information about how customers use its products and what innovations it could develop to address their needs.

Source: Petro (2016).

---

## Seller Relationship Marketing Performance Outcomes

Ultimately, companies undertake relationship marketing investments to enhance firm performance. The performance impact of relationship marketing investments on **seller relationship marketing performance outcomes** is mediated by customer relational mechanisms. If these investments effectively spark favorable emotional, cognitive, conative, and behavioral customer responses, financial and nonfinancial performance enhancements likely result.

## Financial Relationship Marketing Performance Outcomes

The category of **financial relationship marketing performance outcomes** consists of sales-based and profitability-based measures. The sales-based category predicts that loyal purchase behaviors increase sales revenue, so it features measures such as annual sales growth, sales diversity (i.e., selling various products and services to the same customer), sales volatility (variability over time), and share of wallet (sales penetration for each customer). In addition, sales-based metrics can address the overall portfolio of customers, such as the number of new customers generated or retention and churn rates. However, sales effects might not be sufficient to reveal the comprehensive influences of relationship marketing investments. Therefore, three prominent profitability-based measures address both sales and costs associated with a customer to determine the effectiveness of relationship marketing tactics. Specifically:

1.  Customer lifetime value (CLV) might be the best measure of customer value; it captures "the present value of all future profits obtained from a customer over the life of his relationship with a firm" (Gupta and Zeithaml 2006, p. 724). By discounting future cash flows and selling costs, CLV accounts for both sales and cost effects and reveals a customer's precise, present value to the firm (Kumar and Reinartz 2016). However, it is difficult to gather the data needed to support these calculations, which also are highly sensitive to imposed assumptions (e.g., margins, future growth rates, allocation of costs). Relationship marketing initiatives can positively affect both customer loyalty and overall CLV (Venkatesan and Kumar 2004), and customer cognitions (e.g., perceptions of quality, price, convenience, and preferential treatment) also strongly determine CLV (Rust, Lemon, and Zeithaml 2004).
2.  Recent extensions of the CLV concept coincide with the emergence of the customer engagement construct in the digital age. They seek to quantify additional elements of this concept: customer referral value (CRV), or the value produced when existing customers help the firm acquire new customers, in response to firm-initiated and incentivized referral programs; customer influencer value (CIV), referring to customers' intrinsically motivated word-of-mouth activity that converts prospects into customers or encourages the expansion of existing customers; and customer knowledge value (CKV), reflecting the value of feedback customers provide to the company that helps it develop innovations and improvements. Together, these assessments produce an overall customer engagement value (CEV) measure (Kumar et al. 2010; Kumar and Reinartz 2016; Kumar 2017).

3. Rather than focusing on individual customers, the return on investment (ROI) can assess different relationship marketing investments (e.g., financial, social, or structural programs) rather than individual customers. Combining the investments in and returns on financial, social, and structural relationship marketing programs, this measure of incremental profits offers pertinent insights. In particular, it appears that immediately following the investments, social programs offer the highest payoff, structural programs break even, and financial programs do not benefit the firm (Palmatier, Gopalakrishna, and Houston 2006).

Even with these appealing measures, though, the effects of relationship marketing investments on customer relational mechanisms and performance are complex and contingent on many factors (e.g., relationship marketing programs, dynamics, customer characteristics). Therefore, the actual returns on the various relationship marketing investments, as well as the value generated from relationships, remain difficult to measure. The only consensus is that customer–company relationships influence a firm's financial performance, and relationship marketing investments can pay off, in the form of short- and long-term financial returns, but that positive returns are never guaranteed.

---

### Example 3.6  Apple (USA)

According to one Goldman Sachs study, Apple enjoys strong customer relationships that substantially contribute to its financial performance. In a survey of current Apple customers, 94% indicated they were likely or highly likely to stick with Apple for their next smartphone or tablet. More than one in five even said there is no discount high enough to persuade them to switch to a non-Apple device. The average lifetime value to Apple of each iOS customer is $1,053. Multiplying customer lifetime value with 281 million iOS users gets at the value of Apple's installed customer base, summing up to about $295 billion. That is, Apple's customer relationships at that point accounted for about 55% of its market capitalization.

Source: Elmer-DeWitt (2012).

---

### *Nonfinancial Relationship Marketing Performance Outcomes*

Financial performance obviously is critical, but it would be short-sighted to ignore the ways in which relationship marketing investments can produce nonfinancial benefits for the seller, off its balance sheet. **Nonfinancial relationship marketing performance outcomes** might increase knowledge, accrued through customers' relational behaviors. That is, loyal and engaged customers often willingly share information with companies, granting those firms novel insights into potential new markets, product opportunities, and product concepts that should be more appealing when launched, because they reflect customers' input. Imagine, for example, that a loyal customer describes a preference for an added functionality, which the company develops and then makes available for sale to multiple markets. The added function likely appeals to many customers, so the company earns profitable sales on this innovation. Typical financial metrics would not attribute these benefits to the company's strong relationship with its loyal customer, which pertains to a different time and location than the actual sales. Although such outcomes thus are especially difficult to measure, companies should track them by measuring knowledge-based achievements, such as patents, the time required to get to market, or new product success rates. Knowledge-based outcomes are especially pertinent to firms that rely strongly on innovation-based strategies.

## Summary

As with all marketing strategies, relationship marketing does not represent a goal in itself but rather is an important means to achieve the superordinate goal of enhanced company performance. Relationship marketing research consistently reveals that understanding relationship marketing's performance impact requires a three-stage causal model: seller relationship marketing investments → customer relational mechanisms → seller relationship marketing performance outcomes. That is, customer relational mechanisms mediate the investment–performance linkage. Through their relationship marketing investments, companies seek to spur favorable relational emotions, cognitions, conations, and behaviors among customers (i.e., gratitude, commitment, trust, reciprocity norms, relationship breadth, relationship composition, relationship velocity, experience, media richness, parasocial interaction, flow, loyalty, and engagement). These customer responses in turn constitute researchers' most common explanations for the positive influence of relationships on firm performance. Also, relationship marketers seek to avoid negative emotions such as customer perceptions of unfairness.

Relationship marketing investments consist of dedicated relationship marketing strategies or programs, designed and implemented to build, grow, and maintain strong relationships with customers. The three broad categories of relationship marketing investments are financial, social, and structural relationship marketing programs. Financial relationship marketing investments offer customers some kind of economic benefit, such as special discounts, giveaways, free shipping, or extended payment terms, in exchange for their loyal behaviors. Social relationship marketing investments employ social engagements (e.g., meals, sporting events) or frequent, customized communication to personalize the customer relationship and convey the customer's elevated status. Structural relationship marketing investments are relational investments designed to enhance customer efficiency and/or productivity, which customers likely would not undertake on their own, such as an electronic order-processing interface or customized packaging. These different types of investments exert differential effects on customers and induce varying returns. In the short term, social programs have the highest payoff, structural programs break even, and financial programs fail to pay off.

Through these financial, social, or structural relationship marketing investments, sellers seek to stimulate relational mechanisms, capturing customers' emotions, cognitions, conations, and behaviors resulting from their interactions with the seller. Establishing a causal sequence among emotional, cognitive, conative, and behavioral processes, short-term emotions typically affect longer-term cognitions; jointly, emotions and cognitions influence conations. Emotions, cognitions, and conations in turn affect short- and long-term relational behaviors. Key relational emotions are customer gratitude and unfairness. Customer commitment, trust, and reciprocity norms, as well as assessments of relationship breadth and composition, represent central cognitive mechanisms. Relationship velocity, customer experience, media richness, parasocial interaction, and flow reflect relevant conations of the relational bond, as perceived by customers. Ultimately, customers' favorable emotions, cognitions, and conations toward the firm should promote customer loyalty and engagement, which are important behavioral manifestations that carry the relationship forward. Relational mechanisms reflect the intangible value that a firm receives from its relational bonds with a customer; they mediate the effect of relationship marketing investments on performance.

Strong relationships with customers likely bring about increased financial and nonfinancial performance for the seller. Financial relationship marketing performance outcomes consist of sales-based and profitability-based performance indicators. Sales-based outcomes refer to revenues, by measuring annual sales growth, diversity, volatility, or share of wallet, for example. Profitability-based outcome measures are more comprehensive and acknowledge both sales and cost effects on relationship marketing performance. Customer lifetime value (CLV), customer engagement value (CEV), and return on investment (ROI) represent three key concepts for evaluating the profit ramifications of relationship marketing investments. The nonfinancial benefits for the seller might not have direct or immediate implications for the seller's balance sheet, but they remain important, because they imply increased knowledge gained by the seller from customers who are loyal to and engaged with it.

## Takeaways

- Relationship marketing investments affect firm performance by stimulating relational mechanisms among customers.
- Three generic types of relationship marketing investments are financial, social, and structural relationship marketing programs, each with differential effects and performance implications.
- Customer relational mechanisms integrate customers' responses to sellers' relationship marketing efforts and encompass emotional, cognitive, conative, and behavioral processes.
- Customer gratitude and unfairness represent the key emotional mechanisms in customer–company relationships, acting as opposing twin pillars. Customer commitment, trust, reciprocity norms, relationship breadth, and relationship composition jointly reflect a customer's cognitions when evaluating a relational bond with a seller. Relationship velocity, customer experience, media richness, parasocial interaction, and flow reflect customers' conative assessments. Customer loyalty and engagement capture their behavioral manifestations toward the firm.
- Typically, customers' short-term emotions influence their longer-term cognitions, which together affect conations. Emotions, cognitions, and conations all affect customers' behavior toward the seller.
- If effective, relationship marketing investments result in enhanced seller performance, as indicated by superior financial and nonfinancial performance.
- Financial relationship marketing performance can be assessed by measuring sales-based or profitability-based outcomes; nonfinancial performance is reflected in sellers' superior knowledge gained from customers who share important information.
- Customer lifetime value (CLV), customer engagement value (CEV), and return on investment (ROI) represent comprehensive, profitability-based indicators of relationship marketing performance.

## References

Anderson, Erin, and Baron A. Weitz (1992), "The Use of Pledges to Build and Sustain Commitment in Distribution Channels." *Journal of Marketing Research* 29 (February), 18–34.

Anderson, James C., and James A. Narus (1990), "A Model of Distributor Firm and Manufacturer Firm Working Partnerships." *Journal of Marketing* 54 (January), 42–58.

Bagozzi, Richard P. (1995), "Reflections on Relationship Marketing in Consumer Markets." *Journal of the Academy of Marketing Science* 23 (4), 272–7.

Barksdale, Hiram C., Jr., Julie T. Johnson, and Munshik Suh (1997), "A Relationship Maintenance Model: A Comparison Between Managed Health Care and Traditional Fee-For-Service." *Journal of Business Research* 40 (3), 237–47.

Bendapudi, Neeli, and Robert P. Leone (2002), "Managing Business-to-Business Customer Relationships Following Key Contact Employee Turnover in a Vendor Firm." *Journal of Marketing* 66 (April), 83–101.

Berry, Leonard L. (1995), "Relationship Marketing of Services-Growing Interest, Emerging Perspectives." *Journal of the Academy of Marketing Science* 23 (4), 236–45.

Berry, Leonard L. (1996), "Retailers With a Future." *Marketing Management* 5 (Spring), 39–46.

Bettencourt, Lance A. (1997), "Customer Voluntary Performance: Customers as Partners in Service Delivery." *Journal of Retailing* 73 (3), 383–406.

Blau, Peter (1964), *Exchange and Power in Social Life*. New York: John Wiley & Sons.

Bolton, Ruth N., P. K. Kannan, and Matthew D. Bramlett (2000), "Implications of Loyalty Programs Membership and Service Experiences for Customer Retention and Value." *Journal of the Academy of Marketing Sciences* 28 (Winter), 95–108.

Bolton, Ruth N., Amy K. Smith, and Janet Wagner (2003), "Striking the Right Balance: Designing Service to Enhance Business-to-Business Relationships." *Journal of Service Research* 5 (May), 271–91.

Brodie, Rodeick J., Linda D. Hollebeek, Biljana Juric, and Ana Ilic (2011), "Customer Engagement: Conceptual Domain, Fundamental Propositions, and Implications for Research." *Journal of Service Research* 14 (3), 252–71.

Cannon, Joseph P., Ravi S. Achrol, and Gregory T. Gundlach (2000), "Contracts, Norms, and Plural Form Governance." *Journal of the Academy Marketing Science* 28 (Spring), 180–94.

Cao, Yong, and Thomas S. Gruca (2005), "Reducing Adverse Selection Through Customer Relationship Management." *Journal of Marketing* 69 (October), 219–29.

Chang, Ya Ping, and Dong Hong Zhu (2012), "The Role of Perceived Social Capital and Flow Experience in Building Users' Continuance Intention to Social Networking Sites in China." *Computers in Human Behavior* 28 (3), 995–1001.

Cialdini, Robert B. (2001), *Influence: Science and Practice*. Boston: Allyn and Bacon.

Crosby, Lawrence A., Kenneth R. Evans, and Deborah Cowles (1990), "Relationship Quality in Services Selling: An Interpersonal Influence Perspective." *Journal of Marketing* 54 (July), 68–81.

Csikszentmihalyi, Mihaly (1975), *Beyond Boredom and Anxiety: Experiencing Flow in Work and Play*, 36. San Francisco: Jossey-Bass Publishers.

Daft, Richard L., and Robert H. Lengel (1986), "Organizational Information Requirements, Media Richness and Structural Design." *Management Science* 32 (5), 554–71.

Dahl, Darren W., Heather Honea, and Rajesh V. Manchanda (2005), "Three Rs of Interpersonal Consumer Guilt: Relationship, Reciprocity, Reparation." *Journal of Consumer Psychology* 15 (4), 307–15.

Day, George S., and Robin Wensley (1988), "Assessing Advantage: A Framework for Diagnosing Competitive Superiority." *Journal of Marketing* 52 (April), 1–20.

De Wulf, Kristof, Gaby Odekerken-Schröder, and Dawn Iacobucci (2001), "Investments in Consumer Relationships: A Cross-Country and Cross-Industry Exploration." *Journal of Marketing* 65 (October), 33–50.

Dick, Alan S., and Kunal Basu (1994), "Customer Loyalty: Toward an Integrated Conceptual Framework." *Journal of the Academy of Marketing Science* 22 (2), 99–113.

Doney, Patricia M., and Joseph P. Cannon (1997), "An Examination of the Nature of Trust in Buyer-Seller Relationships." *Journal of Marketing* 61 (April), 35–51.

Elmer-DeWitt, Philip (2012), "Goldman Sachs Puts the Value of Apple's iPhone and iPad Customer Base at Nearly $295 Billion." Available at: http://fortune.com/2012/06/29/goldman-sachs-puts-the-value-of-apples-iphone-and-ipad-customer-base-at-nearly-295-billion/ (accessed 24 July 2018).

Forgas, Joseph P., and Jennifer M. George (2001), "Affective Influences on Judgments and Behavior in Organizations: An Information Processing Perspective." *Organizational Behavior and Human Decision Processes* 86 (September), 3–34.

Garbarino, Ellen, and Mark S. Johnson (1999), "The Different Roles of Satisfaction, Trust, and Commitment in Customer Relationships." *Journal of Marketing* 63 (April), 70–87.

Garnefeld, Ina, Andreas Eggert, Sabrina Helm, and Stephen S. Tax (2013), "Growing Existing Customers' Revenue Streams Through Customer Referral Programs." *Journal of Marketing* 77 (July), 17–32.

Giles, David C. (2002), "Parasocial Interaction: A Review of the Literature and a Model for Future Research." *Media Psychology* 4 (3), 279–305.

Gilliland, Nikki (2017), "How Disney World Has Mastered Customer Experience." Available at: www.econsultancy.com/blog/69458-how-disney-world-has-mastered-customer-experience (accessed 24 July 2018).

Gundlach, Gregory T., Ravi S. Achrol, and John T. Mentzer (1995), "The Structure of Commitment in Exchange." *Journal of Marketing* 59 (January), 78–92.

Gupta, Sunil, and Valarie Zeithaml (2006), "Customer Metrics and Their Impact on Financial Performance." *Marketing Science* 25 (November–December), 718–39.

Harmeling, Colleen M., Jordan W. Moffett, Mark J. Arnold, and Brad D. Carlson (2017), "Toward a Theory of Customer Engagement Marketing." *Journal of the Academy of Marketing Science* 45 (3), 312–35.

Harmeling, Colleen M., Robert W. Palmatier, Mark B. Houston, Mark J. Arnold, and Stephen A. Samaha (2015), "Transformational Relationship Events." *Journal of Marketing* 79 (September), 39–62.

Henderson, Conor, Joshua T. Beck, and Robert W. Palmatier (2011), "A Review of the Theoretical Underpinnings of Loyalty Programs." *Journal of Consumer Psychology* 21 (July), 256–76.

Hennig-Thurau, Thorsten, Kevin P. Gwinner, and Dwayne D. Gremler (2002), "Understanding Relationship Marketing Outcomes: An Integration of Relational Benefits and Relationship Quality." *Journal of Service Research* 4 (February), 230–47.

Hewett, Kelly, and William O. Bearden (2001), "Dependence, Trust, and Relational Behavior on the Part of Foreign Subsidiary Marketing Operations: Implications for Managing Global Marketing Operations." *Journal of Marketing* 65 (October), 51–66.

Hewett, Kelly, Bruce R. Money, and Subhash Sharma (2002), "An Exploration of the Moderating Role of Buyer Corporate Culture in Industrial Buyer-Seller Relationships." *Journal of the Academy of Marketing Sciences* 30 (Summer), 229–39.

Hibbard, Jonathan D., Frederic F. Brunel, Rajiv P. Dant, and Dawn Iacobucci (2001), "Does Relationship Marketing Age Well?" *Business Strategy Review* 12 (4), 29–35.

Horton, Donald, and R. Richard Wohl (1956), "Mass Communication and Para-Social Interaction: Observation on Intimacy at a Distance." *Psychiatry* 19, 215–29.

Houston, Mark B., Michael D. Hutt, Christine Moorman, Peter H. Reingen, Aric Rindfleisch, Vanitha Swaminathan, and Beth A. Walker (2004), "A Network Perspective on Marketing Strategy." In *Assessing Marketing Strategy*

*Performance*, eds. Christine Moorman and Donald R. Lehman, 247–68. Cambridge: Marketing Science Institute.

Howard, John A., and Jagdish Sheth (1969), *The Theory of Buyer Behavior.* New York: John Wiley & Sons.

Jacoby, Jacob, and Robert W. Chestnut (1978), *Brand Loyalty.* New York: John Wiley & Sons.

Jap, Sandy D., and Shankar Ganesan (2000), "Control Mechanisms and the Relationship Life Cycle: Implications for Safeguarding Specific Investments and Developing Commitment." *Journal of Marketing Research* 37 (May), 227–45.

Johnson, Jean L. (1999), "Strategic Integration in Industrial Distribution Channels: Managing the Interfirm Relationship as a Strategic Asset." *Journal of the Academy of Marketing Science* 27 (1), 4–18.

Johnson, Michael D., and Fred Selnes (2004), "Customer Portfolio Management: Toward a Dynamic Theory of Exchange Relationships." *Journal of Marketing* 68 (April), 1–17.

Johnson, Tara (2016), "Amazon B2B Selling." Available at: www.cpcstrategy.com/blog/2016/03/amazon-b2b/ (accessed 24 July 2018).

Klaus, Philipp (2015), *Measuring Customer Experience: How to Develop and Execute the Most Profitable Customer Experience Strategies.* New York: Palgrave Macmillan.

Klaus, Philipp, and Stan Maklan (2012), "EXQ: A Multiple-Item Scale for Assessing Service Experience." *Journal of Service Management* 23 (1), 5–33.

Klaus, Philipp, and Stan Maklan (2013), "Towards a Better Measure of Customer Experience." *International Journal of Market Research* 55 (2), 227–46.

Kumar, V. (2013), *Profitable Customer Engagement: Concept, Metrics and Strategies.* New Delhi: SAGE Publications.

Kumar, V. (2017), "A Theory of Customer Valuation: Concepts, Metrics, Strategy, and Implementation." *Journal of Marketing* 82 (January), 1–19.

Kumar, V., Lerzan Aksoy, Bas Donkers, Rajkumar Venkatesan, Thorsten Wiesel, and Sebastian Tillmanns (2010), "Undervalued or Overvalued Customers: Capturing Total Customer Engagement Value." *Journal of Service Research* 13 (3), 297–310.

Kumar, Nirmalya, Jonathan D. Hibbard, and Leonard D. Stern (1994), *The Nature and Consequences of Marketing Channel Intermediary Commitment.* Report No. 94–115. Cambridge: Marketing Science Institute.

Kumar, V., and Anita Pansari (2016), "Competitive Advantage Through Engagement." *Journal of Marketing Research* 53 (4), 497–514.

Kumar, V., and Werner Reinartz (2016), "Creating Enduring Customer Value." *Journal of Marketing* 80 (November), 36–68.

Lee, Ming-Chi, and Tzung-Ru Tsai. (2010), "What Drives People to Continue to Play Online Games? An Extension of Technology Model and Theory of Planned Behavior." *International Journal of Human–Computer Interaction* 26 (6), 601–20.

Leigh, Heather (2005), "If You Get Invited to a Nordstrom 'Private Shopping Event', You Should Definitely Go!" Available at: https://blogs.msdn.microsoft.com/heatherleigh/2005/12/01/if-you-get-invited-to-a-nordstrom-private-shopping-event-you-should-definitely-go/ (accessed 24 July 2018).

Lemon, Katherine N., and Peter C. Verhoef (2016), "Understanding Customer Experience Throughout the Customer Journey." *Journal of Marketing* 80 (6), 69–96.

Luna, David, Laura A. Peracchio, and María D. de Juan (2002), "Cross-cultural and Cognitive Aspects of Web Site Navigation." *Journal of the Academy of Marketing Science* 30 (4), 397–410.

Macintosh, Gerrard, and Lawrence S. Lockshin (1997), "Retail Relationships and Store Loyalty: A Multi-level Perspective." *International Journal of Research in Marketing* 14 (5), 487–97.

Marchand, André, Michael Paul, Thorsten Hennig-Thurau, and Georg Puchner (2016), "How Gifts Influence Relationships With Service Customers and Financial Outcomes for Firms." *Journal of Service Research* 20 (2), 105–19.

McKenna, Katelyn Y., Amie S. Green, and Marci E. Gleason (2002), "Relationship Formation on the Internet: What's the Big Attraction?" *Journal of Social Issues* 58 (1), 9–31.

Moorman, Christine, Gerald Zaltman, and Rohit Deshpandé (1992), "Relationships Between Providers and Users of Market Research: The Dynamics of Trust Within and Between Organizations." *Journal of Marketing Research* 29 (August), 314–29.

Morales, Andrea C. (2005), "Giving Firms an 'E' for Effort: Consumer Responses to High-Effort Firms." *Journal of Consumer Research* 31 (March), 806–12.

Morgan, Robert M., and Shelby D. Hunt (1994), "The Commitment-Trust Theory of Relationship Marketing." *Journal of Marketing* 58 (July), 20–38.

Neslin, Scott A., Dhruv Grewal, Robert Leghorn, Venkatesh Shankar, Marije L. Teerling, Jacquelyn S. Thomas, et al. (2006), "Challenges and Opportunities in Multichannel Customer Management." *Journal of Service Research* 9 (2), 95–112.

Nordstrom (2018), "Your VIP Events." Available at: https://shop.nordstrom.com/c/rewards-vip-event-access (accessed 24 July 2018).

Novak, Thomas P., Donna L. Hoffman, and Yiu-Fai Yung, (2000), "Measuring the Customer Experience in Online Environments: A Structural Modeling Approach." *Marketing Science* 19 (1), 22–42.

Oliver, Richard L. (1999), "Whence Consumer Loyalty?" *Journal of Marketing* 63 (Special Issue), 33–44.

Palmatier, Robert W. (2008), *Relationship Marketing*. Cambridge: Marketing Science Institute.

Palmatier, Robert W., Rajiv P. Dant, Dhruv Grewal, and Kenneth R. Evans (2006), "Factors Influencing the Effectiveness of Relationship Marketing: A Meta-Analysis." *Journal of Marketing* 70 (October), 136–53.

Palmatier, Robert W., Srinath Gopalakrishna, and Mark B. Houston (2006), "Returns on Business-to-Business Relationship Marketing Investments: Strategies for Leveraging Profits." *Marketing Science* 25 (September–October), 477–93.

Palmatier, Robert W., Mark B. Houston, Rajiv P. Dant, and Dhruv Grewal (2013), "Relationship Velocity: Toward a Theory of Relationship Dynamics." *Journal of Marketing* 77 (January), 13–30.

Palmatier, Robert W., Cheryl Burke Jarvis, Jennifer R. Bechkoff, and Frank R. Kardes (2009), "The Role of Customer Gratitude in Relationship Marketing." *Journal of Marketing* 73 (September), 1–18.

Palmatier, Robert W., Lisa K. Scheer, Mark B. Houston, Kenneth R. Evans, and Srinath Gopalakrishna (2007), "Use of Relationship Marketing Programs in Building Customer-Salesperson and Customer-Firm Relationships: Differential Influences on Financial Outcomes." *International Journal of Research in Marketing* 24 (September), 210–23.

Pansari, A., and V. Kumar (2017), "Customer Engagement: The Construct, Antecedents, and Consequences." *Journal of the Academy of Marketing Science* 45 (3), 294–311.

Parasuraman, A., Valarie A. Zeithaml, and Leonard Berry (1988), "SERVQUAL: A Multiple-Item Scale for Measuring Consumer Perceptions of Service Quality." *Journal of Retailing* 64 (1), 12–40.

Petro, Greg (2016), "Nike Just Does It—Keeping an Eye on the Customer." Available at: www.forbes.com/sites/gregpetro/2016/07/08/nike-just-does-it-keeping-an-eye-on-the-customer/#1ea6ce0056da (accessed 24 July 2018).

Pucinelli, Nancy M., Ronald C. Goodstein, Dhruv Grewal, Robert Price, Priya Raghubir, and David Stewart (2009), "Customer Experience Management in Retailing: Understanding the Buying Process." *Journal of Retailing* 85 (March), 15–30.

Rheinberg, Falko, Regina Vollmeyer, and Stefan Engeser (2003), "Die Erfassung des Flow-Erlebens [The Assessment of Flow Experience]." In *Diagnostik von Selbstkonzept, Lernmotivation und Selbstregulation* [Diagnosis of Motivation and Self-Concept], eds. Joachim Stiensmeier-Pelster and Falko Rheinberg. Göttingen: Hogrefe.

Rubin, Alan M., Elizabeth M. Perse, and Robert A. Powell (1985), "Loneliness, Parasocial Interaction, and Local Television News Viewing." *Human Communication Research* 12 (2), 155–80.

Rust, Roland T., Katherine N. Lemon, and Valarie A. Zeithaml (2004), "Return on Marketing: Using Customer Equity to Focus Marketing Strategy." *Journal of Marketing* 68 (January), 109–27.

Samaha, Stephen A., Jordan Moffett, Irina Kozlenkova, and Robert W. Palmatier (2018), "Multichannel Communication Strategies." Working Paper.

Samaha, Stephen A., Robert W. Palmatier, and Rajiv P. Dant (2011), "Poisoning Relationships: Perceived Unfairness in Channels of Distribution." *Journal of Marketing* 75 (May), 99–117.

Schwartz, Barry (1967), "The Social Psychology of the Gift." *The American Journal of Sociology* 73 (July), 1–11.

Sirdeshmukh, Deepak, Jagdip Singh, and Barry Sabol (2002), "Consumer Trust, Value, and Loyalty in Relational Exchanges." *Journal of Marketing* 66 (January), 15–37.

Spekman, Robert E. (1988), "Strategic Supplier Selection: Understanding Long-Term Relationships." *Business Horizons* 31 (July/August), 75–81.

Steinhoff, Lena, and Robert W. Palmatier (2016), "Understanding Loyalty Program Effectiveness: Managing Target and Bystander Effects." *Journal of the Academy of Marketing Science* 44 (January), 88–107.

Van Den Bulte, Christophe, and Stefan Wuyts (2007), *Social Networks and Marketing*. Cambridge: Marketing Science Institute.

Van Doorn, Jenny, Katherine N. Lemon, Vikas Mittal, Stephan Nass, Doreén Pick, Pete Pirner, and Peter C. Verhoef (2010), "Customer Engagement Behavior: Theoretical Foundations and Research Directions." *Journal of Service Research* 13 (3), 253–66.

Venkatesan, Rajkumar, and V. Kumar (2004), "A Customer Lifetime Value Framework for Customer Selection and Resource Allocation Strategy." *Journal of Marketing* 68 (October), 106–25.

Verhoef, Peter C. (2003), "Understanding the Effect of Customer Relationship Management Efforts on Customer Retention and Customer Share Development." *Journal of Marketing* 67 (October), 30–45.

Verhoef, Peter C., Philip Hans Franses, and Janny C. Hoekstra (2002), "The Effect of Relational Constructs on Customer Referrals and Number of Services Purchased From a Multiservice Provider: Does Age of Relationship Matter?" *Journal of the Academy Marketing Science* 30 (Summer), 202–16.

Watson IV, George F., Joshua T. Beck, Conor M. Henderson, and Robert W. Palmatier (2015), "Building, Measuring, and Profiting From Customer Loyalty." *Journal of the Academy of Marketing Science* 43 (6), 790–825.

Wöhler (2018), "Mehr Know-How für Ihr Unternehmen." Available at: www.woehler.de/de/services/power-partner/programm/#issue-4 (accessed 24 July 2018).

# Part II

# Applying Relationship Marketing

# 4 Relationship Marketing Dynamics

## Learning Objectives

- Assess relationships and relationship marketing from a dynamic perspective.
- Retrace the advancement of dynamic relationship marketing by considering three perspectives on incremental relationship change.
- Understand the four different stages of the classic life cycle perspective.
- Acknowledge the contribution of the relationship velocity perspective.
- Synthesize life cycle stage and relationship velocity perspectives into a parsimonious, dynamic perspective on relationship states and migration mechanisms.
- Recognize transformational relationship events as triggers of disruptive relationship change.
- Learn how customer information gathered from market research techniques, CRM database analyses, and big data analytics helps identify the status quo of customer–seller relationships.

## Introduction

Relationships change over time (Palmatier et al. 2013; Zhang et al. 2016). Their fundamental dynamism is hard to deny. But managers often evaluate their customer–seller relationships with a static perspective, and researchers tend to do the same, largely because it is so difficult to capture and analyze relational data over time. During the course of a relationship, it passes through multiple stages, such that the key relational constructs shift and change, yet because they also tend to be unobserved or difficult to measure (e.g., commitment, trust, gratitude), gathering relevant data for thousands of customers in each stage quickly becomes an overwhelming task. If salespeople can interact directly with customers, they might rely on emotional intelligence, adaptive selling, and empathy to recognize important cues about the relationship, track its progress, and dynamically adjust their selling behaviors. If instead the relationships are impersonal, technology-mediated, or less rich, firms have to gather data from various customer interfaces in multiple channels, limit their costs by limiting their use of direct selling, and work to target individual customers. In this latter case, a dynamic view is even more critical, because without a single point of contact (in the form of a dedicated salesperson), the use of intuitive, emotion-based information is no longer viable.

Considering these challenges, the purpose of this chapter is twofold. In the first part, we delineate several approaches for understanding and managing the dynamics of customer–seller relationships. In the second part, building on these approaches, we offer managerial guidance for how to assess and diagnose relational dynamics to optimally design and continuously adapt relationship marketing strategies (as detailed subsequently in Chapters 5 and 6) to reflect the current status of the customer–seller bond.

## Approaches to Managing Relationship Marketing Dynamics

In this section, we synthesize extant research insights into the dynamics of relationships and their implications for a dynamic approach to relationship marketing. We start by delineating findings pertaining to how relationships evolve over time, according to classic relationship life cycle assumptions, as well as more fine-grained concepts, such as relationship velocity, relationship state, and state migration approaches. Then we describe some more disruptive relationship changes, as driven by transformational relationship events.

### Incremental Relationship Change

A widespread but erroneous assumption about relationships, whether social or business, is that they follow smooth, foreseeable paths. But as early as the 1950s, a life cycle perspective, based in biology, suggested that just as living creatures undergo various growth stages, so might customers, products, or industries. The current position of any entity—living being, product, firm—in its life cycle (e.g., birth, growth, death) defines the state of its existence. According to Dwyer, Schurr, and Oh (1987), marketing relationships generally follow a life cycle composed of awareness, exploration, expansion, commitment, and dissolution stages. More dynamic models, which rely less on the notion of a direct path, also have emerged more recently to predict the trajectories of customer–seller relationships.

### Relationship Life Cycle Stages

In the generic life cycle model in Figure 4.1, relationships consist of four path-dependent **relationship life cycle stages**: They begin, develop, solidify, and ultimately dissolve, similar to how individuals tend to go through

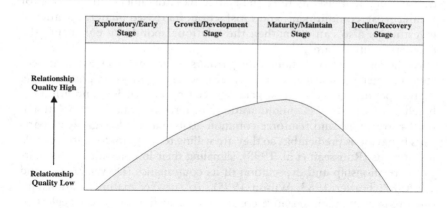

*Figure 4.1* Customer Relationship Life Cycle

life as they age and reach common milestones (e.g., school, marriage, retirement). By applying this human-oriented path to consumers' decision making, behaviors, and spending, marketing researchers seek to predict their future developments and devise the best ways to appeal to an average member of a target market in each stage (Arndt 1979; Rich and Jain 1968; Wagner and Hanna 1983; Wells and Gubar 1966).

The four conventional stages start with the *exploratory or early stage*. At this point, each partner has only limited confidence in the other party's trustworthiness, and any trust or commitment they show is calculative. That is, each party anticipates that the other side will act appropriately to avoid punishment, sanctions, or reputation losses, and those expectations often are enforced through institutional mechanisms such as laws and regulations (Jap and Ganesan 2000; Lewicki and Bunker 1996; Luna-Reyes, Cresswell, and Richardson 2004; Rousseau et al. 1998; Wilson 1995). But each side also is willing to explore the relationship, because they anticipate the potential for benefits that are better than what they currently receive from alternative partners. As these potential partners interact, they can start to develop and achieve synergistic norms and goals through their reciprocated transactions and bilateral investments (Dwyer, Schurr, and Oh 1987; Hibbard, Kumar, and Stern 2001; Jap and Ganesan 2000; Wilson 1995). To retain customers in a relationship, though, sellers must go beyond calculative views and start leveraging gratitude, communication, and competency to establish reciprocity norms that increase the potential for long-term relationships.

Assuming they do so and that the initial interactions produce desired outcomes, along with evidence of each partner's trustworthiness, their relationship enters a *growth or development stage*. Their reciprocated transactions increase, as does their affective attachment, in the form of greater trust, commitment, and satisfaction. Increased bilateral relational investments also can strengthen the relational bonds by enhancing the partners' mutual gains.

As the relationship continues, the partners continue to increase their benefits and interdependence, such that they reach a *maturity or maintain stage*. At this point, calculative trust gets replaced by knowledge- and affective-based forms, even as communication, reciprocity, and other relational norms strengthen and reinforce common goals. Each side regards its partner's behavior as predictable, so they are willing to make mutual, irrevocable investments (Rousseau et al. 1998), signaling their long-term commitments to the relationship and expectation of its continuance (Dwyer, Schurr, and Oh 1987; Frazier 1983; Wilson 1995). To survive, mature relationships often require avoiding negative consequences, such as customer neglect or service failures, even more than pursuing good ones. Accordingly, it is up to sellers to maintain communication, invest in the relationship, and avoid conflict with or perceptions of unfairness among customers.

But even the most successful relationships may enter a *decline stage*, potentially followed by a *recovery stage*. Sellers that exhibit passive neglect fail to communicate sufficiently or else do not make appropriate relational investments, and their ties with customers slowly weaken and break. More problematically, conflict with customers—causing them to perceive that the seller has betrayed them or treats them unfairly—can prompt an immediate end to the relationship. To recover, the seller firms must gather new insights into what customers really want then be flexible enough to provide it. They also should make sure that their customer exchanges provide compelling benefits beyond simply relying on or assuming dependence and that they exhibit mutual appreciation for the link.

---

### Example 4.1  Vodafone (Australia)

To manage its dynamic relationships with contractual mobile customers, the telecommunications provider Vodafone assigns them to different life cycle stages, depending on their relational state: sign-up, consolidation, risk, or loyalty. In each stage, customers receive communications and offers that emphasize aspects typically relevant to a relationship in that stage. For example, during the sign-up stage, customers might receive information about how to find their way around Vodafone's stores or website and where to get answers to their questions. In the consolidation stage, Vodafone calls customers to ask about their satisfaction. If customers enter the risk stage, such as near the end of their contract, the company sends them personalized renewal offers

Source: Williams (2015).

In summary, a relationship life cycle perspective suggests a common developmental process for relationships along a simple trajectory, marked by growth stages for customers. Therefore, relational strategies reflect customers' current positions in the life cycle and the consumption preferences typically associated with that position. The generic, universal nature of the customer life cycle model makes this approach simple and easy for marketers to use. But expecting all customers to follow the same relational trajectory represents a strong and likely inaccurate assumption. A life cycle approach describes average or typical customers; it ignores individual customer heterogeneity. Nor did early relationship life cycle applications offer insights into the origins or causes of customer dynamics, even though understanding the individual dynamics of specific customers and identifying the reasons for them is critical to effective relationship marketing strategies.

## Relationship Velocity

In an effort to explicate these dynamics, some researchers take series of "snapshots" or static conceptualizations of the precise level of relational constructs at each point in time to describe a customer's relationship state (Morgan and Hunt 1994; Palmatier et al. 2006). More recent relationship marketing research instead acknowledges the time-varying nature of relationships explicitly and measures the rate and direction of change in the key relational constructs, summarized in the concept of **relationship velocity** (Palmatier et al. 2013). These analyses rely on latent growth curve assessments of the customer's growth process, according to its level, velocity, and acceleration. By revealing observed growth trajectories, they can predict both antecedents and outcomes of the relevant growth factors.

Consider the sample in Figure 4.2 as an example: For 433 new channel relationships, commitment increases at first, peaks at about year four, and then decays (Palmatier et al. 2013). This commitment velocity construct in turn has a notable impact on relationship performance (i.e., sales growth), more so than do static measures of a commitment level at any particular point in time. In particular, initial commitment affects performance only partially (one effect); commitment velocity instead consistently enhances it across all three effects. An isolated, single-moment-in-time measure of the level of commitment cannot predict how the relationship will change in the future, because there is no consideration of its trajectory, nor do analysts know where the relationship is in its overall trajectory. A new relationship marked by low but increasing levels of commitment should prompt more positive predictions than a longer-term relationship in which the commitment levels have started to decay dramatically, but a static measurement cannot reveal that insight and instead might produce terribly misleading predictions. For example, in

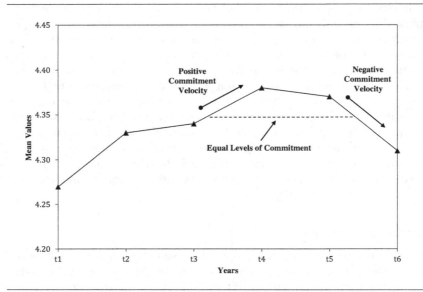

*Figure 4.2* Customer Commitment Velocity
Source: Adapted from Palmatier et al. (2013).

Figure 4.2, the dotted line indicates the same *level* of commitment at two points in time, but the *velocity* (slopes) provides more information about the likely future of the relationship and its performance implications. As Jap and Anderson (2007, p. 271) note, "for the most part, maturity is never better than build-up and is often marginally inferior." Therefore, the rate and direction of change in relational constructs represent crucial information for explaining and predicting relational outcomes.

In addition to determining the commitment velocity of their relationships, relationship managers need insights into how to increase it. As should come as no surprise, trust is key. This relational, governance mechanism encourages continuous adaptation. Furthermore, communication and investments signal the partners' bilateral willingness and ability to explore and exploit value-creation opportunities, which also can speed up commitment velocity. Each driver offers differential effectiveness, depending on the relationship's age, such that trust and communication tend to have weaker influences as the relationship lengthens, but investment capabilities often become more important.

As this section reveals, a relationship velocity perspective has three key implications that help clarify relationship dynamics:

1.  It is not the unique stage in the relationship life cycle that matters but rather its trajectory, reflecting relationship dynamics (i.e., velocity

and acceleration). That is, static and dynamic relational constructs can drive exchange performance, but only the dynamic elements allow for the prediction of future performance. This insight also implies that even a "rocky" early relationship, marked by low levels of initial commitment, can be addressed by increasing relationship velocity and/or acceleration. Accordingly, dynamic variables likely can provide insights into relationship recovery potential as well.

2.  The trajectories and velocities of distinct relational constructs reveal different dynamic patterns (Palmatier et al. 2013). In contrast with a common assumption in prior research, namely, that relational constructs such as commitment and trust develop together, in lockstep, as the relationship advances (Hibbard, Kumar, and Stern 2001; Jap and Anderson 2007), this view acknowledges the unique trajectories of the different relational constructs (commitment, trust, relational norms), depending on the influential time-varying processes that apply to each specific construct.

3.  Relational constructs change; so do the links among them. Cross-sectional studies only capture an average effect and are limited to a sample, often consisting of relationships in their maturity stage, that exhibits generally homogenous relationship trajectories. Consider the impact of trust on commitment velocity: On average, trust drives commitment, but the effect varies for younger versus older relationships. As they mature, trust likely becomes a necessary but not a sufficient condition for relationship growth. In this sense, the connection between trust and commitment appears more complex than previously predicted, and the relationship velocity perspective can better depict that complexity.

## Relationship States and Migration Mechanisms

To weave life cycle stage and relational construct velocity perspectives into a parsimonious framework of relationship dynamics, empirical relationship marketing research relies on hidden Markov models to identify customers' relationship states and migration patterns across states (Zhang et al. 2016). Analyses of data from a longitudinal panel of 552 business-to-business (B2B) customers, describing their relationships with a *Fortune* 500 supplier over a six-year period, indicate four latent **relationship states**. In addition to describing customers' levels of commitment, trust, dependence, and relational norms in each state, this study reveals three positive (exploration, endowment, recovery) and two negative (neglect, betrayal) **relationship migration mechanisms**, as presented in Figure 4.3.

The first *transactional state* accounts for about half of the supplier's customer relationships (54%). It entails low to medium levels of customer commitment, trust, and dependence and relatively low relational norms. These mostly new customer–seller relationships tend to be neutral and

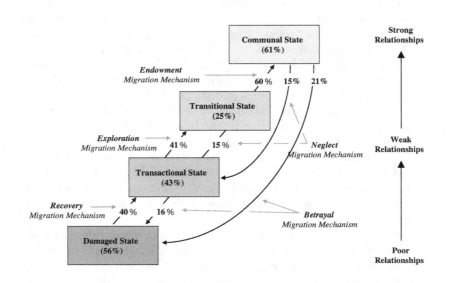

*Figure 4.3* Hidden Markov Model Analysis: Relationship States and Migration
Mechanisms

Note: Percentages represent how many customers migrate or remain in a relationship state
each year.

Source: Adapted from Zhang et al. (2016).

undeveloped, with minimal relational governance. The parties receive
some value from the exchange but continue to evaluate opportunities for
creating more value and rarely invest specifically in the relational bond.
The profits and sales growth that the seller earns from these customers
are moderate. As they move out of this state, customers can go in virtually any direction: 43% of relationships stay transactional, 41% advance
into stronger relational states, and 16% decline into weaker or damaged
states (Zhang et al. 2016).

If they advance, the customer–seller relationships reach a *transitional
state*, in which all the relational constructs increase relative to the transactional state (i.e., medium to high commitment, trust, and relational
norms and low to medium customer dependence). In particular, relational
norms increase approximately three times more than the remaining constructs, likely due to the substantial increase of relational governance in
this transitional state. The higher profits and sales growth also imply the
relationships' performance potential. Finally, this state tends to be brief,

often no more than one period, and mainly consists of relationships that are shifting from a transactional to a more developed state. Each year, 75% of relationships move into to another state (60% strengthening, 15% weakening).

The *communal state* is the ideal (Zhang et al. 2016): It reveals the highest levels of commitment, trust, dependence, relational norms, and profits, along with strong sales growth. Because of these benefits, 61% of customers remain in this state each year, such that the communal state is the "stickiest" one. When these relationship shift, the patterns are generally detrimental, in that they tend to move directly to a damaged relational state (21%) rather than entering a more neutral, transactional state (15%).

Finally, with its low levels of commitment and trust, very low relational norms, and medium to high dependence level, the *damaged state* produces negative sales growth. Yet these relationships might remain profitable, because customers still depend on the seller. Without this high level of dependence, customers likely would terminate the relationship. Due to their negative implications, though, recovering these relationships is difficult, and 56% of relationships in the damaged state stay there, year after year. If they can be recovered, the relationships might move just to the neutral transactional state.

The mix of relational constructs and their levels accordingly determines each relationship's state. Relationship migrations occur with changes in the levels of relational constructs, reflecting their velocity. In Figure 4.3, five prototypical paths, both positive and negative, parsimoniously account for customers' migrations across the four relationship states.

On the positive side, relationships might improve through exploration, endowment, and recovery. *Exploration* means that customer–seller relationships move from a transactional to a transitional state, because the conditions seem favorable for customers to investigate the relationship further. To achieve these promising conditions, sellers must check in periodically with customers and seek opportunities for cross- and up-selling. *Endowment* involves bilateral investments that bring mutual, value-creating opportunities to fruition, which can move relationships from a transitional into the precious communal state. Firms should use dedicated account managers to show their appreciation for the relationship and invest in specific joint infrastructures, through structural relationship marketing programs, to spark endowment. If relationships shift from a damaged to a transactional state, *recovery* mechanisms, such as repairing norms and rebuilding trust, drive this migration. For relational recovery to take place, firms must be ready to change course (e.g., assign a new sales representative to the account) and willing to compromise (e.g., make concessions to alleviate conflict or perceptions of unfairness).

On the negative side, neglect or betrayal can cause customer relationships to deteriorate. *Neglect* represents relational parties' passive abuse, driven by a lack of desire or resources to invest in the relationship. It can diminish relationships, from communal to transactional or from transitional to transactional relational states. To prevent inadvertent neglect-evoked migrations, firms should stay in constant contact with customers to communicate and regularly assess and adapt their resources to serve customers. *Betrayal* occurs when relational partners actively undermine fairness perceptions and reject relational governance mechanisms; these relationships quickly decline from communal or transactional to damaged states. Such betrayal migrations are deeply undesirable, so sellers need to be proactive in identifying potential areas of conflict and clearly establishing and insisting on fairness in their business procedures and profit distributions (Zhang et al. 2016).

Assessing customer–company relationships according to relationship states and migration mechanisms effectively combines and advances both the life cycle stage and velocity conceptualizations. The hidden Markov model can empirically identify relationship states rather than having to assume a generic progression by all customers, as suggested by life cycle theory. Both relationship states and migration mechanisms reflect the levels and also the changes in the levels of the relational constructs, in line with relationship velocity perspectives. Consistent with a dynamic view, it also is apparent that firms' relationship marketing investments are not universally applicable or effective across the entire duration of the relationship. Rather, the effectiveness of specific relationship marketing strategies and programs depends on the relationship's current state and trajectory.

### Disruptive Relationship Change

The previous section outlined the development of increasingly advanced and fine-grained perspectives on dynamic relationship change. As an implicit assumption, all of these views suggest rather smooth relational trajectories and incremental relationship change. Yet it is easy to imagine that a single discrete event might disrupt the gradual evolution of any relationship and serve as a defining moment in its history, such that it substantially and dramatically, rather than incrementally, alters the nature and course of the relationship.

Recent relationship marketing research investigates the consequences of such **transformational relationship events (TREs)**, which are "encounter[s] between exchange partners that significantly disconfirm relational expectations (positively or negatively) and result in dramatic, discontinuous change to the relationship's trajectory" (Harmeling et al. 2015). Various theoretical perspectives on turning points, expectancy disconfirmation, relational norms, sensemaking, and social emotions underscore how a single event can be instrumental in dynamic customer–seller relationships. Specifically, TREs disrupt the relationship's development and serve as moments of truth in a relationship, exerting a disproportional impact on the relational trajectory.

## Example 4.2  United Airlines (USA)

United Airlines forcibly removed a customer from an overbooked domestic flight, resulting in a disturbing experience for both the manhandled flyer and the passengers who observed the incident. The common practice of overbooking flights is not illegal, but this incident created a publicity nightmare for the company. For the removed customer, of course, but for many other customers, the situation represented a negative transformational relationship event: They expressed outrage on social media and protested that such treatment was totally unacceptable. Some even indicated they had canceled existing United flight reservations and would never fly those unfriendly skies again.

Source: Zdanowicz and Grinberg (2018).

Whether an event in a customer–seller relationship is transformational, according to customers, depends on the relational status quo (see Figure 4.4). In early relationships, when expectations are low, partners expect to encounter autonomous behavior that reinforces individual goals. Mild opportunism (e.g., arguing about a contractual detail) is a negative behavior but an unsurprising one and well within the customer's zone of indifference (Point 1). At low levels of relational expectations, these mild disconfirmations reinforce expectations and contribute to incremental development. In more fully developed relationships, though,

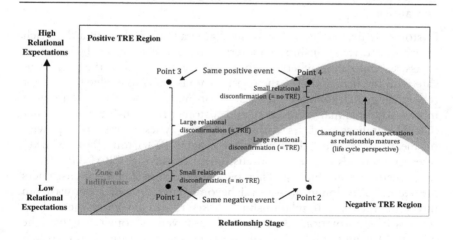

*Figure 4.4* Dynamic Relational Expectations and Disconfirmations
Source: Adapted from Harmeling et al. (2015).

such opportunistic behavior would be nearly unfathomable, because norms of solidarity and trust have developed, and expectations are higher. Therefore, this same behavior falls well below the zone of indifference and creates substantial disconfirmation (Point 2). When relational expectations are high, these disconfirmations can threaten the very foundation of the relationship and become TREs, with detrimental consequences for the relationship. Negative disconfirmations are more (negatively) transformational for strong relationships than for less-established ones (Harmeling et al. 2015).

A positive relational event (e.g., remembering the name of a customer's spouse) in a weakly developed relationship may be strongly disconfirming (Point 3), but in a strong relationship, this behavior reflects the underlying rules guiding the relationship and confirms relational expectations (Point 4). Positive disconfirmations are powerful and transformational for enhancing relationships when relational expectations are still low. Thus, positively disconfirming relational events take underdeveloped relationships to the next level and transform them rather than simply propelling already solidified relationships (Harmeling et al. 2015).

This dynamic perspective on TREs is not contradictory with the insights on incremental relationship change; instead, it reveals how ordinary, continuous relational development can co-occur with extraordinary, discontinuous shocks. The changing relational expectations determine when an event contributes to incremental development and when it dramatically transforms the relationship.

## Guidelines for Managing Relationship Marketing Dynamics

Customer–seller relationships in the digital age take place in a data-rich environment. Relationship marketers can use a plethora of data sources to assess empirically where customers currently stand in their relationship with the firm and how the relationship is likely to evolve then adapt relationship marketing strategies accordingly. Effectively combining more traditional market research and customer relationship management (CRM) database analyses with big data analytics represents a powerful means to generate deep customer insights (Wharton 2014). Market research methods capture what customers are saying; CRM data reveal what customers are buying. Then big data may uncover what customers are feeling and doing, above and beyond what the seller knows from direct interactions. If relationship marketers can integrate these three sources of information to generate data-driven customer insights, the potential for mutually beneficial customer–seller relationships increases substantially.

Imagining the customer–seller relationship as a life cycle of different stages offers a valuable starting point for acknowledging customer dynamics. Rather than assuming that all customers proceed through the same generic, discrete stages at the same pace, though, as suggested by life cycle theory, relationship marketers should apply the more advanced concepts of relationship velocity, states, and migrations to identify segments of customers, together with individual customers' dynamic patterns and tendencies. Observing drastic changes in customers' emotions, cognitions, and behaviors may indicate a TRE that threatens to upset the relational status quo—in either a positive or a negative sense.

### Diagnosing Relationship Change Through Market Research Techniques

Understanding the level and development of customers' relational mechanisms, in terms of the emotional, cognitive, and behavioral manifestations they exhibit toward the company, is key to understanding their relationship velocity, relationship state, and potential migration paths. To assess the battery of relevant relational mechanisms and track changes in relational constructs over time, firms should survey their customers consistently (e.g., once a year), which will increase data availability and quality. To keep track of the most relevant relational indicators, they also can conduct brief telephone interviews more frequently (e.g., once per quarter) or after specific interactions (e.g., after a service provision to resolve a concern). Changes and trends in customers' evaluations of relational constructs would alert firms to the current relationship trajectory and potential customer migrations. With these insights, firms can undertake relationship investments that either enforce positive trajectories or counter negative developments.

---

**Example 4.3  Drive Research (USA)**

As a market research company, Drive Research consults with firms and conducts their continuous customer feedback surveys. Providing clients with tailored approaches to match their unique requirements, the consultancy offers yearly, quarterly, monthly, or ongoing voice-of-customer (VoC) surveys, which it distributes to the clients' customer bases online, via mail, or over the phone. Thus, Drive Research helps its customer companies become more customer-centric.

Source: Palermo (2018).

---

Qualitative market research is particularly helpful in understanding *why* relationships change. Relationship marketing managers should take every chance they get to talk in depth with selected customers to determine which mechanisms might drive them to migrate. Critical incident techniques can be valuable for identifying and digging deep into positive and negative TREs (Bitner, Booms, and Tetreault 1990; Hanagan 1954).

Beyond identifying specific, disruptive events, focus group research also can be valuable for generating in-depth feedback about the seller's products to inform either new product launches or development efforts to improve current products.

---

**Example 4.4  Beats Electronics (USA)**

Before launching its Beats by Dr. Dre headphones, Beats Electronics employed prototypes and invited prospective customers to come test them. During focus groups, people gave constructive, in-depth feedback about what they liked and did not like about the headphones, which the firm used to identify areas for improvement before rolling out the actual product to the market. Beyond product-specific preferences, the company learned a lot about its (prospective) customers' preferences in general, establishing new insights for future innovations.

Source: Tottle (2016).

---

### *Diagnosing Relationship Change Through CRM Database Analyses*

In their CRM databases, companies typically collect demographic information (e.g., name, age, address), purchase transactions, and other relational interactions (e.g., e-mails, customer service requests) for all their customers. The history of customer interactions offers a rich summary of customers' behavior over time. To gain a sense of the current state of the relationship, companies might apply RFM (recency, frequency, monetary value) methods to capture the time elapsed since the customer's last purchase, number of transactions in the previous period, and spending in the previous period. Observing such RFM variables over time can reveal variations or anomalies in customers' usual buying behavior, so that firms can design relationship marketing strategies to direct their purchase behaviors in productive directions.

---

**Example 4.5  Apple (USA)**

The Apple ID is a unique customer identifier, across all Apple devices and touchpoints. Thus, all relevant customer information (e.g., transactions on iTunes and App Store, interactions with customer service, selections and preferences on Apple Music) converge in a huge CRM database. For customers, the result is convenient, seamless content synchronization. For the company, the Apple ID database provides a constantly updated, evolving description of all its customers and their preferences, supporting the firm's seemingly effortless, targeted marketing.

Source: Expert CRM Software (2018).

---

Substantial changes in a customer's purchase behavior (e.g., regular customer suddenly stops buying) may indicate a TRE. If the CRM database includes non–purchase-related customer interactions, such as customer service inquiries, they can provide pertinent insights into why the behavioral changes might be happening (e.g., unresolved customer complaint). If such information is not tracked in the CRM database, qualitative market research techniques should be leveraged to find out what has happened to the relational bond.

### *Diagnosing Relationship Change Through Big Data Analytics*

Big data can be powerful in parallel with market research and CRM data analyses to derive superior insights into where a customer–seller relationship is headed. Many firms gather customer information through social media channels, because customers' personal profiles on Facebook or other sites reveal valuable information about their living circumstances, lifestyles, and major life events (e.g., graduating from college, getting married, having kids). These events have the potential to alter the relationship with the firm, so the firm needs to leverage this information to design and target its effective relational investments. Such psychographic information also can serve to segment customers, such that the firm can design relevant offers for specific lifestyle segments. Beyond social media, customers interact with a company through its website or mobile applications. By tracking customers' omnichannel usage behavior (e.g., frequency of usage, duration of usage, features used), the firm gains insights into their overall relationship engagement.

Furthermore, social media and review sites serve as important platforms for customers to talk to or about a firm. Tracking customers' seller-related conversations on the Internet enriches understanding of why customers behave the way they do. Sentiment analysis, applied to investigate customers' online feedback and reviews, can offer clues about the relationship's status quo. Specifically, a TRE might give customers an occasion to share positive or negative experiences with the company through social media. Identifying strong sentiments in customers' comments helps managers understand what has led to the disruptive relationship change and take appropriate next steps.

---

### Example 4.6  TripAdvisor (USA) and Lexalytics (USA)

TripAdvisor uses Lexalytics's sentiment analysis tools to identify users' consensus opinions on hotels, restaurants, attractions, and so forth. For example, Lexalytics undertook an in-depth comparison of two famous Las Vegas casinos: the Bellagio and Bally's. The general review scores were pretty similar; for location, they were nearly identical, which confirmed the reliability of the method, in that the properties are across the street from each other. But the Bellagio earned lower scores on factors such as cleanliness, service, and overall satisfaction. "Digging deeper into the results, I was surprised to see that Bally's had higher scores than Bellagio because Bellagio is one of the five-star properties in Vegas, so we dug a bit deeper to make sure we weren't scoring the reviews wrong," explains Jeff Catlin, Lexalytics's CEO. "When we dug into the reviews we discovered that people expected more for their money than they were getting at Bellagio" (Groenfeldt 2011). Sentiment analysis on publicly available information such as online reviews can help firms such as TripAdvisor offer more reliable evaluations, at a minimal incremental cost, so that providers in turn can discover new, previously unmeasured categories in which they can meet customers' demands, according to recurring themes in the data.

Source: Groenfeldt (2011).

## Summary

By their very nature, relationships are dynamic and evolve over time. To understand relationship marketing performance, it is vital to acknowledge that relationship marketing strategies vary in their effectiveness across relational development stages. Strategies that are most effective in early stages may not work later, and vice versa. Adapting relationship marketing to the dynamics of the relationship is key for long-term success. Relationship marketing research proposes diverse concepts that delineate how relationships change over time, whether through incremental alterations or substantial disruptions.

In many cases, relational change is assumed to be incremental, with the sense that relationships progress in smooth, predictable trajectories over time. Starting from the seminal relationship life cycle perspective, relationship marketing research has advanced knowledge of relationship dynamics by suggesting less generic and more fine-grained models that capture the dynamic evolution of relationships. According to the relationship life cycle stages view, relationships follow a generic, four-stage trajectory, progressing from exploratory or early stages to growth and development and then to the maturity or maintain stage before entering a decline and possibly a recovery stage. More recent research adopts more dynamic, less path-dependent models to depict the life trajectory of customer–seller relationships. Systematically building on the life cycle approach, relationship velocity, together with relationship state and state migration perspectives, offer more fine-grained assessments. Specifically, a relationship velocity perspective argues that the rate and direction of change in key relational constructs needs to be considered to understand relationship dynamics. In the relationship states and migration mechanisms perspective, the synthesis of life cycle stages and relational construct velocity conceptualizations predicts four typical states (i.e., transactional, transitional, communal, and damaged), together with three positive (i.e., exploration, endowment, and recovery) and two negative (i.e., neglect and betrayal) migration patterns by which relationships move across states.

Not all relationships change incrementally though. Transformational relationship events emerge when discrete encounters between exchange partners significantly disconfirm relational expectations (positively or negatively), resulting in dramatic, discontinuous changes to the nature and course of the relationship. Negative disconfirmations become TREs with detrimental consequences for the relationship if relational expectations are high; they can destroy strong relationships but tend to be less harmful to less well-established relationships. Positive disconfirmations transform and enhance relationships when the expectations are still low, such that they move underdeveloped relationships to the next level.

In today's data-rich relationship marketing environment, companies should consult and combine as many information sources as possible to generate insights about their customers and their relational dynamics. This chapter reviews three key data sources. First, quantitative (e.g., surveys) and qualitative (e.g., critical-incident technique) market research methods enable firms to track the evolution of relational constructs and identify TREs. Second, CRM databases depict the history of customer purchases and other transactions, which can reveal incremental or substantial changes in customers' behavioral patterns. Third, big data collected through the Internet can be converted into valuable customer insights, such as learning about customers' lifestyles or relevant life events through their personal social media profiles or analyzing their seller-related online conversations (e.g., reviews).

## Takeaways

- Most academic research and most managers take a static perspective on customer–seller relationships, despite the undisputed premise that relationships change over time and are fundamentally dynamic.
- Recent relationship marketing research indicates that relationships can change incrementally as well as disruptively.
- Three concepts describe incremental relationship change: (1) relationship life cycle stages, (2) relationship velocity, and (3) relationship states and migration mechanisms.
- The classic relationship life cycle stage perspective argues that all relationships follow a generic four-stage trajectory, progressing from an exploratory or early stage to a growth or development stage to a maturity or maintain stage to a decline or recovery stage.
- Rather than assuming discrete, generic relationship life cycle stages, the more fine-grained relationship velocity perspective argues that the rate and direction of change in key relational constructs (e.g.

commitment) must be considered to understand relationship dynamics.

- The relationship states and migration mechanisms perspective synthesizes insights on life cycle stages and relational construct velocity. Hidden Markov modeling empirically establishes four typical relationship states (transactional, transitional, communal, damaged) and depicts three positive (exploration, endowment, recovery) and two negative (neglect, betrayal) migration patterns by which relationships move between states.

- These insights on relationship marketing dynamics underscore the idea that relationship marketing investments are not universally applicable or effective during the customer's overall relationship with the firm. Rather, the effectiveness of specific relationship marketing strategies or programs depends on the relationship's current state and trajectory.

- Relationship evolution is not always gradual. Transformational relationship events entail discrete encounters between exchange partners that substantially disconfirm relational expectations (positively or negatively) and result in dramatic, discontinuous changes to the relationship's trajectory.

- Relationships in the digital age take place in a data-rich environment. Companies should combine insights from market research techniques, CRM database analyses, and big data analytics to diagnose incremental as well as disruptive relationship change.

## References

Arndt, Johan (1979), "Toward a Concept of Domesticated Markets." *Journal of Marketing* 43 (4), 69–75.

Bitner, Mary Jo, Bernard H. Booms, and Mary S. Tetreault (1990), "The Service Encounter: Diagnosing Favorable and Unfavorable Incidents." *Journal of Marketing* 54 (January), 71–84.

Dwyer, Robert F., Paul H. Schurr, and Sejo Oh (1987), "Developing Buyer-Seller Relationships." *Journal of Marketing* 51 (April), 11–27.

Expert CRM Software (2018), "Big Brand CRM Case Studies." Available at: www.expertmarket.co.uk/crm-systems/customer-relationship-management-case-studies (accessed 19 July 2018)

Frazier, Gary L. (1983), "On the Measurement of Interfirm Power in Channels of Distribution." *Journal of Marketing Research* 20 (May), 158–66.

Groenfeldt, Tom (2011), "Text Analytics Show Why Bellagio Underperforms Bally's." Available at: www.forbes.com/sites/tomgroenfeldt/2011/06/24/text-analytics-show-why-bellagio-underperforms-ballys/#46abfe84184a (accessed 19 July 2018).

Hanagan, John C. (1954), "The Critical Incident Technique." *Psychological Bulletin* 51 (July), 327–57.

Harmeling, Colleen M., Robert W. Palmatier, Mark B. Houston, Mark J. Arnold, and Stephen A. Samaha (2015), "Transformational Relationship Events." *Journal of Marketing* 79 (September), 39–62.

Hibbard, Jonathan D., Nirmalya Kumar, and Louis W. Stern (2001), "Examining the Impact of Destructive Acts in Marketing Channels Relationship." *Journal of Marketing Research* 38 (February), 25–61.

Jap, Sandy D., and Erin Anderson (2007), "Testing a Life-Cycle Theory of Cooperative Interorganizational Relationships: Movement Across Stages and Performance." *Management Science* 53 (February), 260–75.

Jap, Sandy D., and Shankar Ganesan (2000), "Control Mechanisms and the Relationship Life Cycle: Implications for Safeguarding Specific Investments and Developing Commitment." *Journal of Marketing Research* 37 (May), 227–45.

Lewicki, Roy J., and Barbara B. Bunker, eds. (1996), *Developing and Maintaining Trust in Working Relationships*. Thousand Oaks: Sage Publications, Inc.

Luna-Reyes, Luis F., Anthony M. Cresswell, and George P. Richardson (2004), "Knowledge and the Development of Interpersonal Trust: A Dynamic Model." *Proceedings of Hawaii International Conference on System Sciences* 37 (January), 1–12.

Morgan, Robert M., and Shelby D. Hunt (1994), "The Commitment-Trust Theory of Relationship Marketing." *Journal of Marketing* 58 (July), 20–38.

Palermo, Emily (2018), "The Benefits of Continuous Customer Feedback Surveys." Available at: www.driveresearch.com/single-post/2018/01/23/What-Are-the-Benefits-of-Continuous-Customer-Feedback-Surveys (accessed 19 July 2018).

Palmatier, Robert W., Rajiv P. Dant, Dhruv Grewal, and Kenneth R. Evans (2006), "Factors Influencing the Effectiveness of Relationship Marketing: A Meta-Analysis." *Journal of Marketing* 70 (October), 136–53.

Palmatier, Robert W., Mark B. Houston, Rajiv P. Dant, and Dhruv Grewal (2013), "Relationship Velocity: Toward a Theory of Relationship Dynamics." *Journal of Marketing* 77 (January), 13–30.

Rich, Stuart U., and Subhash C. Jain (1968), "Social Class and Life Cycle as Predictors of Shopping Behavior." *Journal of Marketing Research* 5 (1), 41–9.

Rousseau, Denise M., Sim B. Sitkin, Ronald S. Burt, and Colin Camerer (1998), "Not So Different After All: A Cross-Discipline View of Trust." *Academy of Management Review* 23 (3), 393–404.

Tottle, Will (2016), "How Dr. Dre's Beats Became the Most Popular Headphones in the World." Available at: www.referralcandy.com/blog/beats-headphone-marketing-strategy/ (accessed 19 July 2018).

Wagner, Janet, and Sherman Hanna (1983), "The Effectiveness of Family Life Cycle Variables in Consumer Expenditure Research." *Journal of Consumer Research* 10 (3), 281–91.

Wells, William, and George Gubar (1966), "Life Cycle Concept in Marketing Research." *Journal of Marketing Research* 3 (4), 355–63.

Wharton (2014), "Finding a Place for Market Research in a Big Data, Tech-Enabled World, Knowledge@Wharton." Available at: http://knowledge.wharton.upenn.edu/article/finding-place-market-research-big-data-tech-enabled-world-2/ (accessed 19 July 2018).

Williams, Azadeh (2015), "Vodafone Taps into Data Analytics to Improve the Customer Journey." Available at: www.cmo.com.au/article/574444/vodafone-uses-data-analytics-enhance-customer-journey/ (accessed 19 July 2018).

Wilson, David T. (1995), "An Integrated Model of Buyer-Seller Relationships." *Journal of the Academy of Marketing Science* 23 (4), 335–45.

Zdanowicz, Christina. and Emanuella Grinberg (2018), "Passenger Dragged Off Overbooked United Flight." Available at: https://edition.cnn.com/2017/04/10/travel/passenger-removed-united-flight-trnd/index.html (accessed 19 July 2018).

Zhang, Jonathan Z., George F. Watson IV, Robert W. Palmatier, and Rajiv P. Dant (2016), "Dynamic Relationship Marketing." *Journal of Marketing* 80 (September), 53–75.

# 5 Relationship Marketing Strategies

## Learning Objectives

- Understand that building and maintaining relationships are key managerial goals for relationship marketing.
- Review research insights on the diverse strategies that can nurture customer relationships.
- Consider research evidence that delineates how to prevent negative events and retain customer relationships.
- Identify customer-centric structures and loyalty programs as institutionalized, organization-wide programs for managing customer relationships.
- Synthesize best practices for building and maintaining relationships, based on academic and practical evidence.
- Identify emerging strategies for managing customer relationships in the digital age.

## Introduction

In managing their customer relationships, firms employ a plethora of strategies—from rewards and loyalty prizes to special activities and dedicated programs—to reap performance gains by developing and establishing persistent, long-term relational bonds. Dedicated relationship marketing programs constitute a unique promotional effort, though they often rely on strategies and tactics derived from conventional advertising or direct marketing efforts. With a specific relationship marketing program though, a firm can budget with greater specificity and also gain more precise insights into the returns on its investments, in terms of the program's effectiveness. Therefore, to implement dedicated relationship marketing programs, systematically and strategically, managers must answer two critical, seemingly simple, but actually complex questions:

1. How can we build strong customer relationships?
2. How can we maintain strong customer relationships?

The first question informs the design of effective strategies for creating and growing relational exchanges. In a dynamic sense, these strategies constitute the early stages of the customer–seller bond. The second question instead focuses on how to keep customers, even in later relational stages, by ensuring fruitful relations with them. That effort often hinges more on avoiding the bad rather than adding more good to the relationship.

Accordingly, this chapter consists of two parts, reflecting these two key questions. We start by outlining empirical evidence that reveals the concepts and strategies that researchers have identified as relevant for building or maintaining strong customer relationships. We also address customer centricity and loyalty programs as two important forms of institutionalized relationship marketing efforts. Then we adopt a more practical view to detail some established best practices and emerging strategies that should guide relationship marketers' daily operations to enable companies to manage relationships mediated by technological and digital channels.

## Approaches for Managing Relationship Marketing Strategies

To implement relationship marketing strategies, managers first need strong relationships. Strengthening a relationship requires convincing customers of the value of the relationship, due to the relevant benefits and favorable experiences it provides. Continuing the relationship instead requires companies to insulate customers from bad experiences.

### Relationship Marketing Strategies for Building Relationships

Once a customer has been acquired, the seller must seek systematically to develop and nurture that relationship, using some of the many strategies already identified for appealing to customers and growing the relationship over time. In addition to encouraging specific relationship drivers, effective strategies leverage gratitude and reciprocity norms as key relational mechanisms; they also must address the need for signals and reciprocity to form relationships online.

### Understanding Relationship Drivers

In Table 5.1, we present the results of a meta-analysis of empirical articles devoted to understanding which factors produce strong relationships (Palmatier et al. 2006). This list of drivers with the greatest impacts on relationship quality (defined as an aggregate measure of relational mechanisms) reflects findings from 17 years (1987–2004) of research, summarized in 97 publications that investigate 38,077 relationships. Although this meta-analysis, which was published in 2006, effectively clarifies the most effective relationship drivers, without creating limitations based on

*Table 5.1* Relationship Drivers

| Relational Drivers | Definitions | Adjusted r Between Antecedent and Relationship Quality |
|---|---|---|
| Conflict | Overall level of disagreement between exchange partners | −0.67 |
| Seller expertise | Knowledge, experience, and overall competency of seller | 0.62 |
| Communication | Amount, frequency, and quality of information shared between exchange partners | 0.54 |
| Relationship investments | Seller's investment of time, effort, spending, and resources focused on building a stronger relationship | 0.46 |
| Similarity | Commonality in appearance, lifestyle, and status between individual boundary spanners or similar cultures, values, and goals between buying and selling organizations | 0.44 |
| Relationship benefits | Benefits received, including time saving, convenience, companionship, and improved decision making | 0.42 |
| Dependence on seller | Customer's evaluation of the value of seller-provided resources for which few alternatives are available from other sellers | 0.26 |
| Interaction frequency | Number of interactions or number of interactions per unit of time between exchange partners | 0.16 |
| Relationship duration | Length of time that the relationship between the exchange partners has existed | 0.13 |

Note: The results in this table are based on a meta-analysis performed by Palmatier et al. (2006).

the source studies' methods (e.g., researcher, industry, measurements), it pertains only to already-studied factors, so more recent developments are excluded. Still, addressing these well-established drivers, Table 5.1 reveals unequal influences on relationship quality, ranging from a massive negative effect of conflict (−.67) to a relatively smaller positive influence of relationship duration (.13).

The indication that **conflict** exerts the strongest impact, by destroying the various relationship quality elements, should come as no surprise. If they want to prevent corrosive, relationship-damaging arguments, partners must resolve their disagreements. But it seems notable that the strongest effect in this meta-analysis is negative. It is human nature to pay more attention to negative than to positive information, so even long-lasting, seemingly productive relationships can suffer greatly due to conflict (Fiske 1980; Shiv, Edell, and Payne 1997).

Beyond avoiding the negative though, managers can gain information about positive influences from this meta-analysis. In particular, they need to ensure their salespeople and the firm overall appear knowledgeable. A customer who encounters **seller expertise** regards the provided information as reliable and valuable, so it also is persuasive (Dholakia and Sternthal 1977). Furthermore, engaging with a competent seller makes the exchange relationship appear more important, so customers likely devote more effort or resources to it (Lagace, Dahlstrom, and Gassenheimer 1991). Considering that skills and knowledge thus are fundamental—that is, seller expertise has the strongest positive impact on relationship quality in the meta-analysis (Palmatier et al. 2006; Vargo and Lusch 2004)—firms must guarantee that boundary spanners display such skills and knowledge, by training them well and repeatedly. Inexperienced or unskilled employees can be so damaging that they even prompt relationship termination.

Such skills and knowledge are only valuable when shared, though, so the amount, frequency, and quality of information exchanged by the partners has a related positive effect (Mohr, Fisher, and Nevin 1996). Such bilateral **communication** provides benefits in terms of resolving disputes, aligning expectations, and revealing new value-creation opportunities (Anderson and Narus 1990; Mohr and Nevin 1990; Morgan and Hunt 1994). It also enhances relationship trust, because the parties to the exchange gain confidence in their partner's promises; if they can find new value-creation opportunities, they commit more strongly to the relationship. Although not included in the meta-analysis, recent research also notes how communication, especially early in the relationship, increases its velocity, because their bilateral communications enable the partners to identify complementarities and opportunities, which encourages relationship growth (Palmatier et al. 2013). Finally, communication is effective for shifting a customer relationship from transactional to transitional states. However, poor or limited communication can push it from transitional to transactional states (Zhang et al. 2016).

Logically, **relationship investments** and **relationship benefits** are linked: If they invest time, effort, and resources, sellers build strong relationships, which provide time savings, convenience, companionship, and decision-making benefits. Various relationship investments (e.g., gifts, loyalty programs, preferential treatment) offer different levels of effectiveness, but as a general rule, if the investments are irrecoverable, they evoke psychological bonds and reciprocity expectations, which encourage the relationship (De Wulf, Odekerken-Schröder, and Iacobucci 2001; Smith, Brock, and Barclay 1997). More precisely though, social investments (e.g., sharing meals, inviting customers to sporting events) together with frequent, personalized communication powerfully convey a customer's special status, and they accordingly produce a 180% return on investment (Palmatier, Gopalakrishna, and Houston 2006). Customized solutions, which we refer to as structural investments, achieve a 100%–120% return; financial investments, such as discounts, instead evoke negative returns (Palmatier, Gopalakrishna, and Houston 2006). Applying a dynamic view, we also note that relationship investments can speed up commitment velocity to strengthen the customer relationship, especially as the relationship ages (Palmatier et al. 2013). That is, because customers receive increasing benefits, they recognize the value of the relationship, welcome the seller's investments in the relationship, and devote their own resources to the relational bonds. Although most relationships begin with simple opportunities (i.e., low-hanging fruit) and do not require much investment (Kang, Mahoney, and Tan 2009), as they persist, the partners use up all the easy opportunities, so they seek more intensive links and make larger investments then aim to leverage those expanded relationship investments. As this discussion implies, investments often shift relationships from transitional to communal states, whereas a lack of investment could move the relationship backward, from transitional to transactional states (Zhang et al. 2016).

When exchange partners exhibit **similarity**, they enjoy commonalities, such as in their individual appearance and status, or else in their organizational-level cultures and values (Nicholson, Compeau, and Sethi 2001). A similar exchange partner seemingly should help the focal firm achieve its goals, because its goals are similar. Uncertainty about a partner's actions also declines when the partners share common perspectives (Johnson and Johnson 1972). The resulting confidence, spanning interpersonal and organizational levels, likely enhances relationship quality. This empirical evidence in turn implies that some commonalities are required to allow for relationship development; without them, the exchange could remain primarily economic or transactional rather than relational (Boles, Johnson, and Barksdale 2000; Doney and Cannon 1997; Nicholson, Compeau, and Sethi 2001).

Finally, three antecedents identified by the meta-analysis exert relatively small effects, likely because they constitute basic strategies to lock in customers by increasing switching costs or customer dependence. Still, customers often prefer to maintain existing relationships, especially if they depend on the seller, so **dependence** on the seller can increase commitment. In addition, customers appreciate familiarity and convenience and often exhibit inertia in their purchasing habits. Thus, both **interaction frequency**, or the number of partner interactions during a particular span of time, and **relationship duration**, or the length of their relationship, exert weak but still pertinent effects.

Considering the results of this meta-analysis overall, we note that the most effective strategies minimize conflict, but they also seek positive outcomes, such as improved seller expertise, bilateral communication, relationship investments, and relationship benefits. Furthermore, they aim to create a clear match, whether between boundary spanners or across organizations, with customers. Although sometimes necessary, efforts to increase customer dependence and interaction frequency generally produce only minimal effects; just maintaining a relationship over time might not be enough to keep a customer from switching if another, appealing offer pops up in a competitive market.

## *Stimulating Gratitude and Reciprocity Norms*

**Gratitude** is a catalyst of relationships. It stimulates prosocial reciprocal behaviors for as long as the emotion lasts. Then it extends to longer-term effects by building the relationship and creating pressures for customers to reciprocate (Bartlett and DeSteno 2006). In this sense, gratitude initiates ongoing cycles of reciprocation, self-reinforcing reciprocal behaviors, and relationship continuation (Schwartz 1967). In the short run, customers engage in reciprocal purchase behaviors to satisfy their psychological obligation, in response to relationship-marketing-induced feelings of gratitude. In the long run, gratitude promotes the development of **reciprocity norms** and initiates reciprocation cycles, fostering positive long-term customer behaviors (Palmatier et al. 2009).

Relationship marketing managers use different strategies to leverage this gratitude mechanism. Prior research indicates notable influences of customers' perceptions of their own needs, as well as of the seller's free will, its motives, and the amount of risk it takes.

Appreciation results from noticing and acknowledging the value of some item or benefit (e.g., gift, special treatment) then sensing a positive emotional connection (Adler and Fagley 2005). This appreciation should be particularly great when the item offers value, because it is necessary. When in a *need* condition, a person requires or wants something so that desired item takes on more value than if the person were not in a need condition. Receiving an item with such need value accordingly increases appreciation and gratitude (Tesser, Gatewood, and Driver 1968; Tsang 2006). The value, and thus the corresponding debt perception, reflects the urgency and extent of the recipient's need at the time she or he receives the benefit (Gouldner 1960). Managers can leverage this effect by inducing a need condition (e.g., communicating the benefits of an offering) or making sure that they offer a benefit at an appropriate time, just when the customer most needs it.

If people or organizations act on their own accord, they exhibit *free will*, such as offering an unexpected gift or performing a surprising act of kindness, rather than offering those benefits because of some contractual requirement. Investments made with free will have more value and meaning than those required by a formal contract. Employees can expect annual salary increases when their employment contract requires them, so they are less likely to develop a sense of gratitude from receiving such a raise. But an unexpected bonus, granted by management in recognition of the employee's hard work, signals appreciation more powerfully. Therefore, the employee feels and likely expresses more gratitude. In contrast, solely contractual investments or those that exchange partners must demand on their own are unlikely to evoke gratitude (Morales 2005; Tsang 2006). Overall, recipients feel grateful toward benefactors if the granted benefits appear to fall under the benefactors' volitional control (Weiner 1985)—including relationship marketing investments that appear to constitute acts of free will rather than some program requirement or duty-based or contractual obligation (Emmons and McCullough 2004; Palmatier et al. 2009).

---

**Example 5.1  Zappos (USA)**

Shoe and fashion online retailer Zappos has built exceeding customer expectations into its relationship marketing strategy. Out of all regular orders for which customers expect two- to three-day shipping, the firm picks a certain number of orders to be shipped overnight. Receiving their order earlier than expected makes customers grateful, as can be seen from various enthusiastic social media posts in which customers rave about Zappos's surprise overnight shipping.

Source: Jantsch (2014).

---

In assessing free will, people also tend to consider their exchange partner's *motives*, or what has incited their action. A child who comes home and issues a random complement to his mother likely provokes a response like, "Okay, what did you do?" For customers, sellers' inferred motives define their perceptions of the benefits they receive, such that they may sense more gratitude if they believe in the sellers' benevolent intentions but not if they perceive an ulterior motive. In particular, perceiving benevolent versus self-serving motives largely determines the amount of gratitude a benefit recipient feels, such that ulterior motives evoke gratitude levels that are about half the level of benevolent motives (Tesser, Gatewood, and Driver 1968; Tsang 2006). Such drastic differences in turn should produce notably different future behaviors.

Finally, risky investments can evoke more gratitude, especially in noncontractual settings. To build a customer relationship, it is usually the seller that makes some investment (e.g., time, effort) and incurs some cost to do so, which creates *risk*, reflecting the subjective potential that this costly investment fails to evoke reciprocated behavior. By accepting that risk, the seller can prompt a sense of gratitude in customers (Tesser, Gatewood, and Driver 1968; Tsang 2006).

## Forming Relationships Online

Everywhere in the world, e-commerce continues to expand, leading to not just increases in online sales (Forrester Report 2015) but also expanded customer experience with online marketplaces (Nowlin 2014). Exchange partners are moving away from purely transactional exchanges and toward more relational exchanges that, in many ways, mimic conventional retail interactions. For example, regardless of the channel, humans need relationships, so the psychological mechanisms that underlie relationship development often are similar in both offline and online settings (Zhu, Dholakia, Chen and Algesheimer 2012): People seek relationships to reduce uncertainty and establish relational norms, and they prefer to buy from trusted partners (Adjei, Noble, and Noble 2010; Palmatier, Dant, and Grewal 2007). Yet online and offline settings also differ, indicating the need to address tactics for establishing, growing, and retaining success-ful **online relationships** specifically (Kozlenkova et al. 2017; McConnell 2017; Verma, Sharma, and Seth 2016; KPMG 2017). The leaner com-munication, heightened anonymity, weaker reciprocity norms, and less social interconnectedness encountered in online relational exchanges sug-gest a greater risk that online partners will behave opportunistically, as well as a greater need for risk-reducing and trust-building signals.

A recent study of how online relationships form on Taobao.com, the largest e-commerce platform in China (Kozlenkova et al. 2017), offers three notable, practical insights:

1. Anonymity increases the effectiveness of risk-reducing signals, which can encourage relationships, even among dissimilar partners, to develop quickly. Notably, it took only three days for an estimated 96% of the reciprocal relationships to form. Convincing signals help customers identify suitable relationship partners; relational obser-vations provide strong risk-reducing signals. However, signals lose power as consumers gain more experience but remain critical for committed reciprocal relationships.
2. Because it is relatively easy to form ongoing unilateral relationships, online customers often develop extensive relationship portfolios, which determine their purchase decisions. Typical online users main-tain more unilateral than reciprocal relationships.
3. In a finding that resonates with offline research, reciprocity emerges as central to successful online relationships. Reciprocal online rela-tionships, relative to unilateral ones, strongly increase psychological commitment by customers and thus their purchase behaviors. Even seemingly trivial forms of online reciprocity (e.g., clicking "like") can

have significant influences on firm performance. That is, any relationship increases sales, according to this study, but reciprocal relationships provoke the greatest increase (sales lift of $9.93 versus $3.31 for seller-unilateral and $6.29 for buyer-unilateral relationships), with the longest-lasting performance effect (i.e., seven days versus four days for buyer-unilateral and one day for seller-unilateral relationships).

---

**Example 5.2  Facebook (USA)**

A 2009 study by the Facebook Data Team identified the types of relationships users maintained on Facebook and their relative sizes. A Facebook user can maintain three types of relationships among people in their overall list of verified friends. The strongest type of relationship is where reciprocal communication between friends occurs, followed by relationships with unilateral communication. Beyond, maintained relationships exist with no individually targeted communication, but where a focal user clicks on and reads a friend's post or visits a friend's profile. All other friend connections where none of such interactions takes place would not qualify as a relationship. Overall, the study indicates that around the net of active (i.e., reciprocal and unilateral) relationships, there is a net of passive (i.e., maintained) relationships of about 2–2.5 times the size of the number of active relations. Hence, there is quite some potential to transform a user's passive relations into more active relationship formats.

Source: Marlow (2009).

---

## *Relationship Marketing Strategies for Maintaining Relationships*

As we already noted, it is human nature to grant more weight to negative experiences than to positive experiences (Baumeister et al. 2001). In general, negative relationship activities prompt approximately twice the effect of positive activities (Palmatier et al. 2006). Accordingly, the long-term effectiveness of relationship marketing often depends more on preventing the bad rather than adding more good. Relationship marketers must shield customer relationships from negative events or take immediate action in response to those that do happen. Two particularly potent dangers are customer-perceived unfairness and sellers' failures to ensure data privacy. But in addition to preventing such negative outcomes, relationship marketers must maintain at least a base level of positive relationship marketing efforts (e.g., communication, relationship investments).

### *Avoiding Unfairness*

**Customer unfairness** not only undermines positive customer behaviors, cooperation, flexibility, and performance (Samaha, Palmatier, and Dant

2011), but it also aggravates the negative potential effects of regular daily conflict or opportunism. When faced with negative events, consumers actively seek explanations, and unfairness is a clear and obvious one, signaling the seller's negative motives (Folkes 1988). Once they start to believe that the relationship is unfair, customers become sensitive to any conflict, even the standard forms that are inevitable in relationships, and start to hold the seller accountable for "regular" negative interactions. With the belief that even minimal conflict is the direct result of the seller's actions and illegitimate motives, customers who perceive unfairness assign responsibility for any problems to the seller. If one party invests heavily, and then the partner cheats or free-rides on those investments, the relationship is likely to devolve, especially if the former seeks to punish or retaliate against the latter for its failure to reciprocate. Many customers emotionally declare their intentions to exit the relationship, willing to expend the substantial effort and cost required to switch to another firm, when their unfairness perceptions become too great to bear. In such cases, firms must be preemptive, such as by training frontline employees to identify situations that appear likely to provoke unfairness perceptions and address them promptly.

Instead, though, we find that companies often create or even encourage perceptions of unfairness! Consider loyalty programs. The **bystanders** who do not receive the loyalty benefits frequently express their anger in response to the unfair treatment they perceive (Steinhoff and Palmatier 2016). A hotel scene from the movie *Up in the Air* portrays the situation dramatically: George Clooney, a premium customer who gets served instantly, suffers resentful looks from a long line of customers waiting in the queue. In addition to such direct bystander effects, their indirect effects persist beyond the immediate observation, through word-of-mouth or social media communication. Unfairness-evoked anger causes customers to feel compelled to punish the firm, which in turn can restore the unbalanced ratio of benefits to costs. For example, measured in terms of loyalty and annual sales in an airline context, bystanders' perceptions of unfairness produce effects that are approximately 10 times greater than the beneficial effect of gratitude among loyalty program customers (Steinhoff and Palmatier 2016). Arguably, this outcome might be acceptable financially, if the loyalty programs truly reward the most valuable customers who account for most sales, but it cannot be justified from a relational perspective. Unfair treatment likely prevents any relationship from emerging, even if an early stage or prospective customer could be highly valuable in the long run.

Mitigating unfairness perceptions requires revising relationship marketing and loyalty programs. One option is to hide the benefits provided to targeted customers from bystanders, though it is not always possible to do so. In those cases, the firm must issue clear, comprehensive, and (perhaps most important) legitimate explanations for the differential treatment. Contracts for special treatment might be perfectly legal but still appear unfair, so even customers who learn about the contracts might still seek to punish the firm. As cell phone and cable providers in the modern market can readily tell us, it is very difficult to build a good customer relationship based solely on a contract.

---

**Example 5.3  KLM Royal Dutch Airlines (Netherlands)**

For some rewards in their loyalty program, companies have different options on how visible their preferential treatment of target customers should be. For example, at its Amsterdam Schiphol home base, KLM Royal Dutch Airlines has placed its Crown Lounge in a highly visible spot at the airport, with many passengers passing by. Also, the lounge's architecture uses large glass doors and windows, making the facility's appealing interior and the superior treatment of select target customers hence very salient for passersby. This may on the one hand foster aspiration among regular customers to also achieve a higher level in the loyalty program that grants lounge access. However, on the other hand, such open exposure to select customers' preferential treatment may stimulate feelings of unfairness among bystander customers.

Source: Steinhoff and Palmatier (2016).

---

Even among the targets of preferential treatment, unfairness ultimately can produce negative, or at least less positive, effects. For example, if the firm must constantly explain the treatment to bystanders, the targets might no longer feel pleasurable surprise at their treatment, which likely suppresses their sense of gratitude. According to the evidence in Figure 5.1, target customers of airline rewards (e.g., priority boarding, priority check-in, free services) express gratitude that produces approximately 60% of the incremental lift in annual sales, while the bystanders' unfairness perceptions account for 70% of the incremental sales drop. Considering our repeated assertion that bad has a stronger effect than good, it is critical for firms to reduce the negative sentiment that results from relationship marketing programs that lead to perceptions of unfair treatment.

*Protecting Data Privacy*

Companies today have a wealth of data available to help them tailor their offerings to reflect customers' demographics, purchase histories, or browsing histories. The resulting offers, customized for a "market of one," encourage enhanced customer loyalty and purchases, so firms spend vast amounts ($36 billion annually) to gather more of these big

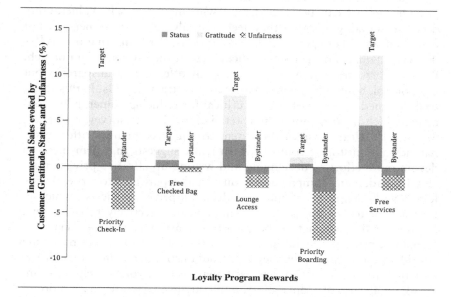

*Figure 5.1* Effects of Airline Rewards on Target and Bystander Customers
Source: Steinhoff and Palmatier (2016, p. 102).

data. According to one study, companies using big data analytics increase their productivity and profits by 5%–6% compared with competitors without such capabilities.

But in addition to supporting customized offers, big data enhance **privacy concerns** (Martin and Murphy 2017), with notable effects for both firms and customers. A firm that suffers a data breach also suffers an average drop in stock performance of -.27% (Martin, Borah, and Palmatier 2017), equivalent to a loss of $130 million in shareholder value on the day of the breach. Such breaches even erode competitor value, by -17% or about $82 million in shareholder value. More extensive breaches lead to greater share price drops. Beyond shareholders though, breaches and privacy failures increase customers' awareness of the risk and decrease their willingness to share information about themselves, especially if the company has earned their distrust through unethical or questionable practices (Martin, Borah, and Palmatier 2018; Martin, Borah, and Palmatier 2017). Even without explicit privacy violations, consumers express a sense of vulnerability any time their data are collected, even if for the most innocuous of purposes (Silverthorne 2016).

To reduce this uncomfortable sense of vulnerability, companies can turn to a ready, easy tool, namely, issuing privacy statements. When companies explain their data collection, use, storage, and protection practices while also granting customers some control over what information they provide, how it can be is used, and who may access it, vulnerability decreases notably. Because they feel less vulnerable, customers do not react as negatively to personal data collections. For firms, that means less dramatic damage to their stock prices, even if they suffer a data breach. But the worst strategy, in which a company offers high transparency but low control, hinders this performance by an estimated 37%. In this sense, well-designed privacy policies are critical for reducing vulnerability concerns, which in turn should limit retaliations. In one survey, customers expressed a clear sense of the extent to which companies offer transparency and customer control, which really suggests that firms need to devote more effort to developing and writing up effective privacy policies. Instead, many companies rely on a legal department to write obtuse, long, overly detailed, difficult-to-understand privacy policies—which in turn are virtually impossible to communicate effectively to customers. Because of their impact on both customer attitudes and financial performance, privacy policies must be informed by relationship marketing considerations. Ultimately, they even could produce a competitive differentiation, in which the firm sets itself apart as trustworthy, helps customers avoid a sense of vulnerability, and convinces them to share more of their data with it.

---

**Example 5.4  Fortune 100 Companies (USA)**

A consumer survey offers insights on the extent of transparency and control provided to customers in Fortune 100 companies' privacy policies. Costco Wholesale, Verizon Communications, and Best Buy attain the top three positions, scoring high on both customer-perceived levels of data transparency and control. These companies explicate in an understandable manner what information they collect and how they collect. At the same time, they concede their customers substantial control or say in the usage of their personal data. A different picture emerges for Morgan Stanley, Energy Transfer Equity, and HCA Holdings. Taking the bottom three ranks among the Fortune 100 companies, these firms receive highly unfavorable ratings when it comes to the transparency of and customer control granted in their privacy policies. It looks like fifth-to-last Citigroup has not even learned from the detrimental effects of a data breach. In 2011, the company experienced a data breach of 146,000 customer records, provoking a $1.3 billion stock value loss. In response, Citigroup invested $250 million in cybersecurity systems and hired 1,000 additional IT professionals. Yet seemingly, customers are still not seeing any improvement in Citigroup's privacy policy, allocating low transparency and control ratings to the firm.

Source: Martin, Borah, and Palmatier (2018).

## Institutionalized Relationship Marketing Programs

Some progressive companies have started to institutionalize their efforts to build and maintain strong customer relationships, whether by installing customer-centric structures or implementing loyalty programs. These companywide relationship marketing programs can reinforce relationship marketing efforts, especially in the digital age. In the anonymous, distant, online environment, interpersonal interactions get replaced by technology-mediated communication, so both customer centricity and loyalty programs represent means for companies to remain close to their customers and provide individually personalized experiences. Both instruments also facilitate the collection of important customer information, which relationship marketers can use to design and continuously adapt relationship management strategies. When used purposefully, customer centricity and loyalty programs represent systematic, next-generation relationship marketing instruments with value for companies that apply them.

### Installing Customer-Centric Structures

A firm's organizational structure refers to how it organizes employees and customer efforts to achieve effective customer relationship management (Lee, Kozlenkova, and Palmatier 2015). Firms with **customer-centric structures** appear to outperform internally oriented peers, by achieving deeper and more satisfactory customer relationships, as well as greater customer value (Kumar, Venkatesan, and Reinartz 2008; Shah et al. 2006). Dell's corporate realignment around customer groups (e.g., large enterprise, public, small and medium business, consumer) sought to understand and address the unique challenges faced by each customer segment (Figure 5.2) (Dell 2010). By actively pursuing seamless operations through this new structure, Dell improved its financial performance. More and more firms are racing to adopt such organizations, such that the proportion of U.S. firms with customer-centric structures appears likely to increase from 32% to 52% (Day 2006), and 30% of *Fortune* 500 firms already have imposed these structures (Lee, Sridhar, and Palmatier 2015). Such trends may be misguided in some cases though. A customer-centric structure failed to benefit Cisco and Xerox; even if it works, companies often suffer through years of struggle.

According to an analysis of *Fortune* 500 firms, customer centricity helps firm divisions focus on specific customer segments, which enhances their knowledge of those groups. But it also introduces complexity and coordination costs, such that communication and decision making become more difficult, and certain redundant functions get duplicated across divisions. Such problems may be less likely if the firm is customer centric from the start. At Tumi, an innovative U.S.-based suitcase manufacturer, each division focuses on a customer segment (e.g., premium,

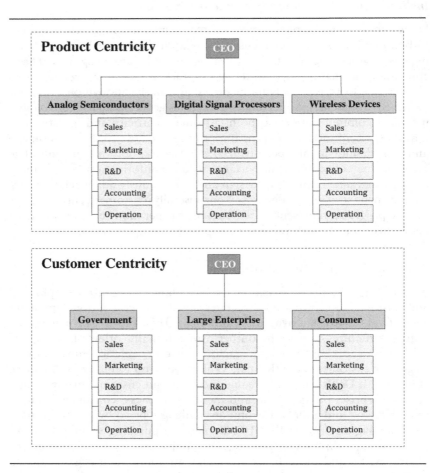

*Figure 5.2* Example Shift From Product-Centric to Customer-Centric Organizational Structures

young adults), then designs products to appeal to it, leading to strongly satisfied customers whose unique needs are met by the targeting product.

With this dedicated approach, a customer-centric structure also creates rich databases, filled with in-depth customer knowledge and expertise, so the firm can uncover unmet needs. For example, when the health care firm Anthem implemented a customer-centric structure, it uncovered and sought to address distinct customer needs (e.g., enhanced transparency, lower costs, enhanced quality), leading to a 36% increase in its return on assets within four years of the restructuring (Lee, Sridhar, and Palmatier 2015). However, in some situations, unmet customer needs are not sufficient to ensure profitable transactions (Lee et al. 2015). When many competitors already have implemented customer centricity, such that they already meet most customer needs, one more company with a customer-centric structure is less likely to accrue value from its efforts. If a customer-centric firm competes in a market with many other customer-centric firms, its performance is 11% lower than that of firms in the same market but that have product-centric structures. When competitive intensity increases, it also impedes the performance of customer-centric firms, relative to product-centric firms, by approximately 69%. Finally, customer centricity is less effective in low-profitability industries, because customers in such sectors do not value customization or responsiveness, so the costs of restructuring cannot be recouped. In these cases, customer-centric firms achieve 20% poorer performance than firms with structures that are not aligned by customers.

---

### Example 5.5  SunGard (USA)

When the software and services firm SunGard installed a customer-oriented structure in 2002, its surrounding competitive environment already was largely customer-centric. Competitors such as Affiliated Computer Services and Leidos Holdings already had effectively discovered and addressed most of the unmet customer needs in the market. Thus its late-stage restructuring offered few incremental benefits, but it strongly increased the firm's costs and complexity. Accordingly, its return on assets fell by a fatal 81% over four years following its initiative.

Source: Lee, Sridhar and Palmatier (2015).

---

As various real-world examples reveal, the outcomes of customer centricity span a simultaneous spectrum, from notable advantages to significant damages, that constantly is subject to change. Thus we previously used Tumi as an example of a customer-centric success story, but more recently the luggage company has struggled due to a lack of consistent corporate brand awareness. Each division focuses only on its dedicated customer segment, creating inconsistent images and high marketing-, coordination-, and complexity-induced costs. By dividing resources, capabilities, and people across departments, Tumi created internal barriers that prevented interdepartmental resource sharing and communications and made economies of scale more difficult to achieve.

Even if customer centricity is appropriate and well supported, it often requires years to produce dividends—more than two years following the restructuring passes before an average firm exceeds its prior performance levels, during which time it faces heightened coordination costs, intense internal conflict, and confusion. Thus for 37 *Fortune* 500 firms that underwent customer-centric restructurings, the damage to their performance averaged 39%, and only after 10 quarters did their performance recover and then exceed the prior performance levels by 11% (Lee, Sridhar, and Palmatier 2015).

Implementing a customer-centric structure requires companies to assess their competitive environment carefully to determine the prevalence of customer centricity already, its competitive intensity, and its profitability. Although there are no simple rules, and every sector differs, when an industry is marked by substantial customer centricity, competitive intensity, and commoditization, with low margins, the benefits of restructuring around customer segments may be minimal. If, after this careful assessment, the firm identifies a customer orientation as viable, it must realize that it will suffer poorer performance before things can get better.

### Implementing Loyalty Programs

Loyalty programs are ubiquitous relationship marketing instruments, spanning diverse industries including retailing, travel and hospitality, and financial services. There are 3.8 billion loyalty program memberships in the United States, and the average household subscribes to more than 30 different programs; companies spend $48 billion annually to manage those programs (Fruend 2017; Gordon and Hlavinka 2011). Encompassing any institutionalized incentive system that attempts to enhance customers' attitudes and behaviors over time, **loyalty programs** can take myriad forms, such as bonus points, gifts, tiered service levels, and dedicated support contacts (Henderson, Beck, and Palmatier 2011). To operate these varied programs, companies rely on different approaches, whether providing simple stamp cards and quick e-mail subscriptions, requiring customers to present identifying cards at store check-outs, or establishing sophisticated mobile apps to enable customers to interact with the program.

Regardless of their format, though, loyalty programs represent complex operations. Not surprisingly, even as they keep proliferating, marketing research provides mixed evidence of their effectiveness (Dowling and Uncles 1997; Shugan 2005; Steinhoff and Palmatier 2016). For example, noting poor financial performance, companies such as Starbucks and Safeway temporarily suspended their programs and undertook complete revamps to iron out design flaws (Allison 2010; Meyer-Waarden 2007). Furthermore, loyalty program members often exhibit a lack of activity, such that 54% of members remain inactive, on average (Fruend 2017). To understand the complex interplay of factors, then design and execute loyalty programs for optimal effectiveness, managers need an overarching, integrated conceptual framework, such as the one in Figure 5.3. In particular, relationship marketing managers should develop in-depth understanding of three building blocks of loyalty programs to stimulate true customer loyalty: their psychological elements, their strategic elements, and their operational elements.

## Example 5.6  Starbucks (USA)

In 2016, Starbucks undertook a major revamp of its loyalty program, "My Starbucks Rewards." Since its implementation in 2009, the program had been based on customer purchases, such that customers could earn one star per transaction. But the simple star collection policy actually turned out to be a substantial flaw that required a complex fix, because it prompted customers to try to game the system to maximize their stars. For example, buying three items in one transaction would give customers one star. Splitting up the three items into three transactions instead earned them three stars. The company estimated that 1% of its customers would break up their baskets this way. Although that may seem like a small amount, encouraging customers to take more time at checkout meant that some stores were suffering increased lines and wait times—inefficiencies and added costs that were directly contrary to its overall corporate goals to create a pleasant experience for consumers. Furthermore, it risked creating perceptions of unfairness, because a $2.42 tall, freshly brewed coffee purchase earned the same rewards as a $12.44 purchase of a venti white chocolate mocha with a ham-and-cheese croissant. By redesigning and relaunching the loyalty program, Starbucks acknowledged the purchase value, rather than mere purchase frequency, in awarding points. Customers earn two stars per each $1 spent on anything—coffee, drinks, food, merchandise. With this new "currency exchange rate," Starbucks assigns rewards more effectively while also offering preferential treatment to high-value customers who buy more and spend more on their visits.

Source: Breen (2016).

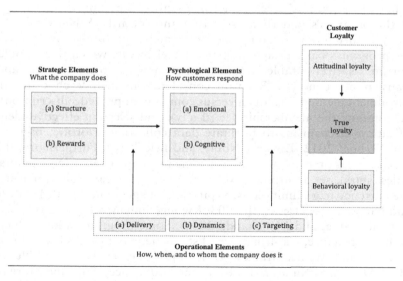

*Figure 5.3* Loyalty Program Framework: Three Key Elements
Source: Adapted from Kim, Steinhoff, and Palmatier (2018).

*Psychological elements* capture how customers respond to loyalty programs by revealing the cognitive and emotional processes, both negative and positive, spurred in customers' minds that also drive loyalty program performance. In response to any single loyalty program, multiple psychological processes come into play, so focusing on only one likely leads to misspecified loyalty program–performance linkages (Steinhoff and Palmatier 2016). Favorable cognitions can be captured by customers' perceptions of the value of the program, satisfaction with it, and motivation to pursue and attain reward goals (Drèze and Nunes 2011; Reynolds and Beatty 1999; Sirdeshmukh, Singh, and Sabol 2002). Other cognitive mechanisms, such as dependence and habit, represent double-edged swords, in that they promote retention but rarely are sustainable if customers encounter opportunities or initiatives to switch (Henderson, Beck, and Palmatier 2011; Liu-Thompkins and Tam 2013; Scheer, Miao, and Palmatier 2015). In addition, customers experience various emotional reactions, including gratitude and status perceptions, to a loyalty program that provides key benefits (Drèze and Nunes 2009; Eggert, Steinhoff, and Garnefeld 2015; Steinhoff and Palmatier 2016). Yet negative emotions are possible too, especially among bystanders who perceive unfairness after observing preferential treatment of others (as we discussed previously). Target customers also can suffer negative emotions, including skepticism or social discomfort at being rewarded in front of others (Eggert, Steinhoff, and Garnefeld 2015; Jiang, Hoegg, and Dahl 2013; Steinhoff and Palmatier 2016). Overall, emotional mechanisms typically outweigh cognitive mechanisms, and negative processes tend to dominate positive ones.

Loyalty programs' *strategic elements* instead pertain to the design of the program's underlying structure and rewards. When establishing a loyalty program, companies must make careful decisions about the program's basic design and strategic elements, which then should remain relatively stable; frequent rule changes create fairness and transparency concerns. Relevant considerations include choosing an enrollment method (i.e., open versus company-approved subscription), determining the membership fee (if any), and selecting effective identification mechanisms to facilitate data collection (Dorotic, Bijmolt, and Verhoef 2012; Esmark, Noble, and Bell 2016). Furthermore, the loyalty program needs to establish some form of currency (e.g., points, miles, stars), set a currency exchange rate, and create rules for using the currency (e.g., limitations, expiration) (Bagchi and Li 2011; Drèze and Nunes 2004; Hsee et al. 2003; Kwong, Soman, and Ho 2011; Van Osselaer, Alba, and Manchanda 2004). Some programs adopt a hierarchical structure, featuring several status tiers, but others instead feature a nonhierarchical framework with just one tier (Drèze and Nunes 2009; Drèze and Nunes 2011; Kim et al. 2009; Lacey, Suh, and Morgan

2007; von Wangenheim and Bayón 2007; Wagner, Hennig-Thurau, and Rudolph 2009). These decisions also might depend on whether managers choose to establish a stand-alone program or team up with industry partners (Capizzi and Ferguson 2005; Dorotic, Bijmolt, and Verhoef 2012; Lemon and von Wangenheim 2009; Sharp and Sharp 1997; Schumann, Wünderlich, and Evanschitzky 2014). Finally, to specify program rewards, the firm needs to determine their value and types, as well as which customer behaviors (purchase, engagement) evoke rewards (Capgemini Consulting 2015; Keh and Lee 2006; Liu, Lamberton, and Haws 2015; Melancon, Noble, and Noble 2011; Roehm, Pullins, and Roehm 2002; Yi and Jeon 2003).

The *operational elements* of loyalty programs are ongoing considerations, such as program delivery, dynamics, and targeting. For example, loyalty program managers need to decide how, when, and to whom to issue rewards, and these contingency factors likely inform their strategic design decisions. Delivery options must ensure rule clarity and reward visibility, for example (Steinhoff and Palmatier 2016). If program rules appear unclear or discretionary, they might enhance targets' gratitude but also increase bystanders' unfairness perceptions, so managers must trade off the complex outcomes of different program designs. An effective balance would establish clear rules for some forms of preferential treatment but still offer a few surprises. Similarly, visibility enhances both the positive effects on target customers, by emphasizing their status, and the negative effects on bystanders (e.g., large glass doors for KLM's Crown Lounges make salient the appealing special offer and the superior treatment offered to target customers). To achieve a balance on this point, managers might evoke visibility temporarily, such as making target customers very visible for selected occasions but not continuously. Discretionary reward endowment (e.g., being gifted rather than earning elevated status in a hierarchical loyalty program) fosters both favorable and unfavorable outcomes for target customers, including gratitude and goal motivation on the one hand but skepticism and social discomfort on the other (Eggert, Steinhoff, and Garnefeld 2015; Jiang, Hoegg, and Dahl 2013; Nunes and Drèze 2006). The contextual timing of the reward also constitutes a critical managerial decision: In contractual settings, early-awarded loyalty rewards stimulate expansion behaviors, but later rewards secure customer retention as the contract nears its expiration date (Steinhoff et al. 2016). Not every customer is an equally appropriate target, though. Depending on their intrinsic loyalty profile, reflecting habit-, dependence-, and relationship-based loyalty, customers' responses to rewards differ, such that mainly habitual customers represent "sleeping dogs" for the firm. Waking them up with a reward can prompt them to start playing (expand), or it might lead them to attack (defect).

## Guidelines for Managing Relationship Marketing Strategies

This section synthesizes theoretical insights and empirical evidence to provide clear, actionable guidance for managers who seek to design and implement relationship marketing strategies. In addition, it provides current, real-world examples to describe how firms have tackled the challenges associated with building and maintaining customer relationships. We start with several generalizations about best practices, building on a rich foundation of extant relationship marketing research and synthesizing our previous discussion. Then we outline some recent approaches to relationship management in digital relational environments, which seem promising but whose overall effectiveness is yet to be substantiated by research.

### Established Best Practices

From extant relationship marketing literature that we discussed in depth in the preceding section, we distill several effective strategies for building and maintaining customer–seller relationships, as summarized in Table 5.2. To avoid detrimental effects, sellers should work to minimize conflict and unfairness perceptions and instead leverage the positive effects of seller expertise, communication, and relationship investments. Stimulating gratitude and reciprocity norms also can strengthen customer relationships. Customer-centric organizational structures may be appropriate; regardless of the structure they choose, managers should consistently assess their relationship marketing programs and efforts.

### Emerging Practices

In the digital age, boundary-spanning personnel, who have long functioned as a selling firm's representatives, increasingly are being replaced by nonhuman, technology-based entities and channels. This shift has

*Table 5.2* Relationship Marketing Strategies: Established Best Practices

---

*Preventing Conflict, Unfairness, and Privacy Concerns*

---

- Do not let conflict go unresolved, because it will overwhelm other relationship-building efforts.

---

- Do not constantly expose bystander customers to target customers' preferential treatment; establish transparent and clear rules for the differential customer treatment to avoid unfairness perceptions.

---

- Cooperate with your legal department on the design of privacy policies. Privacy statements should provide customers with transparency about and control over the use of their personal data.

---

*Table 5.2* Continued

| Leveraging Seller Expertise, Communication, and Relationship Investments |
| --- |

- Assign customers a dedicated contact person, even if they interface through multiple channels (e.g., call center, online).

- Focus the largest portion of relationship marketing investments on selecting, training, and motivating boundary-spanning employees, who represent the most effective means to build and maintain relationships.

- Institute relationship marketing programs focused on increasing the amount, frequency, and quality of communication with customers, especially early in the relationship life cycle, because communication is a strong driver of relationship quality and future relationship growth (relational velocity).

- Relationship marketing investments dedicated to specific programs should be primarily allocated to social and structural programs. Minimize the proactive use of financial relationship marketing programs (e.g., price rebates, points programs) for relationship building; rather, consider these programs as price/volume discounts or competitive responses.

- Boundary spanners should be given allocation control of most social programs, but allocation control of structural and financial programs should not fully reside with boundary spanners. If facing high turnover of boundary spanners, sellers should increase the consistency across boundary spanners, reallocate spending from social to structural programs, and reduce boundary spanners' discretionary control of relationship marketing programs.

### Fostering Gratitude and Reciprocity Norms

- Sellers should leverage relationship marketing investments by designing programs that increase customers' perceptions of the seller's free will, benevolence, risk, and cost in providing the relationship marketing benefit.

- A seller can leverage relationship marketing investments by providing a benefit when the customer's need is the highest and the benefit provides the most value.

- Sellers should give customers opportunities to reciprocate soon after providing them with a relationship marketing benefit (not quid pro quo), which takes advantage of high levels of gratitude, prevents guilt rationalization, and leads to reciprocity norms.

- Sellers should seek to foster reciprocal relationships online with their customers.

### Professionalize Relationship Marketing Throughout the Organization

- Sellers should assess their industry environment (i.e., predominance of customer centricity, competitive intensity, commoditization, profitability) to figure out whether restructuring their organization to center around customers or customer groups may enhance firm performance.

- Sellers should develop loyalty programs that ignite target customers' favorable cognitions and emotions while motivating rather than alienating bystanders.

*Table 5.3* Relationship Marketing Strategies: Emerging Practices

---

**Enhancing Communication Strategies**

---

- Sellers use social media company profiles to enable bilateral rather than unilateral communications with customers.

---

- Companies are implementing their own mobile apps to be constantly accessible, at customers' discretion.

---

- Seller firms employ artificial intelligence–based, embodied virtual agents that can interact individually and in a real-time, humanoid way with customers.

---

**Enhancing Personalization Strategies**

---

- Seller companies make use of machine-learning techniques to turn customer data into highly personalized services.

---

- Sellers communicate with customers in a relevant, personalized way through augmented-reality technologies.

---

**Enhancing Experiential Benefits Strategies**

---

- Gamification is a popular strategy that applies game design elements to nongame contexts to enhance customers' online experience.

---

- Online sellers can use status bestowal to enhance the customer experience.

---

major implications for bilateral communications, efforts to individualize relationships, and pleasurable customer experiences. Table 5.3 compiles some emerging practices pertaining to the digital age.

## Enhancing Communication Strategies

Relationships evolve through effective, individualized communication among the parties, which helps strengthen relational bonds, reduces customer-perceived relational uncertainty, and facilitates relationship formation (Kozlenkova et al. 2017; Weathers, Sharma, and Wood 2007). The anonymity and geographical distance of relational partners that engage in online relationships impedes such communication. Compared with traditional offline relationships, online exchanges are characterized by leaner communication, with limited verbal and nonverbal cues (Kozlenkova et al. 2017). To deepen customer relationships, these communications thus must be tailored to each customer's needs and preferences but also provide a means to humanize online relationships and stimulate bilateral communication. Consider three popular strategies.

First, sellers can use social media profiles to encourage bilateral, seller-initiated communications, and many do so: 84% of *Fortune 500* companies maintain Facebook or Twitter profiles to share content and enhance customer engagement (Barnes and Griswold 2016). Firms use different approaches to enter into dialogs with customers, share information, collect customer feedback, and create a sense of community. For example, Nike couples hashtags reinforcing its main tagline, "Just do it," with specific segmentation approaches such as #NikeWomen, which regularly receive hundreds of thousands of likes and comments from targeted users (Banovic 2017). The MyStarbucksIdea crowdsourced innovation contest resulted in online submissions of 190,000 new product ideas and 300 innovative implementations by consumers (Tolido 2016). Lay's "Do us a flavor" campaign focused on millennial customers' desire for self-expression and brand engagement, resulting in 3.8 million flavor submissions, 2.2 billion impressions on Facebook, and an 8.5% increase in sales (Capgemini 2017).

Second, companies' dedicated mobile apps can accompany their customers and are accessible at customers' discretion. Mobile devices are a widely preferred method of engaging online, and 80% of all time customers spend on the Internet occurs through mobile apps, so the importance of this channel to online relationship marketing is undeniable (Arora, Hofstede, and Mahajan 2017). For example, the popular McDonald's Monopoly promotion now operates through the company's app, which customers use to scan token codes to reveal prizes that are redeemable online or in stores. The app effectively stimulates communication and encourages customers to share their personal information (e.g., sign-up, location data) (Verheul 2017). Approximately half of Airbnb hosts use the company's app to support instantaneous communication, leading to bookings that are eight times faster than those made online (Brown 2014). In this sense, apps help overcome some of the asynchronicity of communication that is common in the online context.

Third, in response to the disadvantages associated with the lack of human interaction in online contexts, marketers have invested in new tools to enhance online customer experiences and respond to people's general desire for human connection (Baumeister and Leary 1995), often centered on the use of "humanizing" virtual reality technologies, such as chatbots, avatars, and virtual assistants (Saad and Abida 2016). The advances of Web 4.0 have enabled companies to anthropomorphize relational communications with their customers. Through artificial intelligence, online sellers may introduce a "human touch" resembling interpersonal interaction to their technology-mediated customer relationships, making customer interactions more interpersonal, real time, and tangible. Often, seller firms employ embodied virtual agents that can interact individually with customers to bond with them and evoke a conspecific presence (van Doorn et al. 2017). Embodied virtual agents are humanlike extensions of online chatbots that act like virtual salespeople to inform and interact individually with customers as they browse a site (Wood, Solomon, and Englis 2005). Reflecting the concept of anthropomorphism, modern embodied virtual agents resemble humans and use naturalistic language processing to facilitate realistic, humanoid conversations, as well as artificial intelligence to learn from series of customer interactions (Hume 1957; Keeling, McGoldrick, and Beatty 2010). Although embodied virtual agents promise efficiency and relational benefits, they have achieved varying levels of success (Mimoun, Poncin, and Garnier 2012). For example, Toshiba's Yoko processes 50,000 after-sales service enquiries daily across 17 countries, reducing human-to-customer contacts by approximately 40% and support e-mails by 50% (Living Actor 2016). But IKEA's assistant Anna was retired from service in 2015, largely due to its inadequate, inefficient service provision and a large volume of inappropriate dialog initiated by online customers (Wakefield 2016). New embodied virtual agents continue to emerge though, and many large companies (e.g., IBM Watson, IP Australia) are investing in artificial intelligence, machine learning, and emotional recognition tools to expand the relationship-building capabilities of embodied virtual agents (Nott 2017).

### Enhancing Personalization Strategies

In the digital age more so than ever, customers have come to expect individually relevant, personalized treatment from companies online, counting on firms' opportunities to use big data to generate enhanced customer insights (Burke 2002; Fruend 2017). Marketers coincide on personalization being key to enhance today's customer relationships (Researchscape International 2018). We present two approaches that help relationship marketers individualize their online relationships with customers.

First, sellers provide tailor-made, subscription-based services through mobile apps or a combination of channels. Technology vastly facilitates one-to-one personalization strategies, such that many relationship marketers rely on machine-learning personalization where algorithms and predictive analytics dynamically propose individually relevant recommendations and experiences to customers (Hyken 2017). Upon sign-up, customer need to provide the necessary data for the focal service. Algorithms operating in the background then use this data to deliver individually targeted, relevant contents to the focal customer. Consider the example of the Berlin-based startup 8fit (8fit 2018; O'Hear 2017). Their app acts as an online personal trainer to accompany people on their way to a healthier lifestyle. Combining meal plans and workout programs fully customized to subscribers' goals and preferences, 8fit takes a more comprehensive approach than many other fitness app providers focusing on either recipes or exercise schedules. When signing up, customers are asked to choose between three overriding goals, i.e. losing weight, getting fitter, or gaining muscle. After that, subscribers indicate detailed personal data related to their current and intended physical measures, their dietary and meal prep preferences, as well as their fitness state and habits. From this data then, 8fit generates a custom agenda for each subscriber. In an effort to provide customers with a holistic omnichannel experience, the firm accompanies its personalized app by their Facebook profile and website, where it engages customers in additional contents such as weekly challenges, meal prep videos for select recipes, or health-related background articles.

Second, firms mimic and even go beyond customers' physical store visits where customers can try out product options by personalizing the shopping experience through augmented-reality technologies. Augmented reality is enabled by interactive technological interfaces that modify physical environments by superimposing multimodal digital elements and thus appeal to a range of human sensory inputs (Javornik 2016). These efforts to enhance customer online experiences are predicted to evoke investments of more than $2.5 billion by 2018 (ABI Research 2013). Such applications allow marketers to mitigate some of the sensory disadvantages customers face online, such as visualizing how specific product offerings will fit into their personal environment (Hilken et al. 2017). Augmented reality can facilitate customers' decision-making process by layering virtual images and content on a person, product, or background (Javornik 2016). For example, L'Oréal's Style My Hair and Makeup Genius apps allow customers to try products and view the results on real photos of themselves prior to purchasing them. Topology Eyewear uses 3D face-scanning technology to give customers a means to try on a variety of customized eyeglasses using a smartphone-based augmented-reality interface (Buhr 2017). The IKEA Place 3D application allows customers to visualize how more than 2,000 products would look in their own homes and thus make more informed product purchases (Lunden 2017). Such visiotactile and haptic imagery also can evoke a psychological state of control and ownership, enabling exploratory engagement, consumer empowerment, and better decision making (Huang and Liao 2017; Marinova et al. 2017; Rafaeli et al. 2017).

### Enhancing Experiential Benefits Strategies

In the digital age, more so than ever before, relationship marketers seek to provide customers with a holistic customer experience. Consumers shop and build relationships with companies not just for utilitarian reasons but also to attain hedonic and fun experiences (Childers et al. 2001). Modern relationship marketing practices can cater to customers' desire for self-enhancing or communal experiences in two main ways.

The first popular strategy is gamification, which applies game design elements to nongame contexts to enhance customers' online experience (Hamari 2013). Gamification positively affects customer attitudes, experiences, and enjoyment, as well as their likelihood of exhibiting task-specific behaviors and adoption of innovations (Leclercq, Poncin, and Hammedi 2017; Kuo and Rice 2015; Müller-Stewens et al. 2017).

Computer games are a ubiquitous form of entertainment, and more than 59% of the U.S. population routinely plays (Entertainment Software Association 2014). By 2020, the gamification market is expected to grow eightfold beyond the 2015 level of US$1.65 billion (Statista 2018). In turn, firms turn to gamification to improve the effectiveness of their relationship marketing efforts. For example, M&M's Facebook-based Eye-Spy Pretzel game promoted its pretzel-flavored candy and prompted 25,000 likes, 6,000 shares, and 11,000 comments (Smart Insights 2015). Buffalo Wild Wings partnered with a location-based gaming platform SCVNGR for a three-month campaign, during which customers participated in customized challenges (e.g., in-store activities such as taking pictures of the sauciest wing) to receive discounts. As a result, customers engaged in 184,000 unique game plays across 740 restaurant locations, with more than 100 million impressions on Facebook and Twitter (Drell 2011). McDonald's Australia enriched its app with "tap and play," "spin and win," and "dice roll" in-app games. On its first day of release, the app reached the top position in Apple's App Store.

A second online mechanism is status bestowal. The pursuit of status has been established as a powerful motivator for customers, such as in hierarchical loyalty programs (Eggert, Steinhoff, and Garnefeld 2015; Lampel and Bhalla 2007). Beyond classic loyalty programs, many online communities use status hierarchies, such that users must meet increasingly challenging goals to achieve higher status levels (Lampel and Bhalla 2007). For example, TripAdvisor delivers badges to customers (e.g., "local expert"), which signal their elevated status and expertise to the rest of the online community (Anderson, Hildreth, and Howland 2015). With the Nike Fuel program, users track and share their training results with other members in the online Nike community and also receive daily feedback, which enhances their engagement with the firm (Muoio 2017). Customers who achieve high status online tend to engage in status-reinforcing behaviors, even if they entail costs (Ivanic 2015).

## Summary

Relationship marketers seek to build and maintain strong, effective customer relationships. Building relationships requires effective strategies for creating and growing relational exchanges with customers. Dynamically speaking, strategies for building relationships are key in early stages of the customer–seller bond. Maintaining relationships in the longer run is more concerned with how to keep established customers happy and continue their fruitful relations. For that purpose, it often is more important to avoid bad outcomes rather than adding more good aspects to the relationship.

A meta-analysis of relational drivers reveals key relationship-building strategies. Conflict has the biggest (detrimental) impact on relationship quality, meaning that the strongest effect is negative, in line with people's tendency to weigh negatives more heavily than positives. The strongest positive determinants of relationship quality are seller expertise, communication, relationship investments, relationship benefits, and similarity between relational exchange partners. Gratitude is a strong catalyst of customer relationships too, stimulating both short- and long-term reciprocal behaviors. Fostering customer perceptions of the seller's free will, benevolent motives, and risky relationship investments can leverage this gratitude mechanism. Customers' need for the relationship investment also can increase their level of gratitude.

Online relationships differ from offline relationships in several ways, which affects the optimal relationship-building strategies. Specifically, online anonymity increases the influence of risk-reducing signals, allows online relationships to form and end quickly, and supports relationship formation and influence among dissimilar partners. The ease of forming and maintaining unilateral relationships also allows customers to develop extensive, diverse portfolios of online, unilateral relationships, which in turn inform their decision making. Consistent with offline relationships, reciprocity remains key for successful online relationships. Reciprocated rather than unilateral online relationships have a stronger effect on customers' psychological commitment and financial behaviors.

To maintain relationships, sellers must avoid the bad, particularly perceptions of unfairness, as is often experienced by bystander customers. Customer-perceived unfairness undermines beneficial customer behaviors while also aggravating negative effects of conflict and opportunism. Specific to online relationships, privacy concerns also are pertinent, and firms need to establish privacy policies that provide customers with transparency and control.

In efforts to institutionalize relationship marketing, two prominent approaches are customer-centric organizational structures and loyalty programs. After amortizing the costs of the restructuring, which may take several years, a customer-centric organizational structure can enhance company performance, especially in industries with few other customer-centric firms, low competitive intensity, low commoditization, and high margins. For loyalty programs, relationship marketers should take a holistic view of their psychological, strategic, and operational elements. Loyalty programs simultaneously spur positive and negative, emotional and cognitive responses; managers must carefully determine what structure to apply over the long term; and managers should strategically use reward delivery, timing, and targeting designs to enhance program effectiveness.

These findings suggest best practices for relationship marketing. To protect relationships, sellers need to circumvent conflict and unfairness perceptions. In turn, leveraging the positive performance ramifications of seller expertise, communication, and relationship investments strengthens relational bonds, as well as fostering gratitude and reciprocity norms among customers. Beyond that, installing customer-centric organizational structures and loyalty programs may boost relationship marketing effectiveness.

The digital age also has brought about some relevant technological developments that can reinforce relationship marketing efforts. To enhance communication with customers in online channels, sellers might employ social media profiles, mobile apps, embodied virtual agents, or augmented reality. They can provide clear data privacy policies and reputation signals to build trust, even among customers in relatively anonymous online environments. Moreover, they can enhance the customer experience by using gamification elements and bestowing elevated status on selected customers.

## Takeaways

- In a meta-analysis of relational drivers, conflict has the biggest (detrimental) impact on relationship quality. Strong positive determinants of relationship quality include seller expertise, communication, relationship investments, relationship benefits, and similarity between relational exchange partners.
- Gratitude catalyzes customer relationships, stimulating both short- and long-term reciprocal behaviors. The seller's free will, benevolent motives, and risk-taking in making relationship investments, as well as the customer's need for the investment, effectively leverage gratitude mechanisms.
- Online relationships differ in several important ways from offline relationships (e.g., geographic distance, anonymity, unilateral structures, lower social interconnectedness), which affects the optimal relationship-building strategies in online environments.
- A substantial threat to relationships is perceived unfairness, which leads customers to reduce their cooperation, flexibility, and performance but also aggravates the negative effects of conflict and opportunism.
- The digital age creates privacy concerns, which in turn can lead to negative performance effects for firms. Privacy policies should provide transparency and control.
- Customer-centric organizational structures may enhance company performance, especially in industries with few other customer-centric firms, low competitive intensity, low commoditization, and high margins. Switching to customer-centric structures takes time to produce benefits though.
- Loyalty programs are complex relationship marketing instruments, so marketers must account for the programs' psychological, strategic, and operational elements.

- Established best practices in relationship marketing recommend avoiding conflict and unfairness; promoting seller expertise, communication, and relationship investments; spurring gratitude and reciprocity norms; implementing overarching relationship marketing programs throughout the firm; and assessing relationship marketing effectiveness.
- Emerging relationship marketing practices include strategies to leverage communication, trust-building efforts, and contributions to the customer experience.

# References

8fit (2018), "Skip the Gym." Available at: https://8fit.com/ (accessed 19 August 2018).

ABI Research (2013), "Developers to Invest \$2.5 Billion in Augmented Reality in 2018; Look for Enterprise to Drive Smart Glasses." Available at: www.abiresearch.com/press/developers-to-invest-25-billion-in-augmented-reali/ (accessed 26 March 2018).

Adjei, Mavis T., Stephanie M. Noble, and Charles H. Noble (2010), "The Influence of C2C Communications in Online Brand Communities on Customer Purchase Behavior." *Journal of the Academy of Marketing Science* 38 (5), 634–53.

Adler, Mitchel G., and Nancy S. Fagley (2005), "Appreciation: Individual Differences in Finding Value and Meaning as a Unique Predictor of Subjective Well-Being." *Journal of Personality* 73 (February), 79–114.

Allison, Melissa (2010), "Starbucks Discontinues Duetto Visa Cards, Another Blow for Some Loyalists." *The Seattle Times*, 11 February. Available at: http://old.seattletimes.com/html/coffeecity/2011050289_starbucks_discontinues_duetto.html (accessed 15 August 2018).

Anderson, Cameron, John A. Hildreth, and Laura Howland (2015), "Is the Desire for Status a Fundamental Human Motive? A Review of the Empirical Literature." *Psychological Bulletin* 141 (3), 574–601.

Anderson, James C., and James A. Narus (1990), "A Model of Distributor Firm and Manufacturer Firm Working Partnerships." *Journal of Marketing* 54 (January), 42–58.

Arora, Sandeep, Frenkel T. Hofstede, and Vijay Mahajan (2017), "The Implications of Offering Free Versions for the Performance of Paid Mobile Apps." *Journal of Marketing* 81 (6), 62–78.

Bagchi, Rajesh, and Xingbo Li (2011), "Illusionary Progress in Loyalty Programs: Magnitudes, Reward Distances, and Step-Size Ambiguity." *Journal of Consumer Research* 37 (5), 888–901.

Banovic, Jovana (2017), "How Nike Use Social Media [Case Study]." Available at: http://jovanabanovic.com/2017/12/16/nike-use-social-media-case-study/ (accessed 26 March 2018).

Barnes, Nora G., and Jessica Griswold (2016), "Use of Popular Tools Remains Constant as Use of Instagram Expands Quickly among the 2016 Fortune 500." Available at: www.umassd.edu/cmr/socialmediaresearch/2016fortune500/ (accessed 26 March 2018).

Bartlett, Monica Y., and David DeSteno (2006), "Gratitude and Prosocial Behavior." *Psychological Science* 17 (April), 319–25.

Baumeister, Roy F., Ellen Bratslavsky, Catrin Finkenauer, and Kathleen D. Vohs (2001), "Bad Is Stronger Than Good." *Review of General Psychology* 5 (4), 323–70.

Baumeister, Roy F., and Mark R. Leary (1995), "The Need to Belong: Desire for Interpersonal Attachments as a Fundamental Human Motivation." *Psychological Bulletin* 117 (3), 497–529.

Boles, James S., Julie T. Johnson, and Hiram C. Barksdale, Jr. (2000), "How Salespeople Build Quality Relationships: A Replication and Extension." *Journal of Business Research* 48 (1), 75–81.

Breen, Marcia (2016), "Starbucks Will Reward How Much You Spend, Not How Often You Visit." Available at: www.nbcnews.com/business/business-news/starbucks-revamps-its-rewards-program-gives-stars-cash-not-visits-n523656 (accessed 2 July 2018).

Brown, Morgan (2014), "Airbnb: The Growth Story You Didn't Know." Available at: https://growthhackers.com/growth-studies/airbnb (accessed 26 March 2018).

Buhr, Sarah (2017), "Topology Lets You Try Before You Buy Glasses Using AR in an App." Available at: https://techcrunch.com/2017/10/02/topology-lets-you-try-before-you-buy-glasses-using-ar-in-an-app/ (accessed 26 March 2018).

Burke, Raymond R. (2002), "Technology and the Customer Interface: What Consumers Want in the Physical and Virtual Store." *Journal of the Academy of Marketing Science* 30 (4), 411–32.

Capgemini (2017), "Loyalty Deciphered—How Emotions Drive Genuine Engagement." Available at: www.capgemini.com/resources/loyalty-deciphered/ (accessed 26 March 2018).

Capgemini Consulting (2015), "Fixing the Cracks: Reinventing Loyalty Programs for the Digital Age." Available at: www.capgemini-consulting.com/reinventing-loyalty-programs (accessed 26 March 2018).

Capizzi, Michael T., and Rick Ferguson (2005), "Loyalty Trends for the Twenty-First Century." *Journal of Consumer Marketing* 22 (2), 72–80.

Childers, Terry L., Christopher L. Carr, Joann Peck, and Stephen Carson (2001), "Hedonic and Utilitarian Motivations for Online Retail Shopping Behavior." *Journal of Retailing* 77 (4), 511–35.

Day, George S. (2006), "Aligning the Organization With the Market." *MIT Sloan Management Review* 48 (1), 41–9.

Dell (2010), "10-K Report for 2009 Fiscal Year." Available at: www.sec.gov/Archives/edgar/data/826083/000095012310025998/d70787e10vk.htm (accessed 02 July 2018).

De Wulf, Kristof, Gaby Odekerken-Schröder, and Dawn Iacobucci (2001), "Investments in Consumer Relationships: A Cross-Country and Cross-Industry Exploration." *Journal of Marketing* 65 (October), 33–50.

Dholakia, Ruby Roy, and Brian Sternthal (1977), "Highly Credible Source: Persuasive Facilitator of Persuasive Liabilities?" *Journal of Consumer Research* 3 (March), 223–32.

Doney, Patricia M., and Joseph P. Cannon (1997), "An Examination of the Nature of Trust in Buyer–Seller Relationships." *Journal of Marketing* 61 (April), 35–51.

Dorotic, Matilda, Tammo H. A. Bijmolt, and Peter C. Verhoef (2012), "Loyalty Programmes: Current Knowledge and Research Directions." *International Journal of Management Reviews* 14 (3), 217–37.

Dowling, Grahame R., and Mark Uncles (1997), "Do Customer Loyalty Programs Really Work?" *Sloan Management Review* 38 (4), 71–82.

Drell, Lauren (2011), "How SCVNGRs First National Brand Partnership Scored Big During March Madness." Available at: https://mashable.com/2011/06/01/scvngr-buffalo-wild-wings-campaign/#Q.RGID50Gqq4 (accessed 26 March 2018).

Drèze, Xavier, and Joseph C. Nunes (2004), "Using Combined-Currency Prices to Lower Consumers' Perceived Cost." *Journal of Marketing Research* 41 (1), 59–72.

Drèze, Xavier, and Joseph C. Nunes (2009), "Feeling Superior: The Impact of Loyalty Program Structure on Consumers' Perceptions of Status." *Journal of Consumer Research* 35 (6), 890–905.

Drèze, Xavier, and Joseph C. Nunes (2011), "Recurring Goals and Learning: The Impact of Successful Reward Attainment on Purchase Behavior." *Journal of Marketing Research* 48 (2), 268–81.

Eggert, Andreas, Lena Steinhoff, and Ina Garnefeld (2015), "Managing the Bright and Dark Sides of Status Endowment in Hierarchical Loyalty Programs." *Journal of Service Research* 18 (2), 210–28.

Emmons, Robert A., and Michael E. McCullough (2004), *The Psychology of Gratitude*. New York: Oxford University Press.

Entertainment Software Association (2014), "Essential Facts About the Computer and Video Game Industry." Available at: www.theesa.com/wp-content/uploads/2017/09/EF2017_Design_FinalDigital.pdf (accessed 26 March 2018).

Esmark, Carol L., Stephanie M. Noble, and John E. Bell (2016), "Open Versus Selective Customer Loyalty Programmes." *European Journal of Marketing* 50 (5/6), 770–95.

Fiske, Susan T. (1980), "Attention and Weight in Person Perception: The Impact of Negative and Extreme Behavior." *Journal of Personality and Social Psychology* 38 (June), 889–906.

Folkes, Valerie S. (1988), "Recent Attribution Research in Consumer Behavior: A Review and New Directions." *Journal of Consumer Research* 14 (March), 548–65.

Forrester Report (2015), "Forrester Research eCommerce Forecast 2014 to 2019." Available at: www.forrester.com/Forrester+Research+eCommerce+Forecast+2014+To+2019+US/fulltext/-/E-res116713 (accessed 02 July 2018).

Fruend, Melissa (2017), *2017 Colloquy Loyalty Census: An In-Depth Analysis of Where Loyalty Is Now . . . and Where It's Headed*. Cincinnati: Colloquy.

Gordon, Nancy, and Kelly Hlavinka (2011), *Buried Treasure: The 2011 Forecast of U.S. Consumer Loyalty Program Points Value*. Cincinnati: Colloquy.

Gouldner, Alvin W. (1960), "The Norm of Reciprocity: A Preliminary Statement." *American Sociology Review* 25 (April), 161–78.

Hamari, Juho (2013), "Transforming Homo Economicus Into Homo Ludens: A Field Experiment on Gamification in a Utilitarian Peer-to-Peer Trading Service." *Electronic Commerce Research and Applications* 12 (4), 236–45.

Henderson, Conor, Joshua T. Beck, and Robert W. Palmatier (2011), "A Review of the Theoretical Underpinnings of Loyalty Programs." *Journal of Consumer Psychology* 21 (July), 256–76.

Hilken, Tim, Ko de Ruyter, Mathew Chylinski, Dominik Mahr, and Debbie I. Keeling (2017), "Augmenting the Eye of the Beholder: Exploring the Strategic Potential of Augmented Reality to Enhance Online Service Experiences." *Journal of the Academy of Marketing Science* 45 (6), 884–905.

Hsee, Christopher K., Fang Yu, Jiao Zhang, and Yan Zhang (2003), "Medium Maximization." *Journal of Consumer Research* 30 (1), 1–14.

Huang, Tseng-Lung, and Shu-Ling Liao (2017), "Creating E-Shopping Multisensory Flow Experience Through Augmented-Reality Interactive Technology." *Internet Research* 27 (2), 449–75.

Hume, David (1957), *The Natural History of Religion*. Stanford: Stanford University Press.

Hyken, Shep (2017), "Recommended Just for You: The Power of Personalization." Available at: www.forbes.com/sites/shephyken/2017/05/13/recommended-just-for-you-the-power-of-personalization/#6b063dba6087 (accessed 19 August 2018).

Ivanic, Aarti S. (2015), "Status Has Its Privileges: The Psychological Benefit of Status-Reinforcing Behaviors." *Psychology & Marketing* 32 (7), 697–708.

Jantsch, John (2014), "How Unexpected Surprises Create Insane Customer Loyalty." Available at: www.americanexpress.com/us/small-business/openforum/articles/how-unexpected-surprises-create-insane-customer-loyalty/ (accessed 19 August 2018).

Javornik, Ana (2016), "Augmented Reality: Research Agenda for Studying the Impact of Its Media Characteristics on Consumer Behaviour." *Journal of Retailing and Consumer Services* 30 (May), 252–61.

Jiang, Lan, JoAndrea Hoegg, and Darren W. Dahl (2013), "Consumer Reaction to Unearned Preferential Treatment." *Journal of Consumer Research* 40 (3), 412–27.

Johnson, David W., and Stephen Johnson (1972), "The Effects of Attitude Similarity, Expectation of Goal Facilitation, and Actual Goal Facilitation on Interpersonal Attraction." *Journal of Experimental Social Psychology* 8 (3), 197–206.

Kang, Min-Ping, Joseph T. Mahoney, and Danchi Tan (2009), "Why Firms Make Unilateral Investments Specific to Other Firms: The Case of OEM Suppliers." *Strategic Management Journal* 30 (February), 117–35.

Keeling, Kathleen, Peter McGoldrick, and Susan Beatty (2010), "Avatars as Salespeople: Communication Style, Trust, and Intentions." *Journal of Business Research* 63 (8), 793–800.

Keh, Hean T., and Yih H. Lee (2006), "Do Reward Programs Build Loyalty for Services? The Moderating Effect of Satisfaction on Type and Timing of Rewards." *Journal of Retailing* 82 (2), 127–36.

Kim, Donghoon, Seung-yon Lee, Kyunghee Bu, and Seho Lee (2009), "Do VIP Programs Always Work Well? The Moderating Role of Loyalty." *Psychology & Marketing* 26 (7), 590–609.

Kim, Jisu J., Lena Steinhoff, and Robert W. Palmatier (2018), "Loyalty Programs in Theory, Research, and Practice: A Dynamic Perspective." Working Paper.

Kozlenkova, Irina V., Robert W. Palmatier, Eric (Er) Fang, Bangming Xiao, and Minxue Huang (2017), "Online Relationship Formation." *Journal of Marketing* 81 (3), 21–40.

KPMG (2017), "The Truth about Online Consumers: 2017 Global Online Consumer Report." Available at: https://assets.kpmg.com/content/dam/kpmg/xx/pdf/2017/01/the-truth-about-online-consumers.pdf (accessed 26 March 2018).

Kumar V, Rajkumar Venkatesan, and Werner Reinartz (2008), "Performance Implications of Adopting a Customer-Focused Sales Campaign." *Journal of Marketing* 72 (5), 50–68.

Kuo, Andrew, and Dan H. Rice (2015), "Catch and Shoot: The Influence of Advergame Mechanics on Preference Formation." *Psychology & Marketing* 32 (2), 162–72.

Kwong, Jessica Y. Y., Dilip Soman, and Candy K. Y. Ho (2011), "The Role of Computational Ease on the Decision to Spend Loyalty Program Points." *Journal of Consumer Psychology* 21 (2), 146–56.

Lacey, Russell, Jaebeom Suh, and Robert M. Morgan (2007), "Differential Effects of Preferential Ttreatment Levels on Relational Outcomes." *Journal of Service Research* 9 (3), 241–56.

Lagace, Rosemary R., Robert Dahlstrom, and Jule B. Gassenheimer (1991), "The Relevance of Ethical Salesperson Behavior on Relationship Quality: The Pharmaceutical Industry." *Journal of Personal Selling and Sales Management* 11 (Fall), 39–47.

Lampel, Joseph, and Ajay Bhalla (2007), "The Role of Status Seeking in Online Communities: Giving the Gift of Experience." *Journal of Computer-Mediated Communication* 12 (2), 434–55.

Leclercq, Thomas, Ingrid Poncin, and Wafa Hammedi (2017), "The Engagement Process During Value Co-Creation: Gamification in New Product-Development Platforms." *International Journal of Electronic Commerce* 21 (4), 454–88.

Lee, Ju-Yeon, Irina V. Kozlenkova, and Robert W. Palmatier (2015), "Structural Marketing: Using Organizational Structure to Achieve Marketing Objectives." *Journal of the Academy of Marketing Science* 43 (January), 73–99.

Lee, Ju-Yeon, Shrihari Sridhar, Conor M. Henderson, and Robert W. Palmatier (2015), "Effect of Customer Centricity on Long-Term Financial Performance." *Marketing Science* 34 (2), 250–68.

Lee, Ju-Yeon, Shrihari Sridhar, and Robert W. Palmatier (2015), "Customer-Centric Org Charts Aren't Right for Every Company." *Harvard Business Review*, July–August. Available at: https://hbr.org/2015/06/customer-centric-org-charts-arent-right-for-every-company (accessed 26 March, 2018).

Lemon, Katherine N., and Florian von Wangenheim (2009), "The Reinforcing Effects of Loyalty Program Partnerships and Core Service Usage—A Longitudinal Analysis." *Journal of Service Research* 11 (4), 357–70.

Liu, Peggy J., Cait Lamberton, and Kelly L. Haws (2015), "Should Firms Use Small Financial Benefits to Express Appreciation to Consumers? Understanding and Avoiding Trivialization Effects." *Journal of Marketing* 79 (3), 74–90.

Liu-Thompkins, Yuping, and Leona Tam (2013), "Not All Repeat Customers Are the Same: Designing Effective Cross-Selling Promotion on the Basis of Attitudinal Loyalty and Habit." *Journal of Marketing* 77 (5), 21–36.

Living Actor (2016), "Yoko, Toshiba Virtual Helpdesk Assistant, Successfully Deployed Across Europe!" Available at: http://blog.livingactor.com/yoko-toshiba-virtual-helpdesk-assistant-deploys-all-across-europe/ (accessed 26 March 2018).

Lunden, Ingrid (2017), "IKEA Place, the Retailer's First ARKit App, Creates Lifelike Pictures of Furniture in Your Home." Available at: https://techcrunch.com/2017/09/12/ikea-place-the-retailers-first-arkit-app-creates-lifelike-pictures-of-furniture-in-your-home/ (accessed 26 March 2018).

Marinova, Detelina, Ko de Ruyter, Ming-Hui Huang, Matthew L. Meuter, and Goutam Challagalla (2017), "Getting Smart: Learning From Technology-Empowered Frontline Interactions." *Journal of Service Research* 20 (1), 29–42.

Marlow, Cameron (2009), "Maintained Relationships on Facebook." Available at: www.facebook.com/notes/facebook-data-science/maintained-relationships-on-facebook/55257228858/ (accessed 19 August 2018).

Martin, Kelly D., Abhishek Borah, and Robert W. Palmatier (2017), "Data Privacy: Effects on Customer and Firm Performance." *Journal of Marketing* 81 (1), 36–58.

Martin, Kelly D., Abhishek Borah, and Robert W. Palmatier (2018), "Research: A Strong Privacy Policy Can Save Your Company Millions." *Harvard Business Review*, 15 February. Available at: https://hbr.org/2018/02/research-a-strong-privacy-policy-can-save-your-company-millions (accessed 26 March, 2018).

Martin, Kelly D., and Patrick E. Murphy (2017), "The Role of Data Privacy in Marketing." *Journal of the Academy of Marketing Science* 45 (March), 135–55.

McConnell, Cody (2017), "How to Build Strong Customer Relationships Online." Available at: www.forbes.com/sites/forbescommunicationscouncil/2017/02/09/how-to-build-strong-customer-relationships-online/#63b8e4421295 (accessed 26 March 2018).

Melancon, Joanna P., Stephanie M. Noble, and Charles H. Noble (2011), "Managing Rewards to Enhance Relational Worth." *Journal of the Academy of Marketing Science* 39 (3), 341–62.

Meyer-Waarden, Lars (2007), "The Effect of Loyalty Programs on Customer Lifetime Duration and Share of Wallet." *Journal of Retailing* 83 (2), 223–36.

Mimoun, Mohammed S. B., Ingrid Poncin, and Marion Garnier (2012), "Case Study—Embodied Virtual Agents: An Analysis on Reasons for Failure." *Journal of Retailing and Consumer Services* 19 (6), 605–12.

Mohr, Jakki J., Robert J. Fisher, and John R. Nevin (1996), "Collaborative Communication in Interfirm Relationships: Moderating Effects of Integration and Control." *Journal of Marketing* 60 (July), 103–15.

Mohr, Jakki J., and John R. Nevin (1990), "Communication Strategies in Marketing Channels: A Theoretical Perspective." *Journal of Marketing* 54 (October), 36–51.

Morales, Andrea C. (2005), "Giving Firms an 'E' for Effort: Consumer Responses to High-Effort Firms." *Journal of Consumer Research* 31 (March), 806–12.

Morgan, Robert M., and Shelby D. Hunt (1994), "The Commitment-Trust Theory of Relationship Marketing." *Journal of Marketing* 58 (July), 20–38.

Müller-Stewens, Jessica, Tobias Schlager, Gerald Häubl, and Andreas Herrmann (2017), "Gamified Information Presentation and Consumer Adoption of Product Innovations." *Journal of Marketing* 81 (2), 8–24.

Muoio, Dave (2017), "Nike Exec Looks Back at FuelBand's Rise and Fall, Talks Lessons of Wearables 1.0." Available at: www.mobihealthnews.com/content/nike-exec-looks-back-fuelband%E2%80%99s-rise-and-fall-talks-lessons-wearables-10 (accessed 26 March 2018).

Nicholson, Carolyn Y., Larry D. Compeau, and Rajesh Sethi (2001), "The Role of Interpersonal Liking in Building Trust in Long-Term Channel Relationships." *Journal of the Academy of Marketing Science* 29 (1), 3–15.

Nott, George (2017), "The Battle for the Brains of the Call Centre Killer Bots." Available at: www.computerworld.com.au/article/615344/battle-brains-call-centre-killer-bots/ (accessed 26 March 2018).

Nowlin, Jordan (2014), "What You Need to Know About the Chinese Consumer: Understanding Taobao." Available at: www.channeladvisor.com/blog/?pn=marketplaces/what-you-need-to-know-about-the-chinese-consumerunderstanding-taobao (accessed 02 July 2018).

Nunes, Joseph C., and Xavier Drèze (2006), "The Endowed Progress Effect: How Artificial Advancement Increases Effort." *Journal of Consumer Research* 32 (4), 504–12.

O'Hear, Steve (2017), "8fit, a Health and Fitness App that Offers Tailored Workout and Meal Plans, Closes $7M Series A." Available at: https://techcrunch.com/2017/09/19/8fit/ (accessed 19 August 2018).

Palmatier, Robert W., Rajiv P. Dant, and Dhruv Grewal (2007), "A Comparative Longitudinal Analysis of Theoretical Perspectives of Interorganizational Relationship Performance." *Journal of Marketing* 71 (4), 172–94.

Palmatier, Robert W., Rajiv P. Dant, Dhruv Grewal, and Kenneth R. Evans (2006), "Factors Influencing the Effectiveness of Relationship Marketing: A Meta-Analysis." *Journal of Marketing* 70 (October), 136–53.

Palmatier, Robert W., Srinath Gopalakrishna, and Mark B. Houston (2006), "Returns on Business-to-Business Relationship Marketing Investments: Strategies for Leveraging Profits." *Marketing Science* 25 (September–October), 477–93.

Palmatier, Robert W., Mark B. Houston, Rajiv P. Dant, and Dhruv Grewal (2013), "Relationship Velocity: Toward a Theory of Relationship Dynamics." *Journal of Marketing* 77 (January), 13–30.

Palmatier, Robert W., Cheryl Burke Jarvis, Jennifer R. Bechkoff, and Frank R. Kardes (2009), "The Role of Customer Gratitude in Relationship Marketing." *Journal of Marketing* 73 (September), 1–18.

Rafaeli, Anat, Daniel Altman, Dwayne D. Gremler, Ming-Hui Huang, Dhruv Grewal, Bala Iyer, A. Parasuraman, and Ko de Ruyter (2017), "The Future of Frontline Research: Invited Commentaries." *Journal of Service Research* 20 (1), 91–9.

Researchscape International (2018), "2018 Trends in Personalization." Available at: www.evergage.com/wp-content/uploads/2018/04/Evergage-2018-Trends-in-Personalization-Survey.pdf (accessed 19 August 2018).

Reynolds, Kristy E., and Sharon E. Beatty (1999), "Customer Benefits and Company Consequences of Customer-Salesperson Relationships in Retailing." *Journal of Retailing* 75 (1), 11–32.

Roehm, Michelle L., Ellen B. Pullins, and Harper A. Roehm Jr. (2002), "Designing Loyalty-Building Programs for Packaged Goods Brands." *Journal of Marketing Research* 39 (2), 202–13.

Saad, Sihem B., and Fatma C. Abida (2016), "Social Interactivity and Its Impact on a User's Approach Behavior in Commercial Web Sites: A Study Case of Virtual Agent Presence." *Journal of Marketing Management* 4 (2), 63–80.

Samaha, Stephen A., Robert W. Palmatier, and Rajiv P. Dant (2011), "Poisoning Relationships: Perceived Unfairness in Channels of Distribution." *Journal of Marketing* 75 (May), 99–117.

Scheer, Lisa K., C. Fred Miao, and Robert W. Palmatier (2015), "Dependence and Interdependence in Marketing Relationships: Meta-Analytic Insights." *Journal of the Academy of Marketing Science* 43 (6), 694–712.

Schumann, Jan H., Nancy V. Wünderlich, and Heiner Evanschitzky (2014), "Spillover Effects of Service Failures in Coalition Loyalty Programs: The Buffering Effect of Special Treatment Benefits." *Journal of Retailing* 90 (1), 111–18.

Schwartz, Barry (1967), "The Social Psychology of the Gift." *The American Journal of Sociology* 73 (July), 1–11.

Shah, Denish, Roland T. Rust, A. Parasuraman, Richard Staelin, George S. Day (2006), "The Path to Customer Centricity." *Journal of Service Research* 9 (2), 113–24.

Sharp, Byron, and Anne Sharp (1997), "Loyalty Programs and Their Impact on Repeat-Purchase Loyalty Patterns." *International Journal of Research in Marketing* 14 (5), 473–86.

Shiv, Baba, Julie A. Edell, and John W. Payne (1997), "Factors Affecting the Impact of Negatively and Positively Framed Ad Messages." *Journal of Consumer Research* 24 (December), 285–94.

Shugan, Steven M. (2005), "Brand Loyalty Programs: Are They Shams?" *Marketing Science* 24 (2), 185–93.

Silverthorne, Sean (2016), "Insights From MSI: How Customers Feel About Your Data Practices." *Marketing Science Institute*, 25 August. Available at: www.msi.org/articles/how-customers-feel-about-your-data-practices/ (accessed 26 March, 2018).

Sirdeshmukh, Deepak, Jagdip Singh, and Barry Sabol (2002), "Consumer Trust, Value, and Loyalty in Relational Exchanges." *Journal of Marketing* 66 (1), 15–37.

Smart Insights (2015), "Gamification as a Content Marketing Tactic." Available at: www.smartinsights.com/content-management/content-marketing-creative-and-formats/gamification-as-a-content-marketing-tactic/ (accessed 26 March 2018).

Smith, J. Brock, and Donald W. Barclay (1997), "The Effects of Organizational Differences and Trust on the Effectiveness of Selling Partner Relationships." *Journal of Marketing* 61 (January), 3–21.

Statista (2018), "Value of the Gamification Market Worldwide in 2015 and 2020 (in billion U.S. dollars)." Available at: www.statista.com/statistics/608824/ gamification-market-value-worldwide/ (accessed 26 March 2018).

Steinhoff, Lena, Eric (Er) Fang, Robert W. Palmatier, and K. Wang (2016), "Dynamic Effects of Loyalty Rewards for Contractual Customers." Marketing Science Institute (MSI) Working Paper Series, 16–121.

Steinhoff, Lena, and Robert W. Palmatier (2016), "Understanding Loyalty Program Effectiveness: Managing Target and Bystander Effects." *Journal of the Academy of Marketing Science* 44 (January), 88–107.

Tesser, Abraham, Robert Gatewood, and Michael Driver (1968), "Some Determinants of Gratitude." *Journal of Personality and Social Psychology* 9 (3), 233–6.

Tolido, Ron (2016), "TechnoVision 2016—No Work." Available at: www.capgemini. com/2016/01/technovision-2016-no-work/ (accessed 26 March 2018).

Tsang, Jo-Ann (2006), "The Effects of Helper Intention on Gratitude and Indebtedness." *Motivation & Emotion* 30 (September), 198–204.

van Doorn, Jenny, Martin Mende, Stephanie M. Noble, John Hulland, Amy L. Ostrom, Dhruv Grewal, and J. Andrew Petersen (2017), "Domo Arigato Mr. Roboto: Emergence of Automated Social Presence in Organizational Frontlines and Customers' Service Experiences." *Journal of Service Research* 20 (1), 43–58.

Van Osselaer, Stijn M. J., Joseph W. Alba, and Puneet Manchanda (2004), "Irrelevant Information and Mediated Intertemporal Choice." *Journal of Consumer Psychology* 14 (3), 257–70.

Vargo, Stephen L., and Robert F. Lusch (2004), "Evolving to a New Dominant Logic for Marketing." *Journal of Marketing* 68 (January), 1–17.

Verheul, Rob (2017), "McDonalds Monopoly—A Promotional Masterclass." Available at: www.graphitedigital.com/blog/mcdonalds-monopoly-promotional-masterclass (accessed 26 March 2018).

Verma, Varsha, Dheeraj Sharma, and Jagdish Seth (2016), "Does Relationship Marketing Matter in Online Retailing? A Meta-Analytic Approach." *Journal of the Academy of Marketing Science* 44 (2), 206–17.

Von Wangenheim, Florian, and Tomás Bayón (2007), "Behavioral Consequences of Overbooking Service Capacity." *Journal of Marketing* 71 (4), 36–47.

Wagner, Tillmann, Thorsten Hennig-Thurau, and Thomas Rudolph (2009), "Does Customer Demotion Jeopardize Loyalty?" *Journal of Marketing* 73 (3), 69–85.

Wakefield, Jane (2016), "Would You Want to Talk to a Machine?" Available at: www.bbc.com/news/technology-36225980 (accessed 26 March 2018).

Weathers, Danny, Subhash Sharma, and Stacy L. Wood (2007), "Effects of Online Communication Practices on Consumer Perceptions of Performance Uncertainty for Search and Experience Goods." *Journal of Retailing* 83 (4), 393–401.

Weiner, Bernard (1985), "An Attributional Theory of Achievement Motivation and Emotion." *Psychological Review* 92 (4), 548–73.

Wood, Natalie T., Michael R. Solomon, and Basil G. Englis (2005), "Personalisation of Online Avatars: Is the Messenger as Important as the Message?" *International Journal of Internet Marketing and Advertising* 2 (1–2), 143–61.

Yi, Youjae, and Hoseong Jeon (2003), "Effects of Loyalty Programs on Value Perception, Program Loyalty, and Brand Loyalty." *Journal of the Academy of Marketing Science* 31 (3), 229–40.

Zhang, Jonathan Z., George F. Watson IV, Robert W. Palmatier, and Rajiv P. Dant (2016), "Dynamic Relationship Marketing." *Journal of Marketing* 80 (September), 53–75.

Zhu, Rui, Utpal M. Dholakia, Xinlei (Jack) Chen, and René Algesheimer (2012), "Does Online Community Participation Foster Risky Financial Behavior?" *Journal of Marketing Research* 49 (3), 394–407.

# 6 Relationship Marketing Targeting

## Learning Objectives

- Define purposeful targeting as key to relationship marketing effectiveness.
- Understand how customers differ in their level of relationship orientation, which makes them more or less appropriate targets for sellers.
- Describe the diverse customer-, industry-, and culture-specific drivers of customer relationship orientation.
- Explain how field experiments can help companies optimize their relationship marketing targeting.
- Identify which groups of customers represent new targets of relationship marketing efforts in the digital age.

## Introduction

The notion of purposeful targeting, which requires differential customer treatment, is at the heart of relationship marketing (Homburg, Droll, and Totzek 2008; Zeithaml, Rust, and Lemon 2001). Investing in customer relationships does not pay off equally for every individual customer or each relationship. Instead, relationship marketing effectiveness varies according to how customers value and respond to sellers' efforts to build and maintain strong relationships in particular customer-specific, market-specific, or culture-specific contexts. Thus seller expertise might be a critical, positive antecedent of relationship quality (as we discussed in Chapter 5) in most settings and on average, but this factor has little impact in straight rebuy situations, such as when customers consistently purchase the same commodity. For customers buying expensive technical equipment, especially in business-to-business settings, an expert seller instead is highly valuable and a strong relationship driver. Thus the buying situation determines customers' relationship orientations, but so do other notable factors. In the first part of this chapter, we therefore delineate several determinants, identified by prior research, of this relationship orientation. Recognizing these determinants can help relationship marketers deal with the challenge of effectively targeting their relational investments, identify appropriate target customers, and design relationship marketing activities that provide optimal returns on investments. Then in the second part of this chapter, we make a further case for using field experiments with limited samples of customers to learn the effects of specific relationship marketing programs before rolling out the initiatives to an overall customer base.

## Managing Relationship Marketing Targeting

Only certain customers prefer relationship marketing efforts; others do not find them valuable or even actively work to avoid them. It therefore is up to sellers to identify which customers are most receptive to their relationship marketing efforts (Anderson and Narus 1991; Dwyer, Schurr, and Oh 1987), then allocate their budgets and other resources accordingly (Berry 1995; Cao and Gruca 2005; Crosby, Evans, and Cowles 1990; Reichheld and Teal 1996; Reinartz and Kumar 2000). Instead of simply assigning these resources to the biggest or highest potential customers—a tactic that might appear reasonable but that actually ignores customers' preferences—good marketers seek information about whether each customer wants to establish a relationship. Three types of customers tend to be receptive to relationship marketing and thus are good targets for relevant initiatives: those that suffer from specific governance issues (e.g., dependence, uncertainty) that can be resolved with a relational governance structure, those with problems that cannot be predicted or dealt with fully in advance, and those that lack protection from other forms of governance (Heide 1994; Pfeffer and Salancik 1978; Williamson 1985). Such traits likely encourage customers' relationship orientation, to varying levels, which in turn determine the effectiveness of the seller's relationship marketing attempts.

### The Concept of Customer Relationship Orientation

If a customer prefers a strong relationship with a partner, its customer **relationship orientation** is high, such that it likely responds positively to requests for information from the seller, is willing to meet regularly and communicate broadly with seller representatives, aligns its goals with the seller's, and avoids conflict (Palmatier et al. 2008). When customers are receptive to relationship marketing efforts, efforts by the seller gain in effectiveness. Optimal relationship marketing outcomes emerge when sellers' specific relationship marketing activities match each customer's preferred relationship orientation. That assertion means that the seller also needs to consider those customers that exhibit low relationship orientations. They prefer transactional interactions and even might actively work to avoid suppliers that insist on a relationship approach.

Why might customers develop such negative views of relationship marketing activities? Primarily, they do so in response to the perceived costs of relational involvement.

First, for customers with low relationship orientations, relationship marketing involves painful opportunity costs, in that they must devote time and effort to communicating intensively with the seller or analyzing and applying the benefits offered through the relationship marketing program. If they have little interest in these programs, little impetus to communicate intensively, and no particular need for relationship-based governance, such investments are costly and even unnecessary—or at least inefficient. They would prefer instead to avoid the hassle, time, and costs required to nurture a relationship. It is not difficult to imagine a situation in which a customer calls into a call center solely to request a product sample or simple quote. When the sales rep comes to deliver the sample or quote, she or he might try to develop a relationship by making small talk, asking probing questions, or suggesting add-on products, beyond what the customer requested. But the customer just wants to get a sense of what is available and has no desire or immediate need for a relational exchange. A chatty, extended, time-consuming interaction with the salesperson feels deeply inefficient to this customer, potentially creating so much annoyance that the customer refuses to place an order.

Second, reciprocity obligations constitute another type of cost. Especially when those obligations emerge from interpersonal relationships, they leave the recipient of relationship marketing efforts uncomfortable. That is, reciprocity norms involve not just the cost of repaying the favor but also the personal discomfort the customer feels due to a sense of (unwanted) psychological debt owed to the seller. Those same psychological processes and reciprocity norms that benefit relationships with relationally oriented customers thus can alienate customers without such a relationship orientation, such that they purposefully avoid apparently generous sellers that shower them with benefits. Even despite their lack of interest in these benefits, such customers likely feel guilty or worry that they will appear impolite if they fail to reciprocate (Cialdini 2001).

Third, the customer might assume that relationship marketing efforts must raise the prices that the seller charges, because it needs some way to pay for these resource-consuming activities. Even if frequent calls, visits, or other communications do not entail direct costs for customers, less relationally oriented customers likely view these efforts as wasteful and unnecessary, which may lower their evaluations of such an inefficient supplier. Such perceptions degrade the value of existing relational assets and also tend to diminish seller performance (Palmatier et al. 2008).

The costs also accrue to the seller. If it offers an inappropriate level of relationship marketing—either more or less than the customer wants—it risks making insufficient investments that leave relationship-oriented customers dissatisfied or overblown investments that waste scarce

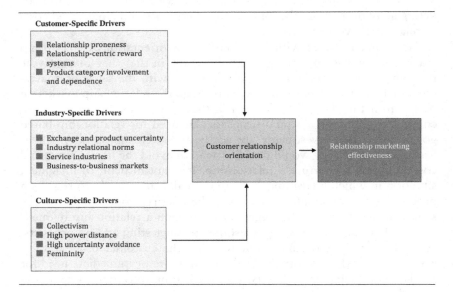

*Figure 6.1* Drivers of Customer Relationship Orientation

marketing resources on customers that resent the associated costs. But if it can match each customer's relationship orientation, the seller can effectively leverage its relationship marketing activities to achieve better relationships and financial performance.

A seller also might seek to encourage factors that promote customers' desire for relational governance. Figure 6.1 details customer-, industry-, and culture-specific factors, which we detail in the following sections. Briefly, though, customer-specific drivers of a customer relationship orientation include individual-level elements, such as relationship proneness or product category involvement. Industry-specific drivers include macro-level factors that reflect the context in which relationships take place, such as service versus product markets. Then macro-level, culture-specific aspects influence the usual relationship orientations in different countries or international regions.

### Customer-Specific Drivers of Customer Relationship Orientation

The customer-specific factors that determine overall relationship orientation include the individual customer's relationship proneness, relationship-specific reward systems, and product category involvement and dependence. If a customer indicates *relationship proneness*, it tends to engage in relationships in general (De Wulf, Odekerken-Schröder, and Iacobucci 2001). This difference tends to be stable, similar to interpersonal relationship proneness, so in various settings, relationally prone customers consistently exhibit stronger relationship orientations toward sellers (Johnson 1999; Johnson and Sohi 2001; Schutz 1992). Such proneness also might lead the customer firm to establish *relationship-centric reward systems* that feature evaluations, compensation rules, and policies that consistently encourage strong supplier relationships and thus produce a relationship orientation overall. In contrast, a system that rewards customer representatives for obtaining price reductions or more transactions with multiple sellers likely prompts a low relationship or transaction-focused orientation.

Finally, when customers are more involved in the product category or exchange, they seek relationships, because such links produce opportunities to generate value (De Wulf, Odekerken-Schröder, and Iacobucci 2001). *Product category involvement and dependence* is specific to a product category that is important or even foundational for a customer; such involvement may reflect the needs and interests of the individual representative, the firm, or the role, all of which can heighten the customer firm's relationship orientation (Mittal 1995).

### Industry-Specific Drivers of Customer Relationship Orientation

Customer relationship orientation also varies across industries or markets. Specifically, in contexts that feature high exchange and product uncertainty, strong industry-level relational norms, service (versus product) industries, and business-to-business (versus business-to-consumer) settings, customers typically exhibit stronger relationship orientations.

Beyond the customer firm's boundaries, uncertain environments can cause customers to prefer relationship-based exchanges, with their enhanced options for adaptability and flexibility. Such *exchange and product uncertainty* stems from three main causes: volatility in the market, challenges associated with monitoring changes in the industry, and rapid technological advancements (Celly and Frazier 1996). Transaction cost economic theory predicts that exchange uncertainty demands more adaptability, and when exchange partners share relational bonds (Noordewier, John, and Nevin 1990; Williamson 1985), they adapt more readily and willingly to unpredictable changes (Cannon and Perreault, Jr. 1999, Noordewier, John, and Nevin 1990). Uncertainty also demands more flexibility and behavioral confidence from exchange partners, which they can develop through relational exchanges, not from transactional ones (Cannon and Perreault, Jr. 1999; Dahlstrom and Nygaard 1995). Even as uncertainty makes the positive effects of commitment, trust, and relational norms more pertinent for encouraging cooperation and firm performance (Palmatier, Dant, and Grewal 2007), stronger relational bonds can reduce conflict and the need for extensive negotiations, thereby overcoming the threat of extended disagreements due to uncertain or turbulent environments.

---

### Example 6.1  Toyota (Japan)

The world's largest automotive company, Toyota, enjoys a strong reputation for its supplier relationship management. Today's car industry in general represents a volatile market which is, in addition, heavily impacted by advances in technology. Beyond, Toyota invented and heavily relies on a just-in-time production approach. All these factors make solid, reliable, and mutually trustful relationships with suppliers key to long-term success. Toyota regards its suppliers as strategic partners rather than just vendors. In 2017, the company underscored its claim with the opening of new purchasing and prototype-development centers on its Toyota Technical Center campus in Michigan. With these centers, Toyota aims at making its supplier relations even more fruitful in the future. To show its appreciation to its supplier partners, the buildings' first floor is fully dedicated to welcoming and hosting visiting suppliers. Rather than having suppliers wait for their meeting in the lobby, they are invited to spend time in the first-floor area, where they can access cubicles, for example, to work in private.

Source: Sutton (2018).

---

In the presence of *industry-level relational norms* that prioritize customer–supplier relationships, nearly every member of the industry agrees about what constitutes working relationships, and that agreement reflects strongly relational strategies, whether implicitly or explicitly (Anderson and Narus 1991; Heide and John 1992; Macaulay 1963). These norms and conventional practices accordingly lead customers to anticipate relationship-building efforts by sellers and respond receptively to them, signaling their strong customer relationship orientation (Palmatier et al. 2008).

Such norms also are especially likely if the industry predominantly sells *services*, which are unpredictable, intangible, and perishable—unlike products. To produce services, the customer and the seller (or their representatives) must work together. Then to evaluate these intangible services, they often have little choice but to rely on trust-based interactions. Accordingly, they likely need and have developed stronger relationships than might be the case for customers and sellers in product markets (Zeithaml, Parasuraman, and Berry 1985), which should make relationship marketing more effective (Palmatier et al. 2006).

Another realm in which industry-based relational norms tend to emerge is in *business-to-business markets*. In a sense, relationship importance even differentiates consumer from business markets: A business-to-business firm depends explicitly on effective working relationships to achieve sustainable advantages and success (Anderson and Narus 2004), implying that relationship marketing can exert a greater impact on the exchange outcomes than is true in business-to-consumer markets. Consider channel relationships as a classic example: When channel partners enter into exchanges, they accept substantial interdependence and coordinate their activities to ensure the channel functions efficiently and effectively, without opportunism. But direct customer–seller transactions, as are more common in business-to-consumer markets, have less need of such coordination to achieve successful outcomes, so they might not develop strong relationship orientations (Anderson and Weitz 1989; Kumar, Scheer, and Steenkamp 1995a).

### Culture-Specific Drivers of Customer Relationship Orientation

Four key tenets describe how culture determines relationship marketing orientations. Such considerations are critical, because few modern firms can avoid entering into at least some international relationships. Accordingly, international relationship marketing research recently has expanded, moving beyond the early studies focused in the West (e.g., United States, Europe). A meta-analysis of this research stream, involving 170 studies that cover 36 countries and test 47,864 relationships, establishes the four tenets that in turn provide recommendations for whether and when sellers should adapt their relationship marketing efforts to various cultures, distinguished according to Hofstede's well-known dimensions (Samaha, Beck, and Palmatier 2014).

First, individualistic cultures make it more difficult to form long-term, social relationships or dependence. Whereas *individualism* implies that people expect to be self-reliant and distinct from others, *collectivism* indicates that people are mutually dependent and closely tied (Hofstede, Hofstede, and Minkov 2010). Accordingly, relationship marketing may tend to offer fewer benefits in individualistic cultures that encourage the prioritization of self-interested behaviors but better outcomes in collectivist cultures that embrace the idea that relationships inherently define social structures. As the most influential cultural dimension—its impact magnitudes exceed those of power distance by 14%, uncertainty avoidance by 90%, and masculinity by 109%—individualism limits the effectiveness of various relationship-building strategies (e.g., communication, dependence, expertise, duration) then mitigates the positive influences of relationships on performance (Samaha, Beck, and Palmatier 2014).

Second, a culture that accepts and embraces high levels of *power distance* regards inequalities in society, between powerful and less powerful members, as reasonable and appropriate (Hofstede, Hofstede, and Minkov 2010). Therefore, people generally are perfectly willing to form status-based relationships, which in turn implies that relationships have more compelling benefits for status-based outcomes. In the presence of normative, hierarchical systems that mandate interpersonal inequalities, the governments, organizations, and policies present in high-power-distance cultures already establish status differences, often by using symbols of prestige (e.g., executive dining rooms, assigned parking places). In relationship marketing terms, seller expertise becomes more important in high-power-distance cultures; the hierarchical relationships also exert stronger influences on word-of-mouth behaviors.

Third, *uncertainty avoidance* describes the degree to which members of a culture dislike and try to avoid uncertain, ambiguous situations (Hofstede, Hofstede, and Minkov 2010). Entering into a new exchange with different partners is generally risky, with uncertain outcomes. Therefore, in high-uncertainty-avoidance cultures, relationship marketing efforts that reduce uncertainty are popular and encourage those relationships to form. Here again, seller expertise is salient; if they can trust an expert seller, customers can mitigate their discomforting sense of uncertainty, which should evoke stronger relationship orientations (Samaha, Beck, and Palmatier 2014).

Fourth, *masculinity (versus femininity)* as a cultural dimension may hinder the effectiveness of relationship marketing, because in societies marked by this trait, people seek a reputation for being assertive, dominant, competitive, and outcome driven, which makes them less likely to pursue relationships. In a more feminine society, people prioritize nurturance, with less competitiveness (Hofstede, Hofstede, and Minkov 2010), so they should be more willing to devote time and effort to establish and maintain stable, long-term relationships. Because members of these feminine cultures also tend to be empathetic, their relational ties likely develop more effectively. Overall, though, this cultural dimension has a relatively smaller impact on relationship-building efforts and performance. In the meta-analysis we described at the start of this section, masculinity merely moderates and diminishes the effect of relationships on word-of-mouth behaviors.

Beyond that meta-analysis, another country- and region-level study indicates that relationship marketing is more effective outside the United States, as Table 6.1 reveals. Such insights should encourage country-specific relationship marketing strategies that optimize the allocation of international relationship marketing resources to the most profitable customer relationships worldwide. For example, addressing just the BRIC nations, in Brazil, relationships are 28% more effective than in the United States; similarly, they enhance business performance by 20% more in Russia, 71% in India, and a notable 100% in China (Samaha, Beck, and Palmatier 2014). Thus, customers in different nations and cultures likely require customized relationship-building strategies. Consider Russia: Dependence prompts a 118% increase in the ability to build relationships, but relationship investments are 50% less effective, compared with the United States.

Even regionally, the United States and Western Europe represent the areas in which relationships are least effective for establishing performance outcomes. In Asia in particular, relationships can exert approximately 70% greater impacts on performance, compared with the United States—a finding that resonates with our four tenets, in that Asia tends to be collectivist. It also aligns with research that highlights how relationships in Asia historically have been key determinants of business success (e.g., *guanxi* in China, *keiretsu* in Japan) (Lee and Dawes 2005; Sambharya and Banerji 2006; Samaha, Beck, and Palmatier 2014).

---

### Example 6.2  China Entrepreneur Club (China)

The China Entrepreneur Club (CEC), an exclusive, not-for-profit network of 46 Chinese top entrepreneurs and business leaders, is a good example of how relationships, or *guanxi*, work in China. Membership in the club encompasses various activities, such as visits to each other's workplaces, nights out, and yearly trips abroad together. All of these activities are targeted at building and strengthening close personal relationships among members. Such bonding helps in difficult times, for example, when a member receives support of all other members of the club. Reciprocity is key in these relationships, such that a person receiving support from another will reciprocate at some point in the future. As a manager, disposing of good *guanxi*, a wide network of mutually beneficial relationships nurtured outside the formal work setting (e.g., over joint dinners), is often key to the business's success.

Source: Hope (2014).

---

*Table 6.1* Effects of Relational Mediators on Performance and Cultural Scores, by Country and Region

| | Performance | | | Cultural Dimension Scores | | | |
|---|---|---|---|---|---|---|---|
| | Esti-mated Effect | Rank | Relative to U.S. | Individ-ualism | Power Distance | Uncertainty Avoidance | Mascu-linity |
| *Country* | | | | | | | |
| Brazil | .46 | 6 | 28% | 38 | 69 | 76 | 49 |
| Canada | .36 | 15 | –2% | 80 | 39 | 48 | 52 |
| China | .73 | 1 | 100% | 20 | 80 | 30 | 66 |
| France | .30 | 22 | –17% | 71 | 68 | 86 | 43 |
| Great Britain | .41 | 11 | 12% | 89 | 35 | 35 | 66 |
| Germany | .32 | 18 | –11% | 67 | 35 | 65 | 66 |
| India | .62 | 3 | 71% | 48 | 77 | 40 | 56 |
| Japan | .41 | 10 | 13% | 46 | 54 | 92 | 95 |
| Mexico | .55 | 4 | 50% | 30 | 81 | 82 | 69 |

(*Continued*)

*Table 6.1* (Continued)

| | Performance | | | Cultural Dimension Scores | | | |
| --- | --- | --- | --- | --- | --- | --- | --- |
| | Esti-mated Effect | Rank | Relative to U.S. | Individ-ualism | Power Distance | Uncertainty Avoidance | Mascu-linity |
| Russia | .44 | 8 | 20% | 39 | 93 | 95 | 36 |
| United States | .36 | 13 | 0% | 91 | 40 | 46 | 62 |
| ... | | | | | | | |
| Country Averages | .40 | | 11% | 55 | 57 | 66 | 50 |
| *Region* | | | | | | | |
| Africa | .51 | 2 | 40% | 36 | 67 | 65 | 49 |
| Asia | .62 | 1 | 70% | 24 | 73 | 50 | 53 |
| Eastern Europe | .43 | 6 | 19% | 46 | 66 | 74 | 47 |
| Latin America | .46 | 4 | 28% | 23 | 71 | 86 | 47 |
| North America | .46 | 5 | 27% | 54 | 49 | 51 | 55 |
| Middle East | .46 | 3 | 28% | 38 | 65 | 71 | 47 |
| Western Europe | .32 | 7 | –11% | 63 | 46 | 69 | 48 |
| Regional Averages | .47 | | 29% | 41 | 62 | 67 | 50 |

Note: This table reproduces selected results from a meta-analysis performed by Samaha, Beck, and Palmatier (2014, p. 91).

## Guidelines for Managing Relationship Marketing Targeting

As we have established, costly, unwanted relationship marketing efforts can undermine the very existence of a relationship. Only if customers gain value from the relationship is it likely to endure, irrespective of its closeness. Transactional customers might be just as profitable as relational ones (Reinartz and Kumar 2000). Therefore, aligning with customers' relationship needs ultimately is more critical for ensuring the seller's performance than is blindly pursuing ever-closer links (Cao and Gruca 2005; Colgate and Danaher 2000; Dowling and Uncles 1997), which cannot guarantee strong performance anyway (Cannon and Perreault, Jr. 1999). By matching relationship marketing efforts with a customer's relationship orientation, the seller helps the customer trade off benefits it receives (e.g., flexibility, monitoring, safeguarding) against the costs it accrues to enter into and maintain relationships. If the customer exhibits a strong relationship orientation, receiving relationship marketing investments and engagement enhances the quality of the relationship, the efficiency of the exchange, and the value of relational assets, with positive implications for seller performance (Palmatier et al. 2008). Defining a customer's relationship orientation establishes whether it will be receptive to relationship marketing and request a relational governance structure—or not.

Such efforts take on particular relevance in the modern digital age, which is marked by efficiency initiatives that leave customer representatives with far less time to chat with sellers' agents, even as those sellers expand their time-consuming efforts to build stronger relationships. In research into business-to-business exchanges, one study found that less relationship-oriented customers—for whom, by definition, past patronage does not guarantee future business—would move 21% of their purchases to a supplier that provided them with totally automated transactions that never required them to interact with a salesperson (Palmatier et al. 2008). If sellers can accurately identify customers with low relationship orientations, they seemingly would hit the sales lottery: They could give customers exactly what they want, at a lower cost, while also poaching competitors' low-relationship-oriented customers, simply by providing easy, (at least) partially automated, arm's-length transactions. As long as sellers segment their business customers according to relationship orientation, they can position themselves appropriately as a transactional partner for those customers that prefer such distance while also devoting relationship marketing investments to those customers that appreciate the benefits of intensive relationships.

But along with creating these unique relationship marketing challenges, the digital age also offers two routes to improve targeting capabilities. First, from a methodological standpoint, digital tools facilitate field experiments, enabling relationship marketers to test new programs with a limited sample of customers and identify the varying effectiveness of these programs for different customer segments. Second, more substantively, targets in the digital age—even in business-to-consumer markets—often are no longer single individuals but instead involve groups of customers. By leveraging the power of group norms, companies can simultaneously build and nurture relationships with a wide range of customers.

## Using Field Experiments to Improve Targeting

Recent marketing research recommends and demonstrates the use of field experiments to understand customer behavior (Gneezy 2017; Meyer 2017). In a field experiment, the experimenter (e.g., academic researcher, manager) manipulates one or several factors in the customers' natural environment, then measures the behaviors and outcomes that result from this manipulation by comparing the behavior of manipulated customers (i.e., treatment group) with the behavior of customers who were not exposed to the manipulation (i.e., control group).

Such experiments have obvious promise for tests of a new relationship marketing investment, such as a rewards program. Before rolling out the rewards program to all customers, the company can test its effectiveness among a limited sample of representative customers. A manager might also seek to determine whether a certain type of reward can stimulate additional revenues or other helpful behaviors. With a random group of, say, several hundred customers defined as the treatment group, the manager can deliver the reward to them then track their buying behavior over a subsequent period. At the same time, the manager defines a comparable, randomly selected control group that does not receive the reward and tracks their buying behavior over the same period. Any lift in sales revealed by the comparison of the groups indicates an outcome of the treatment, that is, the reward program. In addition, the manager can review the customers in both groups (e.g., long-term versus short-term customers) to determine which ones respond most strongly to the reward. A similar example emerges from a publication in which the authors conducted a field experiment to determine whether a proactive marketing initiative achieved better outcomes among customers with distinct loyalty profiles (i.e., habit-, dependence-, or relationship-based) (Henderson, Steinhoff, and Palmatier 2014). Conducting such field experiments is an effective method to test the overall impacts of relationship marketing efforts empirically, as well as to identify optimal target customers rather than wasting resources with a full rollout of a potentially ineffective (at least for some customers) program.

---

**Example 6.3  Optimizely (USA)**

A simple yet powerful form of online field experiments is A/B testing. Dan Siroker, co-founder and executive chairman of Optimizely, served as the director of analytics during Barak Obama's 2008 presidential campaign "Obama'08." With his team, he extensively used A/B testing to optimize the "Obama'08" website design and augment the campaign's effectiveness (e.g., sign-up rates, fund raising). The campaign team developed 24 different variations (i.e., combining six different media images with four different call-to-action buttons) of the website's splash page. Each visitor to the webpage was randomly directed to one of these 24 versions. During the testing period, over 300,000 visitors were recorded, such that each splash page variation was presented to over 13,000 people. The winning combination depicted a picture of the Obama family, accompanied by the slogan "Change We Can Believe In" and a "Learn More" button. This emotionally appealing splash page enhanced sign-up rates (i.e., conversion) by 40%, leading to 2.8 million e-mail addresses which were estimated to have resulted in an additional $60 million in donations.

Source: Siroker (2010); Stringfellow (2012).

For example, when existing customers appear complacent or bored, many firms proactively issue dedicated, unique benefits. But such offerings inevitably interact with other, existing mechanisms, such as customer loyalty and engagement. Therefore, the firm-provided, unexpected benefits could lead to unexpected, undesired consequences. Consider the longitudinal field experiment, conducted with a telecommunications service provider, detailed in Figure 6.2. In this study, the researchers sought to determine the effects of proactive marketing initiatives on an existing relationship that featured habit-, dependence-, and relationship-based loyalty. They measured customers' intrinsic loyalty using data from an existing customer relationship management (CRM) database for five months then issued a proactive reward—a free gift of two months' free calling—to the treatment group in the treatment period and subsequently assessed customers' expansion and defection behaviors for nine months after the treatment. The results led the authors to identify four prototypical customer loyalty classifications or profiles, for which proactive marketing initiatives have radically different implications (see Figure 6.3): loyalists, sleeping dogs, dependent partners, and skeptics (Henderson, Steinhoff, and Palmatier 2014).

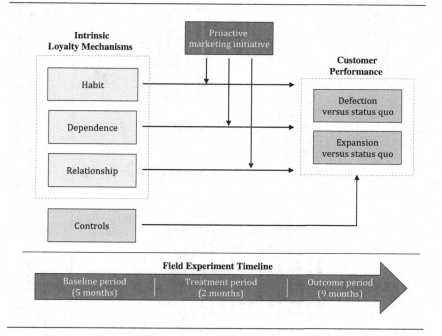

*Figure 6.2*  Field Experiment: Targeting Effectiveness of a Relationship Marketing Initiative

Source: Adapted from Henderson, Steinhoff, and Palmatier (2014).

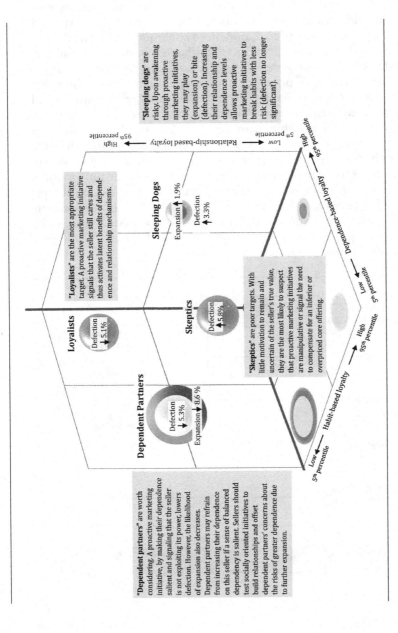

*Figure 6.3* Segmenting and Targeting Customers According to Their Intrinsic Loyalty Profiles

Notes: Bubble sizes correspond with the absolute percentage change in the likelihood of expansion or defection due to a proactive marketing initiative. The spotlight analysis indicates the effects are significant at $p < .05$. The locations for the spotlight analysis were chosen for their managerial relevance and interest.

Source: Adapted from Henderson, Steinhoff, and Palmatier (2014).

- Loyalists are ideal targets: Proactive marketing initiatives prompt benefits with no contrary damage (e.g., 5.1% lower customer defection, no significant effect on expansion). For example, initiatives designed to enhance the relationship signal the seller's devotion, activating dependence and relationship mechanisms that break these loyal customers out of their habits in ways that leverage other activated mechanisms and cause them to be more loyal and less likely to defect.
- Sleeping dogs are mainly habitual in their behaviors. Proactive marketing initiatives might induce them to play (expansion increases by 1.9%), but they also can cause a bite (defection increases by 3.3%). If the seller can clip on a "leash," in the form of greater dependence and stronger relationships, their defection likelihood decreases.
- Dependent partners exhibit high dependence, low habit, and moderate relationship orientations. A proactive marketing initiative makes their dependency more salient, so they are less likely to defect, by 5.3%. But it also makes them less likely to expand the relationship, by 8.6%, likely because they do not want to increase their dependence even further. Thus sellers may want to target these customers, to lower their defection risk, and more socially oriented tactics might be preferable, to avoid creating customer concerns about a risk of being exploited.
- Skeptics score low on all intrinsic loyalty measures, generally have a low relationship orientation, respond negatively to marketing initiatives (5.8% increase in defection, no significant effect on expansion), and have little motivation to stick with the seller. Any relationship marketing efforts thus meet suspicion or rejection, because these customers assume such tactics provide negative signals of the seller's attempt to manipulate them or hide some inferior or overpriced offering.

Research along these lines highlights how defining customers' loyalty profiles then exposing representative samples to proactive marketing initiatives with a field experiment can produce more effective relationship marketing programs. Managers can use the results from their own, similar field experiments to identify the prototypical customer loyalty profiles for their firm and thereby predict for whom proactive marketing initiatives will help, for whom they will hurt, and for which customers they will have mixed performance effects.

### Targeting Groups of Customers

Digital technology enables consumers to function in networks rather than as individuals (Hennig-Thurau et al. 2010; Libai et al. 2010; Verhoef, Reinartz, and Krafft 2010). Reflecting the human need to come together and organize into groups, social networks (e.g., Facebook, Instagram) enable customers to meet, communicate, and interact, such that they can build meaningful relationships with fellow (potential) customers. Each month, more than 1 billion people organize themselves into Facebook groups, which firms arguably could access more readily than they can individual consumers (Guynn 2016). Such relationships also encourage conformity behavior among their members. Therefore, when relationship marketers approach members of these groups, their target might not be a single customer, with individual needs and wants, but rather a collection of customers, whose norms and psychological mechanisms influence their members' consumer behavior.

---

**Example 6.4 Fitbit (USA)**

As a provider of fitness trackers, Fitbit is promoting healthier lifestyles using group-based marketing strategies. In its mobile app, the firm offers a variety of community-focused features, where users can join virtual running competitions, cheer for their friends to be more active, or boast about their own achievements. Through Fitbit Health Solutions, the firm is taking its group marketing approach to the next level, targeting companies to engage their employees in corporate wellness programs. Through group mechanisms and pressures, these programs may effectively foster healthy behavior changes among employees.

Source: Fitbit Health Solutions (2018).

---

In particular, groups drive consistent, conformant purchase behavior (Harmeling et al. 2017), even more strongly than other social influences, by evoking both information appraisal and identity appraisal mechanisms. Even if the group is totally arbitrary, revealing group norms and consensus recommendations causes members to develop a belief that input from another group member will be more diagnostic (information appraisal) and in line with that focal member's self-identity (identity appraisal) than input or recommendations from an outsider. Not only are consumers 1.4 times more likely to choose a product that matches group norms, but they also will pay significantly more for it than for an alternative product (even one that is objectively superior), especially if the products offer social benefits. These influences also depend on whether group members entered the purchase domain recently or not. If they are relatively new to the purchase domain, group norms affect consumers' purchase behaviors according to an inverted U-shape when information appraisals dominate, but they follow a U-shape if identity appraisals dominate. Group norms initially appear weaker, because the new member tries to maintain a personal identity. But eventually, the group increasingly defines the member's social identity, so this consumer becomes willing to pay more (up to three times as much) for a product that matches group norms (Harmeling et al. 2017).

Engaging in relationship marketing with these consumer groups requires some special consideration, as the four steps in Figure 6.4

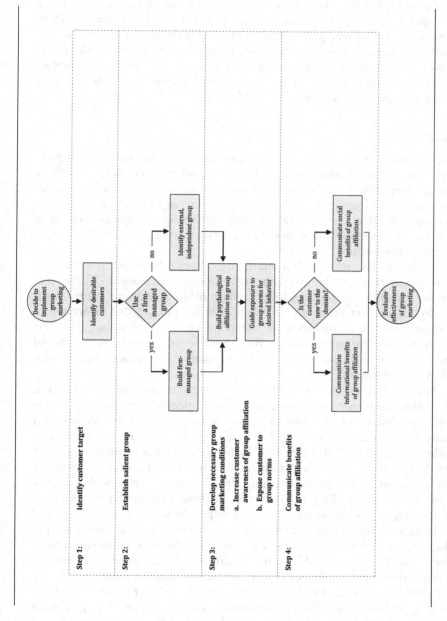

*Figure 6.4* Four Steps for Effective Group Marketing

Source: Adapted from Harmeling et al. (2017).

indicate. After identifying appropriate customers, the relationship manager must encourage them to coalesce into a salient group, whether that means establishing a brand community or leveraging the presence of an independent group. However the group forms, the seller then needs to encourage customers' sense of affiliation with the group and make sure they have been exposed to clear group norms. Finally, assuming these necessary conditions for group marketing are in place, the seller can adapt its relationship marketing strategies to account for customers' traits, such as their time in the purchase domain (Harmeling et al. 2017).

## Summary

Relationship marketing is not effective for all customers; some customers seek to avoid relationships. Therefore, sellers must determine how to allocate their relationship marketing resources across their customer portfolios, and targeting represents a key challenge for relationship marketing. The effectiveness of relationship marketing varies with how much the customers value and respond to sellers' efforts to build and maintain strong relationships.

In particular, relationship marketing should be most effective for customers that exhibit a strong relationship orientation. These customers likely reciprocate a seller's relationship marketing efforts, such as by responding positively to its requests for meetings or information. However, when customers have low relationship orientations, they perceive relationship marketing activities as a waste of time, an unwanted hassle, or an extra cost. They prefer transactional interactions, not relational involvement.

Several factors can promote a customer's relationship orientation, including customer-, industry-, and culture-specific elements. Customer-specific drivers of a relationship orientation include individual-level variations, such that relationship marketing tends to be more effective when targeted to customers with higher relationship proneness, greater exchange and product uncertainty, a higher level of product category involvement and dependence, and already existing relationship-centric reward systems in place. Industry-specific drivers are macro-level factors, reflecting the context in which relationships take place. Relationships and relationship marketing efforts are more effective in industries featuring high relational norms, service industries, and business-to-business markets. Finally, macro-level, culture-specific aspects determine relationship orientation. High levels of collectivism, power distance, and uncertainty avoidance, as well as low levels of masculinity, all favor relationship marketing performance. Thus, for example, relationship marketing is more effective in cultures unlike that of the United States, particularly the set of nations known as the BRIC countries. Effective customer relationship-building strategies demand some amount of cultural customization.

To improve and optimize their targeting decisions, relationship marketing managers also can conduct field experiments and thereby empirically test the impact of new relationship marketing initiatives among a limited sample of customers rather than risking a wasteful implementation of an ineffective program. Field experiments manipulate several factors then measure how people react to this manipulation through a comparison of how customers exposed to the treatment behave versus how control customers act. Field experiments also can reveal why a relationship marketing initiative might achieve mixed effectiveness among existing customers, namely, according to their loyalty profiles. For example, one study shows that relationship marketing initiatives exert positive effects on loyalists, mixed effects on sleeping dogs and dependent partners, and negative effects on skeptics. This approach offers a blueprint for relationship marketers to apply to their own firms and customers.

Because groups of customers, facilitated by digital technology, drive conformity, sellers can apply group marketing strategies to achieve superior performance. If they can tap in to group norms, sellers can evoke parallel mechanisms of information appraisal and identity appraisal and thereby encourage purchase decisions by members of the group, according to the time they have been within the purchase domain. In a four-step process, group marketing efforts should identify desirable customers, establish a salient group, create the necessary conditions for group marketing (e.g., group affiliation, exposure to group norms), and adapt group marketing strategies to the time members have spent in the specific purchase domain.

## Takeaways

- Relationship marketing investments do not pay off equally for each individual customer and each individual relationship; purposeful targeting to customers with high relationship orientations is key to enhance relationship marketing performance.
- Some customers perceive relationship marketing activities as an unwanted waste of time, hassle, or cost. Only customers with a high customer relationship orientation desire strong relationships, which prompts their responsiveness to relationship-building and maintenance efforts.
- Customer-specific drivers of customer relationship orientation include their relationship proneness, exchange and product uncertainty, product category involvement and dependence, and relationship-centric reward systems.
- Industry-specific drivers of customer relationship orientation are industry relational norms, service versus product industries, and business-to-business versus business-to-consumer industries.

- Culture-specific drivers of customer relationship orientation include low individualism, high power distance, high uncertainty avoidance, and low masculinity.
- Field experiments can help relationship marketers avoid wasting resources on the wrong initiatives or the wrong target customers. The comparison of the behaviors and outcomes of sample customers exposed to a manipulation (i.e., treatment group) versus those not exposed to the manipulation (i.e., control group) suggests appropriate, differentiated targeting strategies, especially in combination with analyses of customers' intrinsic loyalty profiles.
- The digital age helps customers organize into groups, and thus groups of customers are relevant targets for relationship marketing efforts. Managers must identify desirable customers, establish a salient group (firm-managed or independent), develop necessary conditions for group marketing (awareness of group affiliation, exposure to group norms), and adapt group marketing strategies to the customer's time in the product domain.

## References

Anderson, Erin, and Barton A. Weitz (1989), "Determinants of Continuity in Conventional Industrial Channel Dyads." *Marketing Science* 8 (Fall), 310–23.

Anderson, James C., and James A. Narus (1991), "Partnering as a Focused Market Strategy." *California Management Review* 33 (Spring), 95–113.

Anderson, James C., and James A. Narus (2004), *Business Market Management: Understanding, Creating, and Delivering Value.* Upper Saddle River: Prentice Hall.

Berry, Leonard L. (1995), "Relationship Marketing of Services-Growing Interest, Emerging Perspectives." *Journal of the Academy of Marketing Science* 23 (4), 236–45.

Cannon, Joseph P., and William D. Perreault, Jr. (1999), "Buyer-Seller Relationships in Business Markets." *Journal of Marketing Research* 36 (November), 439–60.

Cao, Yong, and Thomas S. Gruca (2005), "Reducing Adverse Selection Through Customer Relationship Management." *Journal of Marketing* 69 (October), 219–29.

Celly, Kirti Sawhney, and Gary L. Frazier (1996), "Outcome-Based and Behavior-Based Coordination Efforts in Channel Relationships." *Journal of Marketing Research* 33 (May), 200–10.

Cialdini, Robert B. (2001), *Influence: Science and Practice.* Boston: Allyn and Bacon.

Colgate, Mark R., and Peter J. Danaher (2000), "Implementing a Customer Relationship Strategy: The Asymmetric Impact of Poor Versus Excellent Execution." *Journal of the Academy of Marketing Science* 28 (3), 375–87.

Crosby, Lawrence A., Kenneth R. Evans, and Deborah Cowles (1990), "Relationship Quality in Services Selling: An Interpersonal Influence Perspective." *Journal of Marketing* 54 (July), 68–81.

Dahlstrom, Robert, and Arne Nygaard (1995), "An Exploratory Investigation of Interpersonal Trust in New and Mature Market Economies." *Journal of Retailing* 71 (4), 339–61.

De Wulf, Kristof, Gaby Odekerken-Schröder, and Dawn Iacobucci (2001), "Investments in Consumer Relationships: A Cross-Country and Cross-Industry Exploration." *Journal of Marketing* 65 (October), 33–50.

Dowling, Grahame R., and Mark Uncles (1997), "Do Customer Loyalty Programs Really Work?" *Sloan Management Review* 38 (Summer), 71–82.

Dwyer, Robert F., Paul H. Schurr, and Sejo Oh (1987), "Developing Buyer-Seller Relationships." *Journal of Marketing* 51 (April), 11–27.

Fitbit Health Solutions (2018), "Invest in Healthy Behavior Change." Available at: https://healthsolutions.fitbit.com/employers/ (accessed 19 August 2018).

Gneezy, Ayelet (2017), "Field Experimentation in Marketing Research." *Journal of Marketing Research* 54 (February), 140–3.

Guynn, Jessica (2016), "Facebook Groups Reaches 1 Billion Users." *USA Today*, July 10. Available at: www.usatoday.com/story/tech/news/2016/01/27/facebook-groups-reaches-1-billion-users/79414710 (accessed 26 July 2018).

Harmeling, Colleen M., Robert W. Palmatier, Eric (Er) Fang, and Dianwen Wang (2017), "Group Marketing: Theory, Mechanisms, and Dynamics." *Journal of Marketing* 81 (July), 1–24.

Heide, Jan B. (1994), "Interorganizational Governance in Marketing Channels." *Journal of Marketing* 58 (January), 71–85.

Heide, Jan B., and George John (1992), "Do Norms Matter in Marketing Relationships?" *Journal of Marketing* 56 (April), 32–44.

Henderson, Conor M., Lena Steinhoff, and Robert W. Palmatier (2014), "Consequences of Customer Engagement: How Customer Engagement Alters the Effects of Habit-, Dependence-, and Relationship-Based Intrinsic Loyalty." Marketing Science Institute (MSI) Working Paper Series, 14–121.

Hennig-Thurau, Thorsten, Edward C. Malthouse, Christian Friege, Sonja Gensler, Lara Lobschat, Arvind Rangaswamy, and Bernd Skiera (2010), "The Impact of New Media on Customer Relationships." *Journal of Service Research* 13 (3), 311–30.

Hofstede, Geert H., Gert Jan Hofstede, and Michael Minkov (2010), *Cultures and Organizations: Software of the Mind. Intercultural Cooperation and Its Importance for Survival.* New York: McGraw-Hill.

Homburg, Christian, Mathias Droll, and Dirk Totzek (2008), "Customer Prioritization: Does It Pay Off, and How Should It Be Implemented?" *Journal of Marketing* 72 (5), 110–30.

Hope, Katie (2014), "Doing Business the Chinese Way." Available at: www.bbc.com/news/business-29524701 (accessed 19 August 2018).

Johnson, Jean L. (1999), "Strategic Integration in Industrial Distribution Channels: Managing the Interfirm Relationship as a Strategic Asset." *Journal of the Academy of Marketing Science* 27 (1), 4–18.

Johnson, Jean L., and Ravipreet S. Sohi (2001), "The Influence of Firm Predispositions on Interfirm Relationship Formation in Business Markets." *International Journal of Research in Marketing* 18 (4), 299–318.

Kumar, Nirmalya, Lisa K. Scheer, and Jan-Benedict E. M. Steenkamp (1995a), "The Effects of Perceived Interdependence on Dealer Attitudes." *Journal of Marketing Research* 32 (August), 348–56.

Lee, Don Y., and Philip L. Dawes (2005), "Guanxi, Trust, and Long-Term Orientation in Chinese Business Markets." *Journal of International Marketing* 13 (2), 28–56.

Libai, Barak, Ruth Bolton, Marnix Bügel, Ko de Ruyter, Oliver Götz, Hans Risselada, and Andrew Stephen (2010), "Customer to Customer Interactions: Broadening the Scope of Word-of-mouth Research." *Journal of Service Research* 13 (3), 267–82.

Macaulay, Stewart (1963), "Non-Contractual Relations in Business." *American Sociological Review* 28 (1), 55–67.

Meyer, Robert (2017), "Introduction to the Journal of Marketing Research Special Section on Field Experiments." *Journal of Marketing Research* 54 (February), 138–9.

Mittal, Banwari (1995), "Comparative Analysis of Four Scales of Consumer Involvement." *Psychology & Marketing* 12 (7), 663–82.

Noordewier, Thomas, George John, and John R. Nevin (1990), "Performance Outcomes of Purchasing Arrangements in Industrial Buyer-Vender Relationships." *Journal of Marketing* 54 (October), 80–93.

Palmatier, Robert W., Rajiv P. Dant, and Dhruv Grewal (2007), "A Comparative Longitudinal Analysis of Theoretical Perspectives of Interorganizational Relationship Performance." *Journal of Marketing* 71 (October), 172–94.

Palmatier, Robert W., Rajiv P. Dant, Dhruv Grewal, and Kenneth R. Evans (2006), "Factors Influencing the Effectiveness of Relationship Marketing: A Meta-Analysis." *Journal of Marketing* 70 (October), 136–53.

Palmatier, Robert W., Lisa Scheer, Kenneth R. Evans, and Todd Arnold (2008), "Achieving Relationship Marketing Effectiveness in Business-to-Business Exchanges." *Journal of the Academy of Marketing Science* 2 (June), 174–90.

Pfeffer, Jeffrey, and Gerald R. Salancik (1978), *The External Control of Organizations: A Resource Dependence Approach*. New York: Harper and Row Publishers.

Reichheld, Fredrick F., and Thomas Teal (1996), *The Loyalty Effect*. Boston: Harvard Business School Press.

Reinartz, Werner J., and V. Kumar (2000), "On the Profitability of Long-Life Customers in a Noncontractual Setting: An Empirical Investigation and Implications for Marketing." *Journal of Marketing* 64 (October), 17–35.

Samaha, Stephen A., Joshua T. Beck, and Robert W. Palmatier (2014), "The Role of Culture in International Relationship Marketing." *Journal of Marketing* 78 (September), 78–98.

Sambharya, Rakesh B., and Kunal Banerji (2006), "The Effect of Keiretsu Affiliation and Resource Dependences on Supplier Firm Performance in the Japanese Automobile Industry." *Management International Review* 46 (1), 7–37.

Schutz, Will (1992), "Beyond FIRO-B—Three New Theory-Derived Measures—Elements B: Behavior, Elements F: Feelings, Elements S: Self." *Psychological Reports* 70, 915–37.

Siroker, Dan (2010), "How Obama Raised $60 Million by Running a Simple Experiment." Available at: https://blog.optimizely.com/2010/11/29/how-obama-raised-60-million-by-running-a-simple-experiment/ (accessed 19 August 2018).

Stringfellow, Angela (2012), "5 Businesses That Used A/B Tests to Lift Conversion Rates by up to 216%." Available at: https://unbounce.com/a-b-testing/5-businesses-that-used-ab-tests-to-lift-conversion-rates-by-up-to-216/ (accessed 19 August 2018).

Sutton, Dave (2018), "Remarkable Supplier Relationships are Built on Story, Strategy and Systems." Available at: www.business2community.com/product-management/remarkable-supplier-relationships-are-built-on-story-strategy-and-systems-02105258 (accessed 19 August 2018).

Verhoef, Peter C., Werner J. Reinartz, and Manfred Krafft (2010), "Customer Engagement as a New Perspective in Customer Management." *Journal of Service Research* 13 (3), 247–52.

Williamson, Oliver E. (1985), *The Economic Institute of Capitalism: Firms, Markets, Relational Contracting*. New York: The Free Press.

Zeithaml, Valarie A., A. Parasuraman, and Leonard L. Berry (1985), "Problems and Strategies in Services Marketing." *Journal of Marketing* 49 (Spring), 33–46.

Zeithaml, Valerie A., Roland T. Rust, and Katharine N. Lemon (2001), "The Customer Pyramid: Creating and Serving Profitable Customers." *California Management Review* 43 (4), 118–42.

# Concluding Chapter

# 7 Research and Managerial Guidelines for Relationship Marketing in the Digital Age

## Learning Objectives

- Detail the state of the art and specify research gaps pertaining to relationship marketing research.
- Describe ways to enhance overall understanding of relationship marketing by employing new theoretical approaches.
- Identify additional relational mechanisms that can enhance relationship marketing understanding.
- Improve relationship marketing applications by dynamically timing the deployment of relationship marketing tools and determining relationship states through analyses of big data.
- Describe ways to enhance relationship marketing applications according to the relative effectiveness of emerging relationship marketing tools, balanced with privacy concerns.
- Outline how contingency factors in online relationships, field experiments, and different social effects can improve relationship marketing applications.

## Introduction

For centuries, relationships have been essential to business exchanges, though as we have established, it was not until the early 1980s that the concept of relationship marketing surfaced in marketing literature (Berry 1983). Since then, relationship marketing has remained a central and specific priority for marketing academics and managers, prompting a vast explosion of research papers and popular business books. Such research has illuminated multiple issues that arise out of relationship marketing theory and practice and also established a consensus view: Strong customer relationships are vital to company strategy and performance (Morgan and Hunt 1994; Palmatier et al. 2006). In the digital age, relationship marketing also continues to expand in importance. With the shift to service economies and technological advancements of the digital age, relationships are gaining even greater relevance as premier sources of sustainable competitive advantage, outpacing corporate strategies focused on other marketing mix elements (Palmatier and Sridhar 2017).

Together with this clear importance, research and practice also establish the vast complexity and contingencies associated with the influences of relationships on customers—their emotions, cognitions, conations, and behavior. The preceding chapters in this book have sought to specify what extant research has told us about relationship marketing, as well as where the discipline is headed. With this concluding chapter, we also synthesize the state of the art, in a way that sheds light on the potential avenues and directions that relationship marketing researchers may pursue to advance the domain and gird it for the opportunities and challenges of the digital age. In Table 7.1, we present 14 tenets of relationship marketing, designed to both enhance its understanding (5 tenets) and advance its application (9 tenets).

This plan of action for relationship marketing research reflects the structure of our preceding chapters. That is, we first seek to augment understanding of relationship marketing, in accordance with prior theory and established frameworks. In each area, we briefly review the current state of

*Table 7.1* Relationship Marketing Tenets

| # | Tenets |
| --- | --- |
| **Enhancing Relationship Marketing Understanding** | |
| *Relationship Marketing Theory* | |
| 1. | Beyond interpersonal and interfirm theories explaining relationship marketing effectiveness, online theories that deal with human–technology interactions can make a unique contribution to comprehensive predictions of relationship marketing performance outcomes. |
| 2. | Network theory helps explain relationship marketing effectiveness in consumer markets. Individual customers' decisions and behaviors are affected not just by the focal seller's actions but also by the quality, breadth, and composition of their customer-to-customer networks. |
| *Relationship Marketing Framework* | |
| 3. | The constructs of media richness and parasocial interaction capture customers' cognitive responses to sellers' technology-delivered relationship marketing activities and mediate the impact of such activities on relationship marketing performance. |
| 4. | Experience and flow constructs capture customers' conative responses to sellers' technology-delivered relationship marketing activities and mediate the impact of such activities on relationship marketing performance. |
| 5. | The construct of customer engagement captures customers' behavioral responses to sellers' relationship marketing activities, beyond purchase behaviors. It makes a unique contribution to the overall value of a customer to the firm. |

*Table 7.1* Continued

| # | Tenets |
|---|--------|

**Enhancing Relationship Marketing Applications**

*Relationship Marketing Dynamics*

6. Specific tools used by sellers, such as to communicate with customers or invest in the relationship, feature differential effects over the course of the customer relationship, such that customer journey designers may systematically maximize their performance impacts.

7. Incorporating big data will increase the predictive power of models for determining customer relationship states.

*Relationship Marketing Strategies*

8. Social media company profiles, mobile apps, embodied virtual agents, and augmented reality can enhance customer-perceived seller expertise and communication and drive relational mechanisms, such as commitment, trust, and engagement.

9. Data privacy policies and reputation signals can enhance customer-perceived seller expertise and relationship investments and drive relational mechanisms, such as trust.

10. Gamification and status bestowal can enhance customer-perceived relationship investments and relationship benefits and drive relational mechanisms, such as gratitude, reciprocity norms, and experience.

11. Privacy concerns represent a substantive dark side of relationship marketing in the digital age and may act as existential threats to relationship marketing performance.

*Relationship Marketing Targeting*

12. In online environments, relationship marketing effectiveness is contingent on various customer factors, such as customer age.

13. Testing the effects of relationship marketing programs on different groups of customers with field experiments, prior to full roll-outs, increases programs' return on investments.

14. Relationship marketing strategies that effectively factor in and deliberately manage social effects (e.g., bystander effects, group effects) rather than exclusively focusing on the target customer increase relationship marketing performance.

knowledge, then identify current opportunities and challenges that might be resolved by future inquiry. Then we aim to describe ways to apply relationship marketing for superior performance, which demands insights into how to address the dynamics of customer–seller relationships, develop effective strategies for building and maintaining relations, and identify appropriate target customers for specific relationship marketing programs.

For each area, we start by integrating state-of-the-art insights as a point of departure, revealing the promising directions that relationship marketing researchers should chase to move the domain forward.

## Enhancing Relationship Marketing Understanding

Part I of this book focused on building a sound understanding of relationship marketing, based on a review of the multitude of theories that help explain relationship marketing's effects and a comprehensive causal framework linking relationship marketing investments to performance outcomes. In parallel, in this section, we briefly synthesize state-of-the-art relationship marketing theory and a framework, then proceed to outline fruitful research opportunities in each area.

### Relationship Marketing Theory

Relationship marketing research to date looks back on a rich theoretical landscape. Theories from various disciplines have contributed to our understanding of relationship marketing phenomena. Yet the advances of the digital age are changing how relational interactions take place, laying new avenues for theory, which also can spur insights on relationships in technology-mediated environments.

### Research State

Academics have turned to a multitude of theoretical domains to enhance understanding of relationship marketing phenomena. Insights from diverse disciplines (e.g., economics, sociology, social psychology, psychology) thus inform relationship marketing theory. A review of its historic development depicts a broad pattern, proceeding from the application of institutional, macro-level theories (e.g., economics, sociology) to more individual, micro-level theoretical perspectives (e.g., social psychology, psychology) over time.

Evolutionary psychology, which combines modern psychology with evolutionary biology (Saad 2011; Saad and Gill 2000), also has been valuable for carving out the basic functioning of human relationships, as well as specifying gratitude and unfairness as the two psychological mechanisms that can parsimoniously explain the effectiveness of relationship marketing. Both gratitude and unfairness are universal, hereditary, and deeply ingrained, and they serve to reinforce cooperation within groups to ensure human survival. Due to these characteristics, both mechanisms are indispensable to relationship marketing; gratitude serves to reinforce relationship reciprocity and cooperation (Palmatier et al. 2009), while perceived unfairness can lead to the destruction of relationships as a form of punishment (Samaha, Palmatier, and Dant 2011).

Whether promoting or impeding relationships, gratitude and unfairness represent twin pillars of relationship marketing.

Supported by these pillars, three main types of marketing relationships prevail, with different but complementary theoretical foci and key constructs. First, research on interpersonal relationships (e.g., customer-to-salesperson) relies on social exchange theory and evolutionary psychology and uses customer commitment, trust, gratitude, and reciprocity norms to explain the impact of relationship marketing investments on performance outcomes (Morgan and Hunt 1994; Palmatier et al. 2009). Second, interfirm relationship research (e.g., customer-to-salesperson, customer-to-seller firm, or customer firm-to-seller firm networks) extends beyond interpersonal relationships by using network theory to underscore key roles of relationship quality (i.e., composite of commitment, trust, gratitude, and reciprocity norms), breadth, and composition for explaining relationship marketing performance (Van Den Bulte and Wuyts 2007). Third, online relationships (e.g., individual/firm customer-to-technology) have emerged more recently, in which settings Internet technology acts as a communication transmitter and replaces direct human interactions (Steinhoff et al. 2018). Acquiring a deep understanding of the functioning of online relationships and incorporating online relationships into an overall theoretical framework of relationship marketing requires a broadened theoretical lens, which then opens a panorama of research opportunities.

## Research Avenues

To advance relationship marketing theory, we recommend two main avenues. First, studying online relationships requires fresh, new theoretical lenses. In this developing domain, researchers largely revert to theories that derive from offline relationship marketing, such as commitment–trust theory (Steinhoff et al. 2018). Although commitment, trust, and reciprocity are unlikely to disappear from successful online relational exchanges, other constructs and related theories warrant attention too. The role of Internet technology in mediating interactions between relational partners (partly or fully) suggests the need for theories from domains that study human–technology interactions explicitly, such as computer and communication sciences. In particular, flow (Csikszentmihalyi 1975), media richness (Daft and Lengel 1986), and parasocial interaction (Giles 2002; Horton and Wohl 1956) theories may offer new insights into relationship marketing effectiveness in online settings. Beyond testing these online-specific theories separately, relationship marketing research could compare and contrast their contributions to each theoretical stream (interpersonal, interfirm, and online) and their ability to predict relationship marketing performance outcomes. Customer–seller relationships in the digital age typically involve hybrid constellations that encompass interpersonal, interfirm, and online elements in an omnichannel environment (e.g., web, mobile app, phone, retail, salesperson). Integrating all three relationship types, which build systematically on each other, should produce a more comprehensive relationship marketing theory. Yet researchers also should be aware of the difficulty of gaining acceptance of any such conceptual models, due to the widespread bias against using multiple theoretical perspectives. On the basis of our assessment and review of prior literature, we argue that understanding and integrating the unique contributions of various theoretical perspectives is indispensable for a holistic relationship marketing theory.

> **Tenet 1:** *Beyond interpersonal and interfirm theories explaining relationship marketing effectiveness, online theories that deal with human–technology interactions can make a unique contribution to comprehensive predictions of relationship marketing performance outcomes.*

Second, the scope of network theory (Van Den Bulte and Wuyts 2007) is broadening, from business-to-business-focused theoretical approaches to consumer relational contexts. Even sellers marketing to consumers encounter networks and must develop their relationships accordingly. The digital age facilitates consumer-to-consumer interactions on an unprecedented scale, such as through social networks, and they encompass both interpersonal and online ties. Knowingly or unknowingly, sellers often market to groups of customers rather than individual customers, and the network itself has relevant impacts on consumption decisions and behaviors (Harmeling et al. 2017a). From a theoretical standpoint, relationship marketing should acknowledge findings that derive from sociological network theory, with its notable contributions toward understanding interfirm relationships that always have consisted of networks of relational ties. Network theory, which centers on the relationship quality, breadth, and composition among relational partners, also can inform consumer-based relationship marketing theory. In the digital age, relationship marketers need to understand individual customers' roles in their network, identify key influencers among this network, and limit negative network effects to keep problems with single customers from spreading across a larger network.

> **Tenet 2:** *Network theory helps explain relationship marketing effectiveness in consumer markets. Individual customers' decisions and behaviors are affected not just by the focal seller's actions but also by the quality, breadth, and composition of their customer-to-customer networks.*

## Relationship Marketing Framework

With a foundation in relationship marketing theory and an abundance of empirical research, an overall relationship marketing causal framework has evolved, delineating how seller relationship marketing investments influence customer relational mechanisms, which in turn affect seller relationship marketing performance outcomes. The digital age has added other constructs that may enrich understanding of relational mechanisms and systematically broaden the scope of relationship marketing.

## Research State

Extant relationship marketing research proposes a three-stage causal model to understand relationship marketing effectiveness: seller relationship marketing investments → customer relational mechanisms → seller relationship marketing performance outcomes (Palmatier et al. 2006). Specifically, customer relational mechanisms mediate the investment–performance linkage. With their relationship marketing investments, companies seek to spur favorable relational emotions, cognitions, conations, and behaviors among customers (i.e., gratitude, commitment, trust, reciprocity norms, relationship breadth, relationship composition, relationship velocity, and loyalty). These customer responses represent the most common explanations researchers offer for the positive influence of relationships on firm performance. Relationship marketers also seek to avoid negative emotions, such as customer perceptions of unfairness.

Relationship marketing investments consist of dedicated relationship marketing strategies or programs, designed and implemented to build, grow, and maintain strong relationships with customers. Three broad categories of relationship marketing investments establish financial, social, and structural programs (Palmatier, Gopalakrishna, and Houston 2006; Palmatier et al. 2007). Financial relationship marketing investments offer customers some kind of economic benefit, such as special discounts, giveaways, free shipping, or extended payment terms, in exchange for their loyal behaviors. Social relationship marketing investments employ social engagements (e.g., meals, sporting events) or frequent, customized communication to personalize the customer relationship and convey the customer's elevated status. Structural relationship marketing investments are relational investments in enhanced customer efficiency and/or productivity, which customers likely would not make themselves, such as an electronic order-processing interface or customized packaging. These different types of investments exhibit differential effects on customers and have varying levels of return. In the short term, social programs have the highest payoff, structural programs break even, and financial programs fail to pay off.

Through these financial, social, or structural relationship marketing investments, sellers seek to stimulate relational mechanisms and capture customers' emotions, cognitions, conations, and behaviors as results of their interactions with sellers. Establishing a causal sequence among emotional, cognitive, conative, and behavioral processes, short-term emotions typically affect longer-term cognitions; jointly, emotions and cognitions influence conations. Emotions, cognitions, and conations in turn affect short- and long-term relational behaviors. Relational mechanisms reflect the intangible value that a firm receives from its relational bonds with a customer; they mediate the effect of relationship marketing investments on performance.

Strong relationships with customers likely bring about increased financial and nonfinancial performance for the seller. Among financial relationship marketing performance outcomes, sales- and profitability-based performance indicators can be distinguished. Sales-based outcomes look at revenues, measuring annual sales growth, diversity, volatility, or share of wallet for example. Profitability-based outcome measures are more comprehensive, in that they acknowledge sales and cost effects to establish relationship marketing performance. Customer lifetime value (CLV), customer engagement value (CEV), and return on investment (ROI) represent key concepts for evaluating the profit ramifications of relationship marketing investments (Gupta and Zeithaml 2006; Kumar and Reinartz 2016; Kumar 2017). Effective relationship marketing investments also can evoke nonfinancial benefits for the seller, which may not have direct or immediate implications for the seller's balance sheet. Such nonfinancial relationship marketing performance usually stems from the seller's advanced knowledge, due to customers' engagement and loyalty toward that seller.

*Research Avenues*

To derive a more complete picture of customer–seller relationships and account for the specific characteristics of online relationships, research must expand the constructs used to capture customer relational mechanisms. To date, online relationship marketing research focuses on established relational mechanisms (Steinhoff et al. 2018). Constructs such as gratitude, commitment, trust, reciprocity norms, or loyalty will continue to play primary roles in successful relational exchanges. The digital landscape in which today's relationships take place also broadens and further substantiates the scope of relationship marketing–relevant mechanisms. Several evolving constructs thus demand researchers' attention and profound empirical investigations.

First, media richness (Daft and Lengel 1986) and parasocial interactions (Giles 2002; Horton and Wohl 1956) may contribute additional insights to existing cognitive relational mechanisms. Media richness is particularly well suited to assess customers' evaluation of sellers' uses of omnichannel communication. For example, relationship marketers need to determine which level of media richness customers prefer for any given communication. Likewise, media richness may prove differentially effective at different stages of the customer journey (i.e., dynamic effects). Continued research thus should assess the joint performance impacts of the overall mix of omnichannel communication media, in terms of each channel's unique contribution and synergies across channels. Overall, relationship marketers need insights that describe how they can establish effective omnichannel relationships by encouraging relational mechanisms that span different channels and leverage varied interfaces. Parasocial interaction also is increasingly relevant for customers who interact with nonhuman salespeople or service providers, such as anthropomorphic, embodied virtual agents, chatbots, or robots. Therefore, research needs to investigate the extent to which, and how, technology-driven interactions with customers are able to mimic the feelings evoked by interpersonal interactions. For example, can nonhuman company representatives stimulate gratitude emotions or reciprocal behaviors among customers? Embodied virtual agents likely have both bright and dark sides. Depending on the situation, customers may even prefer a nonhuman counterpart to solve a specific issue. Academic research is needed to establish the ideal level of anthropomorphism in embodied virtual agents. With technological advances, embodied virtual agents become more and more humanoid; the notion of the uncanny valley suggests that too much similarity with humans may decrease their acceptance and likeability though (Mori 2012). In the end, it will be important to determine the performance impact of media richness and parasocial interaction relative to other, more established, emotional, cognitive, conative, and behavioral constructs.

*Tenet 3: The constructs of media richness and parasocial interaction capture customers' cognitive responses to sellers' technology-delivered relationship marketing activities and mediate the impact of such activities on relationship marketing performance.*

Second, customer-perceived experiences (Lemon and Verhoef 2016) and a state of flow (Csikszentmihalyi 1975) may drive relationship marketing effectiveness in a conative sense. In recent research, customer experience provides a comprehensive measure of customers' responses to firms' relationship marketing efforts throughout the customer journey. Most extant research is conceptual in nature; continued research should assess customer experience empirically (Lemon and Verhoef 2016). To start, relationship marketing researchers need to come up with a solid measurement instrument that captures the essence of the customer experience. Thereafter, research agendas should be devoted to the nomological net of the customer experience, identifying its antecedents and performance outcomes. A holistic view reflects how customers judge their overall experience throughout the customer journey, spanning the overall relationship with a seller across all touchpoints. Understanding the drivers that enhance the customer experience can help relationship marketers improve their customer journey and touchpoint design (Lemon and Verhoef 2016). The digital age, and with it fluent customer–technology interactions independent of time or location constraints, increases relationship marketers' interest in the concept of flow. Experiencing fun and pleasurable flow states when interacting online with a seller may heighten customers' bonds with the firm and drive their future behaviors. Researchers thus should seek to identify which online relationship marketing activities (e.g., gamification) are most effective for putting customers into a temporary flow state. Another avenue might determine the effect of flow on customers' behaviors and thus relationship marketing performance. Such studies need to be dynamic too, to reflect how the effectiveness of flow states may vary over the course of the customer journey and relationship life cycle.

> *Tenet 4: Experience and flow constructs capture customers' conative responses to sellers' technology-delivered relationship marketing activities and mediate the impact of such activities on relationship marketing performance.*

Third, customer engagement has broadened the range of relationship-relevant customer behaviors, above and beyond transaction-focused loyalty constructs. Word-of-mouth always has been a prominent feature in relationship marketing, because this customer behavior helps seller firms acquire new customers while simultaneously increasing existing customers' loyalty behaviors (Garnefeld et al. 2013). Yet the traditional focus of relationship marketing has been on stimulating customers' (re)purchase behaviors to drive performance. Recent research institutionalizes seller-related behaviors beyond purchases, using the umbrella term of customer engagement and building on the notion that the digital age facilitates and broadens the reach of non–purchase-related behaviors (Harmeling et al. 2017b; van Doorn et al. 2010). Despite conceptual arguments and empirical evidence of a positive effect of customer engagement on relationship marketing performance for customer engagement value (CEV) (Kumar 2017; Kumar et al. 2010), important research questions remain. For example, which relationship marketing strategies effectively foster either customer loyalty (i.e., repurchase) or customer engagement (i.e., referral, influencer, and knowledge behaviors), or both? What are the returns on investments in loyalty versus engagement marketing strategies? Moreover, it would be valuable to analyze which customer profile (e.g., heavy purchaser and light engager versus light purchaser and heavy engager) is most profitable in terms of overall customer value to the firm.

*Tenet 5: The construct of customer engagement captures customers' behavioral responses to sellers' relationship marketing activities beyond purchase behaviors. It makes a unique contribution to the overall value of a customer to the firm.*

## Enhancing Relationship Marketing Applications

Part II of this book synthesizes current knowledge about how to apply relationship marketing tactics and strategies for optimal effectiveness. Specifically, managers need to acknowledge relationship marketing dynamics, design viable strategies for building and maintaining relationships, and target these strategies appropriately to the customers most likely to respond favorably. Therefore, in this section, we review state-of-the-art relationship marketing dynamics, strategies, and targeting then carve some promising paths for relationship marketing research that aims to advance the science and practice of relationship marketing in the digital age.

### Relationship Marketing Dynamics

Relationships are inherently dynamic. Yet it is only relatively recently that relationship marketing research has developed advanced insights regarding how to deal with these constantly changing relationships. Of course, the digital age brings about new opportunities as well as challenges.

### Research State

Adapting relationship marketing to the inherent dynamics of relationships is key for long-term success. Strategies that are effective in early stages may not work later, and vice versa. Relationship marketing research has identified many diverse concepts to delineate how relationships change over time, whether through incremental alterations or substantial disruptions. Yet a common assumption is that relational change is incremental, such that relationships progress in similar, smooth, predictable trajectories over time. According to the relationship life cycle stages view, for example, all relationships follow a generic four-stage trajectory, from an exploratory or early stage to a growth or development stage to a maturity or maintenance stage to a decline or recovery stage (Dwyer, Schurr, and Oh 1987). More recent relationship marketing research embraces more dynamic, less path-dependent models to describe the trajectory of customer–seller relationships. Systematically building on the life cycle approach, the relationship velocity, relationship state, and state migration perspectives offer more fine-grained assessments. The relationship velocity perspective argues that the rate and direction of change in key relational constructs must be considered to understand relationship dynamics (Palmatier et al. 2013). A perspective that embraces relationship states and migration mechanisms provides a synthesis of life cycle stages and relationship velocity conceptualizations (Zhang et al. 2016). This view suggests four typical relationship states (transactional, transitional, communal, damaged) and five migration patterns—three positive (exploration, endowment, recovery) and two negative (neglect, betrayal)—by which relationships move between states.

Not all relationships change in incremental fashion though. Rather, during transformational relationship events, discrete encounters between exchange partners significantly disconfirm relational expectations (positively or negatively) and result in dramatic, discontinuous changes to the relationship's nature and its course (Harmeling et al. 2015). Specifically, negative disconfirmations become transformational events with detrimental, destructive consequences, especially when relational expectations exist, such that they are more transformational for strong relationships than for less-established ones. Positive disconfirmations instead are most powerful for enhancing relationships marked by low expectations. Positively disconfirming relational events take underdeveloped relationships to the next level and transform them rather than affirming already solidified relationships.

*Research Avenues*

Two promising research avenues—one substantive and one methodological—emerge as effective routes to enhance our understanding of relationship marketing dynamics. On the substantive side, dynamic relationship marketing research should seek to identify viable instruments to manage relational change. Extant research identifies communication, relationship investments, or avoiding conflict as important strategies to drive relationship velocity or foster favorable state migrations (Palmatier et al. 2013; Zhang et al. 2016). In response to calls from both academics and practitioners for better descriptions of sellers' systematic customer journey designs and management across various channels (Lemon and Verhoef 2016; Marketing Science Institute 2018), continued research should turn exciting recent insights into actionable guidelines. In the vast toolbox currently at relationship marketers' disposal, which communication tools (e.g., interpersonal communication, artificial intelligence–based communication) work best in which stage of the relationship? How and when should different investments (e.g., rewards) be deployed over the course of the relationship? A persistent research gap pertains to the dynamic performance ramifications of loyalty programs in particular. Further studies in this domain should investigate how customers in different relational states respond to continuously receiving rewards and how loyalty programs can strengthen the customer–seller relationship over time.

*Tenet 6: Specific tools used by sellers, such as to communicate with customers or invest in the relationship, feature differential effects over the course of the customer relationship, such that customer journey designers may systematically maximize their performance impacts.*

Methodologically, sellers should seek to benefit from the data-rich environments in which customer–seller relationships take place and systematically collect and incorporate additional information sources into their models to estimate and predict relationship dynamics. The combination of subjective customer survey data and objective customer relationship data can reveal dynamic relationship states over time (Zhang et al. 2016). Seller firms then could add in big data to generate even deeper insights about customers and their relational dynamics. For example, firms should turn to social media; customers' personal profiles often provide valuable information about their life circumstances, lifestyles, or major life events (e.g., graduating from college, getting married, having kids), all of which will alter their relationship with the firm—which means they can be used to inform the company's design and targeting of relational investments. Tracking customers' omnichannel usage of company websites or mobile apps (e.g., frequency, duration, preferred features) also can provide insights into customers' overall relationship engagement. Finally, analyzing customers' seller-related conversations on the Internet (e.g., sentiment analysis) can clarify why customers behave the way they do and diagnose potential transformational relationship events. Overall, including big data in dynamic relationship marketing models should improve the predictive power of existing and emerging models.

*Tenet 7: Incorporating big data will increase the predictive power of models for determining customer relationship states.*

### Relationship Marketing Strategies

Empirical relationship marketing research offers in-depth insights into the effectiveness of diverse relationship marketing strategies employed by companies to build and maintain customer relationships. The digital age involves a plethora of new and emerging instruments to pursue these strategies. Their effectiveness for enhancing relationship marketing performance has yet to be determined though, opening up a vast range of research avenues.

*Research State*

Relationship marketers' efforts center on building and maintaining strong customer relationships. A meta-analysis of relational drivers, based on purposeful strategies for relationship building, shows that conflict has the largest impact, even if a detrimental one, on relationship quality (Palmatier et al. 2006). Thus, people weigh negative elements more heavily than positive ones when assessing their relationships with sellers. The strongest positive determinants of relationship quality are seller expertise, communication, relationship investment, relationship benefits, and similarity between exchange partners. Gratitude catalyzes customer relationships, stimulating both short-term and long-term reciprocal behaviors. Fostering customer perceptions about the seller's free will, benevolent motives, and high risk in making a relationship investment can effectively leverage gratitude mechanisms. Customers' own need for the specific investment offered also might increase the level of gratitude they experience (Palmatier et al. 2009). In online environments, the characteristic anonymity makes risk-reducing signals highly influential for relationship formation; it also allows online relationships to form and end quickly and supports relationship formation and influence among dissimilar partners. Due to the ease of forming and maintaining online unilateral relationships, customers can develop extensive, diverse portfolios of unilateral relationships, which then provide important insights for their decision making. Yet similar to offline relationships, reciprocity remains key for successful online relationships. Reciprocated, rather than unilateral, online relationships strongly increase customers' psychological commitment and financially relevant behaviors (Kozlenkova et al. 2017).

To maintain relationships, sellers must avoid the bad rather than just adding more good to the relationship. The most substantial relationship poison is unfairness, such as might be experienced by bystander customers. Customer-perceived unfairness undermines customer cooperation, flexibility, and performance; it aggravates the negative effects of conflict and opportunism (Samaha, Palmatier, and Dant 2011). The digital age also fosters privacy concerns. Especially if companies suffer data breaches, the performance effects are notably negative. To remedy such effects, they need to establish privacy policies that provide customers with transparency and control (Martin, Borah, and Palmatier 2017).

Noting the beneficial performance effects of relationship marketing, many seller firms seek to institutionalize their efforts throughout the organization. Two instruments with particular relevance are customer-centric organizational structures and loyalty programs. After the costs of implementation have amortized, which may take several years, the adoption of customer-centric organizational structures can enhance company performance. Specifically, customer centricity pays off in industries with few other customer-centric firms, low competitive intensity, low commoditization, and a prevalence of high margins (Lee et al. 2015). Loyalty programs are complex relationship marketing instruments, so relationship marketers need to take a holistic view and consider each program's psychological, strategic, and operational elements (Steinhoff and Palmatier 2016). Among psychological elements, it is important to realize that loyalty programs can simultaneously spur positive and negative emotional and cognitive responses. Focusing on one or the other may lead to a misspecification of the loyalty program–performance linkage. In terms of strategic elements, managers need to choose the structure and rewards provided by the program. Such decisions should take a longer-term approach, because frequent rule changes raise fairness and transparency concerns. Finally, the operational elements of loyalty programs reflect how the program is conducted; managers should design reward delivery, timing, and targeting to enhance the program's effectiveness.

In turn, several best practices emerge from extant relationship marketing research and practice. To shelter the customer relationship from detrimental forces, sellers should work to avoid conflict and unfairness. Instead, if they leverage the positive forces of seller expertise, communication, and relationship investments, they can propel relationship performance. In addition, stimulating gratitude and reciprocity norms among customers effectively strengthens relationships in both the short and long runs. To pursue and achieve these strategies systematically, seller firms should use customer-centric organizational structures, if appropriate in their specific industry setting, and loyalty programs. To monitor and ensure effectiveness, managers should assess their relationship marketing programs constantly and consistently.

## Research Avenues

The digital age brings about technological innovations that relationship marketers may use to drive their relationship marketing effectiveness. Established best practices—emphasizing the primary roles of seller expertise, communication, relationship investments, and benefits for driving relational mechanisms—still are key; relationship marketers' toolboxes for building these outcomes are growing ever more expansive. For example, to foster communication with customers through online channels and stimulate their engagement, seller companies use corporate social media profiles, mobile apps, embodied virtual agents, and augmented reality. They therefore need data privacy policies and reputation signals to build trust among their customers in more anonymous online environments. If they want to spark gratitude and reciprocity norms and enhance customers' experience, sellers can provide relational benefits, such as gamification elements or status bestowal for select customers. Most current research into the efficacy of these instruments focuses on a single relational instrument, seeking an in-depth understanding of that particular tool. Future relationship marketing research should go beyond the isolated designs of the different tools to determine the relative efficacy of different instruments across relational constructs. For example, if managers' goal is to increase customers' sense of gratitude, flow, or engagement, which relationship marketing tools are best suited for the specific purpose?

*Tenet 8: Social media company profiles, mobile apps, embodied virtual agents, and augmented reality can enhance customer-perceived seller expertise and communication and drive relational mechanisms, such as commitment, trust, and engagement.*

*Tenet 9: Data privacy policies and reputation signals can enhance customer-perceived seller expertise and relationship investments and drive relational mechanisms, such as trust.*

*Tenet 10: Gamification and status bestowal can enhance customer-perceived relationship investments and relationship benefits and drive relational mechanisms, such as gratitude, reciprocity norms, and experience.*

Although relationship marketing research has primarily focused on the intended positive effects of relationship marketing, academic insights on the dark sides of these relationships (e.g., unfairness) also have increased (Samaha, Palmatier, and Dant 2011; Steinhoff and Palmatier 2016). Acknowledging the unintended, negative effects of relationship marketing and learning how to circumvent them remains a priority for research. Specifically, the digital age has brought about substantial threats to customer–seller relationships in the form of privacy concerns. Building on initial insights that underscore the roles of transparency and perceived control (Martin, Borah, and Palmatier 2017), researchers might consider and investigate privacy policies as strategic relationship marketing tools rather than as a mere legal duty. Documented policies should be designed systematically and from a customer perspective, and then studies should test which privacy policy designs most effectively dissipate and mitigate customer reservations. Ultimately, if sellers cannot overcome customers' concerns and distrust when it comes to data privacy, even the best-intended relationship marketing efforts are doomed.

> **Tenet 11:** *Big data and concurrent privacy concerns represent a substantive dark side of relationship marketing in the digital age and may act as existential threats to relationship marketing performance.*

## Relationship Marketing Targeting

Some customers represent better targets for relationship marketing efforts than others. Extant research lists multiple factors that can enhance relationship marketing effectiveness. The digital age makes relationship marketing targeting both easier (i.e., field experiments to test efforts) and more complex (i.e., customers purchasing in groups rather than as individuals), and both implications constitute interesting opportunities for further inquiry.

### Research State

Because relationship marketing is not effective for all customers, and some customers seek to avoid relationships, sellers must determine where to allocate their relationship marketing resources across their customer portfolios. Targeting thus is a key challenge. The effectiveness of relationship marketing varies with how much customers value and respond to sellers' efforts to build and maintain strong relationships.

A common view is that relationship marketing should be most effective for customers who display high relationship orientations (Palmatier et al. 2008). These customers likely reciprocate the seller's relationship marketing efforts by, for example, responding positively to its requests for a meeting or information. When customers have a low relationship orientation, though, they perceive relationship marketing activities as a waste of time, unwanted hassle, or extra cost. As a consequence, these customers typically prefer transactional sellers and want to avoid relational involvement. To promote a customer's desire for relational governance, sellers might leverage various customer-, industry-, and culture-specific aspects.

Customer-specific drivers of relationship orientation include individual-level elements that differ for any specific customer. Specifically, relationship marketing tends to be more effective if targeted to customers with greater relationship proneness and a higher level of product category involvement and dependence, as well as when those customers have relationship-centric reward systems in place. Industry-specific drivers represent macro-level factors, pertaining to the overall context in which relationships take place. Overall, relationships and thus relationship marketing efforts are more powerful in industries featuring a higher degree of exchange and product uncertainty, high relational norms, in service industries, and in business-to-business industries (Palmatier et al. 2006).

Finally, macro-level, culture-specific aspects determine relationship orientations and relationship marketing performance in different countries and international regions. High levels of collectivism, power distance, and uncertainty avoidance, as well as low levels of masculinity, favor relationship marketing performance. Overall, relationship marketing is more effective outside the United States for increasing business performance (Samaha, Beck, and Palmatier 2014).

*Research Avenues*

Further research can specify when and for which customers relationship marketing works. To date, research on online relationships in the digital age mostly has focused on the main effects of relationship marketing strategies, typical of the early stages in any research field. Yet the specific characteristics of relationships in online settings (e.g., anonymity, more channels) suggest that, even beyond the already established contingencies, different customers demand different digitally supported relational approaches. For example, some customers may choose to provide feedback through an e-mail; others prefer to comment on social media. Some customers still want to receive a printed invoice in the mail, and others favor paperless formats. One driver of such preferences might be customers' age, which typically correlates with their technological aptitude. Relationship marketing to younger versus older customers may be equally effective if sellers cater to their specific needs and wants. Younger customers may favor quick, technology-mediated interactions (e.g., consulting a chatbot via a mobile app); older customers might gain more pleasure from interpersonal relationships (e.g., talking to a service manager on the phone). Marketers need to know precisely how to adapt these approaches, so further research should examine customer contingencies with respect to the evolving landscape of online relationships.

> **Tenet 12:** *In online environments, relationship marketing effectiveness is contingent on various customer factors, such as customer age.*

Recent research makes the case for conducting field experiments to help relationship marketing managers improve and optimize their targeting decisions (Gneezy 2017; Meyer 2017). These experiments offer an effective method to test the overall impact of relationship marketing efforts empirically and to identify optimal target customers by investigating a limited sample of customers before rolling out a potentially ineffective (i.e., at least to some customers) program worldwide. Relationship marketers should rely more on field experiments, due to their unquestionable benefit of treatment randomization. That is, random customer assignments powerfully circumvent the endogeneity issues that hinder studies that rely on nonexperimental data. Researchers also should seek to substantiate the effectiveness of field experiments for enhancing relationship marketing performance. For example, studies could compare the performance effects of a relationship marketing program pretested in a field experiment with a program that was rolled out fully without prior testing. Findings from such studies may help quantify the effectiveness of field experiments. Another path to pursue would be to develop field experimental blueprints that both academics and managers can use, distilling the "dos and don'ts."

*Tenet 13: Testing the effects of relationship marketing programs on different groups of customers with field experiments, prior to full roll-outs, increases programs' returns on investments.*

Customer–seller relationships do not happen in isolation. The digital age vastly facilitates customer-to-customer interactions and connections, so social relationship marketing is gaining in relevance. Recent research prioritizes such social phenomena, investigating bystander effects in loyalty programs, social network effects of one-time reward campaigns, and group conformity effects in product purchasing (Steinhoff and Palmatier 2016; Ascarza et al. 2017; Harmeling et al. 2017a). Sellers must be aware of and ready to manage these social effects to their advantage. Relationship marketing research in turn should provide a comprehensive summary of social effects in marketing relationships, broadening traditional one-to-one approaches to acknowledge that individual customers always are embedded in larger networks of close and distant ties and connections with fellow customers. Furthermore, reviewing both bright and dark sides of customer networks can reveal a battery of group-related mechanisms (e.g., social comparison, status, envy, unfairness, conformity, differentiation, solidarity, identification), which relationship marketers can use to refine their strategies: those targeting focal customers but also those that affect observers, to mitigate detrimental and promote favorable social effects.

*Tenet 14: Relationship marketing strategies that effectively factor in and deliberately manage social effects (e.g., bystander effects, group effects) rather than exclusively focusing on the target customer increase relationship marketing performance.*

## Summary

This chapter summarizes the insights we have established throughout this book by covering both what we know thus far about relationship marketing (theory, frameworks) and its applications (strategies, targeting), as well as where continued research needs to shine new light. In particular, the digital age is marked by new and substantive questions, demanding profound efforts by relationship marketing researchers to understand both how technology mediates relationships and how network structures are redefining them.

From a theoretical standpoint, the partial or full mediation by Internet technologies can be understood by introducing concepts from other research domains, especially those that put a priority on understanding human–technology interactions. Media richness, parasocial interaction, and flow theories likely can inform predictions about which relationship marketing tactics will be most effective for online connections. In addition to testing each online-specific theory, relationship marketing researchers should compare the predictions and contributions obtained from various theoretical streams (i.e., interpersonal, interfirm, and online). Furthermore, as networks grow more prominent and more complex, network theory can help explicate how and why digitally mediated, consumer-to-consumer interactions continue to expand to encompass interpersonal and online ties, as well as define the roles of individual customers in various networks (e.g., key influencers, those likely to spread negative word-of-mouth).

In addition to integrating more theories, another extension of research could apply more diverse, alternative constructs that reflect the unique characteristics and traits of online relationships. In accordance with our recommendations for theoretical extensions, media richness (e.g., evaluations of omnichannel communications) and parasocial interaction (e.g., with robots, chatbots, embodied virtual agents) constructs likely can add insights to current views on cognitive relational mechanisms. Furthermore, customer experience and flow are conative constructs that might enhance relationship marketing effectiveness, reflecting how customers respond to relationship marketing efforts during their entire interaction with the seller. Such interactions also might lead to customer engagement, which implies a broad span of relevant customer behaviors, not just transactional loyalty or repurchases. Customer engagement is particularly resonant in the digital age, when technology facilitates and broadens the influence of customers' non–purchase-related behaviors, such as reviews or word-of-mouth.

More substantively, relationship marketers need better tools to manage relationships as they change, with varying velocity, so that they can maintain beneficial relationships across the entire customer journey design and reinforce it across a variety of channels. To support these efforts, sellers should exploit the data-rich environments surrounding today's customer–seller relationships, incorporate big data into their estimation models, and predict relationship dynamics using all the data at their disposal. As these recommendations indicate, relationship marketers' options for managing customer relationships keep expanding, to include social media, mobile apps, embodied virtual agents, and augmented reality. To evoke gratitude and reciprocity while also improving customer experiences, relational benefits can come through gamification elements and status bestowal, but at the same time, sellers must issue clear data privacy policies and reputation signals to build trust and mitigate customers' legitimate concerns in anonymous online environments. These novel instruments have relatively well-studied individual effects; their combined efficacy for reinforcing relational mechanisms is less clear.

This combined efficacy likely depends on various contingencies that determine whether relationship marketing will be effective, or instead evoke negative effects, among various target customers. In particular, relationship marketing research should uncover different social influences (e.g., bystander, social network, group conformity) on customer–seller relationships to help managers avoid the bad while augmenting the good. One way to identify relevant contingencies, as well as the best customer relationship targets, is to conduct field experiments.

## Takeaways

- An abundance of research generates knowledge about how relationship marketing works, yet in the digital age, new substantial issues arise that need to be explained more profoundly by relationship marketing researchers.
- Theories that deal with human–technology interactions can enrich relationship marketing; networked customer-to-customer relations in the digital age also extend the theoretical scope to business-to-consumer relationships.
- Media richness, parasocial interaction, experience, flow, and engagement constitute an expanded battery of relevant relational mechanisms that might mediate the impact of relationship marketing investments on relationship marketing performance.
- Insights on the differential effects of relationship marketing tools over the course of the customer relationship can help marketers design customer journeys with more positive performance impacts.
- Incorporating big data should improve the predictive validity of relationship models.
- Emerging relationship marketing tools can stimulate different relational mechanisms.
- Privacy concerns represent a pressing dark side of relationship marketing in the digital age.

- Customers differ in their affinity toward online relationships, so sellers should develop targeted online approaches for various segments.
- Field experiments can increase the return on investments in relationship marketing programs.
- Social effects, such as bystander effects in loyalty programs, social network effects of a one-time reward campaigns, and group conformity effects for product purchases, have greater relevance for relationship marketing in the digital age.

## References

Ascarza, Eva, Peter Ebbes, Oded Netzer, and Matthew Danielson (2017), "Beyond the Target Customer: Social Effects of Customer Relationship Management Campaigns." *Journal of Marketing Research* 54 (June), 347–63.

Berry, Leonard L. (1983), "Relationship Marketing." In *Emerging Perspectives on Services Marketing*, eds. Leonard L. Berry, G. L. Shostack, and G. D. Upah, 25–8. Chicago: American Marketing Association.

Csikszentmihalyi, Mihali (1975), *Beyond Boredom and Anxiety: Experiencing Flow in Work and Play*. San Francisco: Jossey-Bass Publishers.

Daft, Richard L., and Robert H. Lengel (1986), "Organizational Information Requirements, Media Richness and Structural Design." *Management Science* 32 (5), 554–71.

Dwyer, Robert F., Paul H. Schurr, and Sejo Oh (1987), "Developing Buyer-Seller Relationships." *Journal of Marketing* 51 (April), 11–27.

Garnefeld, Ina, Andreas Eggert, Sabrina V. Helm, and Stephen S. Tax (2013), "Growing Existing Customers' Revenue Streams Through Customer Referral Programs." *Journal of Marketing* 77 (July), 17–32.

Giles, David C. (2002), "Parasocial Interaction: A Review of the Literature and a Model for Future Research." *Media Psychology* 4 (3), 279–305.

Gneezy, Ayelet (2017), "Field Experimentation in Marketing Research." *Journal of Marketing Research* 54 (February), 140–3.

Gupta, Sunil, and Valarie Zeithaml (2006), "Customer Metrics and Their Impact on Financial Performance." *Marketing Science* 25 (November–December), 718–39.

Harmeling, Colleen M., Jordan W. Moffett, Mark J. Arnold, and Brad D. Carlson (2017a), "Toward a Theory of Customer Engagement Marketing." *Journal of the Academy of Marketing Science* 45 (3), 312–35.

Harmeling, Colleen M., Robert W. Palmatier, Eric (Er) Fang, and Dianwen Wang (2017b), "Group Marketing: Theory, Mechanisms, and Dynamics." *Journal of Marketing* 81 (July), 1–24.

Harmeling, Colleen M., Robert W. Palmatier, Mark B. Houston, Mark J. Arnold, and Stephen A. Samaha (2015), "Transformational Relationship Events." *Journal of Marketing* 79 (September), 39–62.

Horton, Donald, and Richard Wohl (1956), "Mass Communication and Parasocial Interaction: Observation on Intimacy at a Distance." *Psychiatry* 19, 215–29.

Kozlenkova, Irina V., Robert W. Palmatier, Eric (Er) Fang, Bangming Xiao, and Minxue Huang (2017), "Online Relationship Formation." *Journal of Marketing* 81 (3), 21–40.

Kumar, V. (2017), "A Theory of Customer Valuation: Concepts, Metrics, Strategy, and Implementation." *Journal of Marketing* 82 (January), 1–19.

Kumar, V., Lerzan Aksoy, Bas Donkers, Rajkumar Venkatesan, Thorsten Wiesel, and Sebastian Tillmanns (2010), "Undervalued or Overvalued Customers: Capturing Total Customer Engagement Value." *Journal of Service Research* 13 (3), 297–310.

Kumar, V., and Werner Reinartz (2016), "Creating Enduring Customer Value." *Journal of Marketing* 80 (November), 36–68.

Lee, Ju-Yeon, Shrihari Sridhar, Conor M. Henderson, and Robert W. Palmatier (2015), "Effect of Customer Centricity on Long-Term Financial Performance." *Marketing Science* 34 (2), 250–68.

Lemon, Katherine N., and Peter C. Verhoef (2016), "Understanding Customer Experience Throughout the Customer Journey." *Journal of Marketing* 80 (6), 69–96.

Marketing Science Institute (2018), *Research Priorities 2018–2020*. Cambridge, MA: Marketing Science Institute.

Martin, Kelly D., Abishek Borah, and Robert W. Palmatier (2017), "Data Privacy: Effects on Customer and Firm Performance." *Journal of Marketing* 81 (1), 36–58.

Meyer, Robert (2017), "Introduction to the Journal of Marketing Research Special Section on Field Experiments." *Journal of Marketing Research* 54 (February), 138–9.

Morgan, Robert M., and Shelby D. Hunt (1994), "The Commitment-Trust Theory of Relationship Marketing." *Journal of Marketing* 58 (July), 20–38.

Mori, Masahiro (2012), Translated by MacDorman, Karl F. and Norri Kageki, "The Uncanny Valley." *IEEE Robotics and Automation* 19 (2), 98–100.

Palmatier, Robert W., Rajiv P. Dant, Dhruv Grewal, and Kenneth R. Evans (2006), "Factors Influencing the Effectiveness of Relationship Marketing: A Meta-Analysis." *Journal of Marketing* 70 (October), 136–53.

Palmatier, Robert W., Srinath Gopalakrishna, and Mark B. Houston (2006), "Returns on Business-to-Business Relationship Marketing Investments: Strategies for Leveraging Profits." *Marketing Science* 25 (September–October), 477–93.

Palmatier, Robert W., Mark B. Houston, Rajiv P. Dant, and Dhruv Grewal (2013), "Relationship Velocity: Toward a Theory of Relationship Dynamics." *Journal of Marketing* 77 (January), 13–30.

Palmatier, Robert W., Cheryl Burke Jarvis, Jennifer R. Bechkoff, and Frank R. Kardes (2009), "The Role of Customer Gratitude in Relationship Marketing." *Journal of Marketing* 73 (September), 1–18.

Palmatier, Robert W., Lisa K. Scheer, Kenneth R. Evans, and Todd Arnold (2008), "Achieving Relationship Marketing Effectiveness in Business-to-Business Exchanges." *Journal of the Academy of Marketing Science* 2 (June), 174–90.

Palmatier, Robert W., Lisa K. Scheer, Mark B. Houston, Kenneth R. Evans, and Srinath Gopalakrishna (2007), "Use of Relationship Marketing Programs in Building Customer-Salesperson and Customer-Firm Relationships: Differential Influences on Financial Outcomes." *International Journal of Research in Marketing* 24 (September), 210–23.

Palmatier, Robert W., and Shrihari Sridhar (2017), *Marketing Strategy: Based on First Principles and Data Analytics*. London: Palgrave.

Saad, Gad (2011), "The Missing Link: The Biological Roots of the Business Sciences." In *Evolutionary Psychology in the Business Sciences*, ed. Gad Saad, 1–16. Berlin: Springer.

Saad, Gad, and Tripat Gill (2000), "Applications of Evolutionary Psychology in Marketing." *Psychology & Marketing* 17 (12), 1005–34.

Samaha, Stephen A., Joshua T. Beck, and Robert W. Palmatier (2014), "The Role of Culture in International Relationship Marketing." *Journal of Marketing* 78 (September), 78–98.

Samaha, Stephen A., Robert W. Palmatier, and Rajiv P. Dant (2011), "Poisoning Relationships: Perceived Unfairness in Channels of Distribution." *Journal of Marketing* 75 (May), 99–117.

Steinhoff, Lena, Denni Arli, Scott Weaven, and Irina V. Kozlenkova (2018), "Online Relationship Marketing." Working Paper.

Steinhoff, Lena, and Robert W. Palmatier (2016), "Understanding Loyalty Program Effectiveness: Managing Target and Bystander Effects." *Journal of the Academy of Marketing Science* 44 (January), 88–107.

Van Den Bulte, Christophe, and Stefan Wuyts (2007), *Social Networks and Marketing*. Cambridge, MA: Marketing Science Institute.

Van Doorn, Jenny, Katherine N. Lemon, Vikas Mittal, Stephan Nass, Doreén Pick, Peter Pirner, and Peter C. Verhoef (2010), "Customer Engagement Behavior: Theoretical Foundations and Research Directions." *Journal of Service Research* 13 (3), 253–66.

Zhang, Jonathan Z., George F. Watson IV, Robert W. Palmatier, and Rajiv P. Dant (2016), "Dynamic Relationship Marketing." *Journal of Marketing* 80 (September), 53–75.

# Glossary

**Brand-based sustainable competitive advantage:** Relies on brand awareness and the brand image built up in consumers' minds, which makes brands hard to imitate, promotes habitual buying, and offers identity benefits to customers.

**Bystanders:** The customers not targeted by a firm's relationship marketing or loyalty program.

**Commitment:** An enduring desire to maintain a valued relationship (see Customer commitment also).

**Communication:** Amount, frequency, and quality of information shared between exchange partners.

**Conflict:** Overall level of disagreement between exchange partners.

**Customer centricity:** An organization-wide philosophy that places customers' needs at the center of a company's strategic process and uses the resultant insights to make decisions.

**Customer-centric structures:** Organizational design where business units are aligned to distinct customer groups.

**Customer commitment:** An enduring desire to maintain a valued relationship (see Commitment also).

**Customer dependence:** Customer's evaluation of the value of seller-provided resources for which few alternatives are available from other sellers (see Dependence also).

**Customer engagement:** A customer's voluntary resource contribution to a firm's marketing function, going beyond financial patronage (see Engagement also).

**Customer experience:** A multidimensional construct focusing on a customer's cognitive, emotional, behavioral, sensorial, and social responses to a firm's offerings during the customer's entire journey (see Experience also).

**Customer gratitude:** Feelings of gratefulness, thankfulness, or appreciation for a benefit received (see Gratitude also).

**Customer loyalty:** A collection of attitudes aligned with a series of purchase behaviors that systematically favor one entity over competing entities (see Loyalty also).

**Customer reciprocity norms:** Internalized patterns of behaviors and feelings that regulate the balance of obligations between exchange partners (see Reciprocity norms also).

**Customer relational mechanisms:** Customers' emotions, cognitions, conations, and behaviors stemming from their interactions with the seller; they mediate or transmit the effect of relationship marketing investments on performance.

**Customer relationship management:** The managerially relevant, organization-wide, customer-focused application of relationship marketing, using information technology to achieve performance objectives.

**Customer trust:** Confidence in an exchange partner's reliability and integrity (see Trust also).

**Customer unfairness:** A customer's view of the degree to which the ratio of his or her received outcomes relative to inputs, compared with the corresponding input–outcome ratios of other customers, seems unacceptable or inequitable (see Unfairness also).

**Dependence:** Customer's evaluation of the value of seller-provided resources for which few alternatives are available from other sellers (see Customer dependence also).

**Digital age:** The present time, when most information is in a digital form, especially when compared to the time when computers were not used.

**Engagement:** A customer's voluntary resource contribution to a firm's marketing function, going beyond financial patronage (see Customer engagement also).

**Experience:** A multidimensional construct focusing on a customer's cognitive, emotional, behavioral, sensorial, and social responses to a firm's offerings during the customer's entire journey (see Customer experience also).

**Financial relationship marketing investments:** Provision of direct economic benefits in exchange for past or future customer loyalty, includes special discounts, free products to generate incremental sales, and other incentives that easily may be converted to cost savings (e.g., free shipping; extended payment terms).

**Financial relationship marketing performance outcomes:** Performance measures related to revenue enhancements or profit enhancements (i.e., driven by revenue enhancements or cost reductions).

**Flow:** The holistic experience that people feel when they act with total involvement.

**Gratitude:** Feelings of gratefulness, thankfulness, or appreciation for a benefit received (see Customer gratitude also).

**Interaction frequency:** Number of interactions or number of interactions per unit of time between exchange partners.

**Interfirm relationships:** Multiple interactions among many people at multiple levels in the organization—in effect, a network of multilevel relationships.

**Interpersonal relationships:** Exchange dyads of two individuals, one representing the customer side (i.e., individual customer) and the other representing the company side (i.e., individual salesperson).

**Loyalty:** A collection of attitudes aligned with a series of purchase behaviors that systematically favor one entity over competing entities (see Customer loyalty also).

**Loyalty programs:** Any institutionalized incentive systems that attempt to enhance customers' attitudes and behavior over time, such as bonus points, gifts, tiered service levels, and dedicated support contacts.

**Media richness:** Ability to change understanding within a time interval.

**Nonfinancial relationship marketing performance outcomes:** Performance measures related to enhanced market knowledge that are difficult to capture in (short-term) financial terms.

**Offering-based sustainable competitive advantage:** Builds on investments in research and development and resulting innovations, such that the offered products and services substantially improve the customer's experience through cost benefits, performance advantages, or supplementary services.

**Online relationships:** Relational exchanges that are mediated by technology (e.g., Internet, computer) and take place in a non–face-to-face (individual/firm customer-to-technology) environment.

**Parasocial interaction:** A customer's communication and identification with a nonhuman, technological entity (e.g., website, embodied virtual agent) that acts in place of a seller's human representatives.

**Privacy concerns:** Customers' beliefs, attitudes, and perceptions about their privacy.

**Reciprocity norms:** Internalized patterns of behaviors and feelings that regulate the balance of obligations between exchange partners (see Customer reciprocity norms also).

**Relationship-based sustainable competitive advantage:** Relies on strong relationships between customers and salespeople, other boundary-spanning personnel, or the firm as a whole, which evoke hard-to-copy and high levels of trust, commitment, and reciprocal bonds.

**Relationship benefits:** Benefits received, including time saving, convenience, companionship, and improved decision making.

**Relationship breadth:** Number of relational ties with an exchange partner.

**Relationship composition:** Decision-making capability of the relational contacts at an exchange partner.

**Relationship duration:** Length of time that the relationship between the exchange partners has existed.

**Relationship investments:** Seller's investment of time, effort, spending, and resources focused on building a stronger relationship.

**Relationship life cycle stages:** The average change or migration among customers along four path-dependent relational stages (i.e., exploratory or early, growth or development, maturity or maintain, decline and potentially recovery stages), independent of any product or industry differences.

**Relationship marketing:** The process of identifying, developing, maintaining, and terminating relational exchanges with the purpose of enhancing performance.

**Relationship migration mechanisms:** Three positive (i.e., exploration, endowment, recovery) and two negative (i.e., neglect, betrayal) relational migration mechanisms between four relationship states, reflecting the velocity of the levels of customers' commitment, trust, dependence, and relational norms.

**Relationship orientation:** Desire to engage in a strong relationship.

**Relationship quality:** Composite construct capturing the diverse interaction characteristics required to create a high-caliber relational bond, such as commitment, trust, gratitude, reciprocity norms, and exchange efficiency.

**Relationship states:** Four latent relational states (i.e., transactional, transitional, communal, damaged states) reflecting different levels of customers' commitment, trust, dependence, and relational norms.

**Relationship velocity:** The rate and direction of changes in relational constructs.

**Seller expertise:** Knowledge, experience, and overall competency of seller.

**Seller relationship marketing investments:** Seller's investment of financial, social, or structural resources into the customer relationship.

**Seller relationship marketing performance outcomes:** Financial or nonfinancial performance measures to assess the effectiveness of the seller's relationship marketing efforts.

**Similarity:** Commonality in appearance, lifestyle, and status between individual boundary spanners or similar cultures, values, and goals between buying and selling organizations.

**Social relationship marketing investments:** Efforts to personalize the relationship and convey special status; entail social engagements such as meals and sporting events and therefore may vary from ad hoc, low-cost interactions to expensive, formal recognitions.

**Structural relationship marketing investments:** Offer tangible, value-added benefits that are difficult for customers to supply themselves; may include electronic order-processing interfaces, customized packaging, or other custom procedural changes.

**Sustainable competitive advantage (SCA):** An advantage that a firm has when it is able to generate more customer value than the competitor firms in its industry and when these competitor firms are unable to duplicate its effective strategy.

**Transformational relationship events (TREs):** Encounters between exchange partners that significantly disconfirm relational expectations (positively or negatively) and result in dramatic, discontinuous change to the relationship's trajectory.

**Trust:** Confidence in an exchange partner's reliability and integrity (see Customer trust also).

**Unfairness:** A customer's view of the degree to which the ratio of his or her received outcomes relative to inputs, compared with the corresponding input–outcome ratios of other customers, seems unacceptable or inequitable (see Customer unfairness also).

**Web 1.0:** The implementation and dissemination of the World Wide Web and the spread of e-commerce during the 1990s.

**Web 2.0:** The development of a "read and write web," enabling bilateral communication between users through social media, from the early to mid-2000s.

**Web 3.0:** The semantic web emerging in the late 2000s to the mid-2010s, which introduced smartphones and mobile apps, the Internet of Things (IoT), and big data.

**Web 4.0:** The current developmental stage of the digital age, based on artificial intelligence and augmented reality as major technological advances.

# Index

Printed in the United States
by Baker & Taylor Publisher Services